Enterprise and Labour

THE NATURE OF INDUSTRIALIZATION

Series editors: *Peter Mathias and John A. Davis*

This series is based on the graduate seminars in economic history that have been sponsored by the *Istituto Italiano per gli Studi Filosofici (Naples)* and held annually at the Centre for Social History in the University of Warwick.

Published

In preparation

The Nature of Industrialization

Edited by
Peter Mathias and John A. Davis

Volume 3

Enterprise and Labour:
from the Eighteenth Century to the Present

BLACKWELL
Publishers

Copyright © Blackwell Publishers Ltd, 1996

First published 1996
2 4 6 8 10 9 7 5 3 1

Blackwell Publishers Ltd
108 Cowley Road
Oxford OX4 1JF
UK

Blackwell Publishers Inc.
238 Main Street
Cambridge, Massachusetts 02142
USA

British Library Cataloguing in Publication Data
A CIP catalogue record for this book is available from the British Library.

Library of Congress Cataloging-in-Publication Data
Enterprise and labour: from the eighteenth century to the present
/edited by Peter Mathias and John A. Davis.
p. cm. —(Nature of industrialization; v. 3)
Includes bibliographical references and index.
1. Labor—History—Congresses. 2. Industrialization—History—Congresses.
3. Entrepreneurship—History—Congresses. 4. Economic history—Congresses.
5. Labor movement—Case studies—Congresses. 6. Industrial relations—Case studies—Congresses. I. Mathias, Peter. II. Davis, John Anthony. III. Series.
HD4851.E57 1996   95–23055
331'.09—dc20   CIP

ISBN 0–631–17407–9

Typeset in 10 on 12pt Garamond by Pure Tech India Ltd, Pondicherry
Printed in Great Britain by Hartnolls Limited, Bodmin, Cornwall.
This book is printed on acid-free paper

Contents

Preface

This volume is based on revised and expanded versions of papers first given at the third economic history summer school held at the Centre for Social History in the University of Warwick in July 1987, in collaboration with the *Istituto Italiano per gli Studi Filosofici*. The editors wish to take this opportunity to thank the President of the Institute, Avvocato Gerardo Marotta, its Secretary, Professor Antonio Gargano and Professor Luigi De Rosa for their continuing and generous support both for the original conference and for the publication of this volume.

Introduction

why this pairing?

Enterprise and labour cover an immensely wide range of themes and issues that have always been central to the concern of economic historians. Entrepreneurs, managers, the company or firm, the organization of production, labour in general and the work-force in more specific circumstances, the experience of work and the forms of collective organization and culture that have been shaped by that experience are only the most important of these. But above all, enterprise and labour embrace a set of relationships between entrepreneurs and enterprise, between managers and workers, companies and employees, capitalists and proletarians that a multitude of observers from the earliest phases of the industrial era have considered central to the modern process of economic growth and that lie at the heart of the notion of 'industrial relations'.

It is hardly surprisingly, therefore, that the theme of enterprise and labour should bring the economic historian face to face with a wide variety of different disciplines and perspectives – from macro-economic theories of innovation, labour economics and the firm, to industrial relations and sociology, labour history, social history and, most recently, new researches in the field of company and business history. Each of these approaches has its own particular identity, each its own agenda of questions and debates. In recent years, however, there has been a marked tendency for specialists in these different fields to try to communicate more closely and to seek to build common agendas that bridge the limitations and perspectives of their different disciplines.

This trend towards an *histoire integrale* became prominent in the extensive flow of publications in the field of 'proto-industrialization', predominantly for early-modern Europe, which stems from the seminal article of Franklin

Mendels published in the *Journal of Economic History* in 1972. The momentum of change in these contexts was seen to derive from the integration of economic and commercial opportunities with demographic stimuli through the encouragement of marriage and the formation of new households which enhanced employment opportunities made possible. The 'household and family economy' with gender divisions of labour, seasonal integration between work on the land and industrial processing, together with other complex interrelationships was also seen to be critical to the full understanding of the analysis of social and economic structures, together with the processes of change.

A similar logic has prevailed in recent historiography for the nineteenth and twentieth centuries, studying social and family relationships in the context of work. The new methodology has required an emphasis on local and regional studies to allow all the main aspects of the context to be brought into the analysis. Legal, institutional and political relationships are also involved. Detailed investigation into the *microcosm* can thus reveal the sources of momentum for change governing the wider context of the macrocosm. The result has been to remove research and publications from the traditional historiographical thematic subject specializations of economic, industrial, technological, demographic, family specialisms which were increasingly acquiring independent traditions of research, publications and bibliography, becoming separately institutionalized. As this volume indicates, such a tradition of research is now in retreat, and one of its principal aims is to contribute to the process of bridge building between the study of economic history, social history and the history of industrial relations.

It used to be the case, for example, that historians studied either the captains of industry or the workers but rarely, if ever, the two together. But there have been important changes in recent years. On the one hand, social historians have become increasingly aware of the need to document and study the middle classes and managerial groups. On the other, the study of contemporary industrial relations has become more sensitive to the empirical tests of historical experience and historical context. New interest in business history and research on single companies that embrace both management and labour is also indicative of a concern to reconstruct the ways in which industrial relations have historically been shaped in the workplace.

As this enterprise develops, the boundaries between economic history, social history and industrial relations have become particularly fluid (as can be seen in the academic and teaching specialisms of the contributors to this volume). The essays in this volume offer examples of these trends, for a series of selected cases, and provide students and specialists with critical overviews of particular features of the history of industrial relations in the United Kingdom, France, Italy, Germany, Japan and the United States over time periods ranging from the eighteenth to the late twentieth centuries. But they also provide a jumping-off point for some wider reflections. As in previous volumes in this series, the essays here seek to show how the study of entrepreneurship, company organization, labour and industrial relations have been influenced and shaped by shifts in broader historical interpretations and methodological debates.

The first and most general of these are the shifts in the interpretation of the process of industrialization that were the subject of the first volume in this series (*The First Industrial Revolutions*). These debates do not need to be rehearsed again at length here, other than to say that the idea that Britain's eighteenth-century industrial revolution was the mother of all subsequent modern economic growth is now increasingly open to question. Economic historians have for some time been arguing that the British pattern of industrial development was unique rather than typical, that different countries and economies experienced different patterns of growth and followed different paths to establish modern economies.

Nonetheless, the earlier heroic image of the first British industrial revolution that emphasized the cleanness of the break with the past has continued to influence the ways in which the historical role and behaviour of both entrepreneurs and workers have been interpreted. As Peter Mathias shows in the first of the essays in this volume, the image of the industrial entrepreneur has always been deeply inseparable from the notion that Britain's industrial revolution constituted a clean leap into a new age and a paradigm for all subsequent forms of industrialization. In the classical formulations of Max Weber and Schumpeter, the entrepreneur was a vector of modernizing forces and innovation – a creative deviant, ready to break out into new and unexplored fields.

But that image is in many ways misleading because it disguises both the degrees of continuity with the past and also the relatively slow and patchy adoption of new technologies and new forms of production. Many of the questions that were posed in these pioneering sociological essays (for example, those bearing on the prevalence of Nonconformists among Britain's early industrial leaders and innovators) retain their validity, but Mathias's essay emphasizes how the specific skills and attributes of the typical eighteenth-century entrepreneur acquired an importance because of the specific contexts and conditions of enterprise in eighteenth-century England. When those contexts changed, as they did of necessity with the advance of the industrial economies, with changing institutional, political, and social contexts of enterprise, then those original skills and attributes might not only lose their relevance but even become dysfunctional.

Working from the example of eighteenth-century Britain, Mathias's essay challenges the notion that there are timeless values and qualities that make for effective 'entrepreneurship' and shows instead how the skills that facilitated success were contingent on conditions that were specific to time and place, and were in turn shaped by that context. He also demonstrates that the emphasis on innovation has overshadowed the degree to which the new industrial economy in Britain grew out of what already existed, carrying forward forms of production and organization from the past.

This also constitutes the central theme in his chapter on labour in eighteenth-century England, which demonstrates how the realities of industrial labour differed from the stereotypes that surround the classical image of the First Industrial Revolution. In many cases, the organization of industrial labour in the eighteenth century simply continued and built on earlier pre-industrial forms of organization. Mathias also argues that both the novelty of, and resistance to, the new forms of industrial production have been exaggerated, that capitalist forms of exploitation predated industrialization and cannot be considered synonymous with it. Luddism, for example, was by no means the only, or indeed the most widespread, cause of discontent and protest among industrial workers whose grievances were shaped by more immediate, and in general more ephemeral, causes that were specific to time, place and to specific enterprises.

The two essays by Peter Mathias emphasize the need to reconsider conventional images of the history of enterprise and labour in the light of historical contexts, historical reality and historical research. Despite the apparent abundance of studies on the nineteenth-century British labour force, Pat Thane's essay on the participation of women in the British labour force in the late nineteenth-century shows there are still enormous gaps that make it difficult to sustain hard and fast generalizations about the composition of the work force, its collective organizations, attitudes and so forth. It has long been recognized that women and children made up the bulk of the labour force in many industries, but only recently have women's industrial employment and women's work in general in the nineteenth century been studied systematically.

Drawing on recent research to reconstruct the history of women's paid work and employment in Britain between 1870 and World War I, Thane shows that this was much more extensive than has previously been thought, and almost certainly greater than elsewhere in Europe (which poses interesting comparative questions about relative rates of women's paid employment in nineteenth century France, Germany and Italy). She also challenges the idea that women were relegated to less desirable jobs with limited opportunities for advancement because of the stratification of the labour market or the existence of a dual (male and female) labour market. Conditions varied enormously from industry to industry, location to location and, if women were in general assigned subordinate, poorly paid and unskilled jobs, this was by no means always the case. Challenging the notion that women workers were unable to organize collectively or to defend their interests effectively, Thane argues also that the trade unions were less insensitive to the need to defend the rights of women to work than has often been suggested. If women's employment opportunities in nineteenth-century Britain remained limited, she argues that the cause had less to do with women's supposed inability to organize or the disinterest of the trade unions than with 'the strategies and decisions of the employers'. She also shows that World War I brought fewer and less lasting changes to the opportunities for women to obtain paid work with good prospects, and cannot therefore be seen as a major turning point in the history of women's paid employment in Britain.

Pat Thane's essay indicates how traditional approaches to the history of labour in nineteenth-century Britain have in some respects been distorted by an exclusive focus on organized labour and the trade union movement – perspectives that overlook the presence and importance of women in the labour force. Richard Whipp's essay on managerial strategies and wage bargaining in the English pottery industry in the late nineteenth and early twentieth centuries develops a parallel critique of labour history written exclusively in institutional terms. Working from a detailed reconstruction of the organization and development of one of the major industrial concentrations in early twentieth-century Britain, Whipp's analysis emphasizes again the gap between historical reality and the broader interpretations that have shaped theories and interpretations of British industrial relations in the twentieth century.

Illustrating the complex and refractory structure of the ceramic industries and the differences that, as a result, prevented the employers and the workers from establishing compact collective-bargaining procedures, Whipp argues that the pottery industry provides little evidence to support the notion that the history of industrial relations in twentieth-century Britain has been characterized by a transition from informal to formal bargaining, from local to national agreements, from shop-floor negotiations to the collective bargaining between trades unions and employers' associations. The historical realities – that can only be recaptured by reconstructing the historical processes of management strategies and wage bargaining in their historical contexts – suggest a much less tidy situation, in which industrial relations have continued to be dominated by local issues as much as by broader contextual contingencies (the different impacts of periods of expanding demand and employment or contracting orders and unemployment on the respective aims and strategies of employers and workers), and in which the institutionalization of industrial relations seemed no closer at the end than at the beginning of the period studied.

One reason for this, Whipp argues, is that both labour historians and historians of industrial relations have tended to focus too exclusively on strike action, neglecting more commonplace forms of industrial action such as spontaneous short stoppages that were the primary instrument of worker-bargaining. These were, and have remained, localized in origin and impact, and have effectively resisted attempts at institutionalization either by employees or by the unions themselves. Contrary to the widely accepted view that industrial relations in Britain have been characterized by a precocious level of collective organization among employers and workers, Whipp stresses the continuing impact and consequences of 'the want of union' among both groups.

These four essays offer a critical reconsideration of key features of entrepreneurship, labour and the historical development of industrial relations in Britain from the eighteenth to the mid-twentieth centuries. Each perspective underlines the critical importance of historical context and takes this as a starting point for a wider critical evaluation of the interpretations and theories that have guided previous research. As well as suggesting ways in which those interpretations need to be reformulated, these essays also have a particular relevance for the still relatively understudied comparative history of enterprise and industrial relations.

Much of what has been written in this field has been guided by the concept of a single, model process of industrialization that developed around the imitation of Britain's First Industrial Revolution. Until very recently, the analysis of entrepreneurship, company organization and labour in other Western European countries in the nineteenth century has taken British examples and models as a yardstick. But, if the British industrial revolution is taken as one among a variety of possible paths of modern economic growth, then it must follow that, historically, there will also have been a variety of different relations between enterprise and labour.

At the start of his essay on management, labour and the state in France from 1871 to 1939, Roger Magraw points out that much of the literature on French entrepreneurship and management has been dominated by the notion that French entrepreneurs somehow remained 'backward' with respect to their more 'modern' British counterparts. But, as Magraw's essay demonstrates, abstract comparisons of this sort draw attention away from the specific contexts within which French enterprise developed. Not surprisingly, these were different from Great Britain, and, with a more decentralized industrial structure in which older luxury manufactures like silk continued to play an important role, where trade union organization and membership was much weaker than in Britain, and where the primary sector continued to retain a much higher proportion of the labour force than in Britain, French industrialists followed different strategies from the British counterparts.

Their attitudes to their workers remained more authoritarian and paternalist, and, as in other parts of Europe, the French factory masters remained jealous of their autonomy and resisted attempts to erode this, whether they came from the state or from the workers. Emile Zola referred to the new factory-towns and villages as 'new types of Bastille', and Le Creusot's works have been described as 'an Oceania with Schneider as Big Brother'.

This did not mean that French industrialists were uninterested in new ideas. As in Britain, the United States and elsewhere in Europe, scientific management and Taylorism found many enthusiastic advocates in France (notably H. Le Chatelet and Fayol), but few French industrialists did more than pay lip-service to these ideas in practice. But this was probably also true in Britain and the United States at least until the inter-war period. Like Richard Whipp, Magraw also emphasizes the relative failure of French employer associations and challenges the belief that collective bargaining was gaining significant ground in French industries before World War I. Like Thane and Whipp for Britain, Magraw also dismisses the idea that World War I marked a major turning point in the history of industrial relations in France, showing that, despite the hopes of Thomas and Clemenceau, state interventionism was in large part dismantled in France after 1918 and had few strong supporters. Throughout the 1920s and 1930s, French industrial relations continued to be shaped at a local level and in the exchanges between individual employers and their workers. It was only when Blum's Popular Front government introduced the Matignon Agreement in 1937 that large sections of the French *patronat* began to mobilize resources to combat the concessions made to the workers and showed growing approval for the corporatist solutions to industrial relations that had been pioneered in Mussolini's Italy and perfected in Nazi Germany.

There, too, image and reality may have differed. Davis's essay on Italian entrepreneurship reveals many similarities with developments in France, and suggests that Mussolini's regime played little part directly in shaping the internal organization of enterprise in Italy. In many respects, managerial strategies in nineteenth-century Italy reflected the autonomist and paternalist outlook of the French industrialists, but Davis's essay suggests that generalizations may be deceptive because they disguise practices and outlooks that ran the full gamut from pre- to post-modern.

As in the case of France, recent work on entrepreneurship, industrial management and industrial relations in Italy has tended to move away from the issues of 'relative backwardness' – or what in the Italian case is often referred to as 'lazy capitalism' – to emphasize instead the rationality of entrepreneurial strategies in the context of prevailing conditions, markets, resources and opportunities. Seen in the context of the relatively subordinate and vulnerable position of Italy in the international economy, many aspects of management strategies that have hitherto been taken as examples of the 'backwardness' of Italian entrepreneurship (for example, the retention until well into the twentieth century of rural locations for industrial production) can be seen as rational attempts to exploit inelastic resources and narrow comparative advantages. Emphasis on the prevailing conditions of uncertainty and dependence on foreign markets in which Italian industrialists and exporters were forced to operate may modify many accepted judgments of entrepreneurial strategies in Italy, while it is clear that in the most technologically advanced sectors of the Italian economy before 1914, entrepreneurial and managerial objectives and policies were derived directly – and consciously – from the best and most advanced practice of the day. In engineering, chemicals, electricity and electrical engineering, Italian entrepreneurs and managers studied and adopted the latest practices of their German and American (as well as British and French, but these were perhaps second choices) competitors. If this represented a thin stratum of Italian industries, this would also be true for Germany, France and Britain – and indeed the United States – before 1914. And if those strategies did not work in Italy – or at least did not achieve the desired results – the reasons were to be found above all in the very limited market opportunities open to Italian producers in these fields, to the instability of export markets in general, exacerbated in this case by the long recession before 1914.

Italian historians have tended to see World War I as a more permanent turning point, both in the organization of Italian industry and in managerial strategies. Many have argued that the wartime Industrial Mobilization programme, which introduced state control of production quotas and raw materials and suspended free wage bargaining in war industries, set the example which fascist industrial policies would simply perpetuate in Italy. But, as in France, state controls over industrial management were abandoned after 1918, while, until 1926, the fascist movement was stridently neo-liberal in its economic policies. Intervention in the economy was directed primarily at curbing the labour movement (something that upset few industrialists), but the regime encountered much greater opposition when it tried to challenge managerial autonomy. Many Italian industrialists rode in close alliance with the regime, and many key industries remained crucially reliant on government orders and contracts. But, as in France, sympathy for corporatist solutions to industrial relations rarely translated into support among industrialists either for fascist ideas about industrial management or for greater state intervention in the running of industrial concerns. Despite the close ties between many industrialists and the regime, that intimacy affected managerial and productive strategies much less than the regime's propaganda suggested. As in earlier periods, entrepreneurial and managerial strategies in Italy in the 1930s were more closely determined by market conditions and the structure of labour markets than by ideology. As a result, the industries most closely associated with the regime included both 'modernizers' and more traditional enterprises.

National Socialism, on the other hand, may have had a greater impact on accelerating the 'modernization' of German industrial enterprises as Stephen Salter argues, but again the reasons were more closely related to markets and the structure of the labour market than to the regime's industrial ideologies which remained ambiguous and unclear. Stephen Salter emphasizes in particular the ways in which changes in the structure of the labour market played a critical role in the development of German industrial relations in the inter-war period. German workers acquired important concessions under Weimar, but Salter shows how rising unemployment had eroded much of these gains even before 1929. The impact of the Depression meant that the German labour movement was effectively broken before the Nazis came to power, but even the first Nazi challenges to the unions were tentative. While the Law for the Ordering of National Labour (1934) marked the first step towards strengthening the powers of employers, it was not until rising employment rates and prosperity after 1936 gave rise to problems of rapid labour turnover that the regime attempted to intervene to limit labour mobility. These attempts were not very effective, Salter shows, until Albert Speer took control of the programme to co-ordinate war production and introduced much more coercive measures to discipline workers.

The 1930s however did see a marked acceleration in the rationalization of the organization of production in German industries. Salter argues that before 1933 rationalization was actually much less widespread in German industry than is often supposed (in practice, it was limited to companies in coal mining, iron and steel, railway locomotive construction, electrical goods and chemicals). But, in the 1930s, Taylorism became fashionable, and companies were able to take advantage of the absence of a free labour force to experiment with new technologies and organization of production. The introduction of company-based welfare schemes designed to encourage employee loyalty and individualistic achievement orientation (characteristic of the post-war 'affluent' worker) began to increase.

Salter warns that it would be wrong, however, to identify in the Nazi era the origins of the spirit of co-operation and levelling that would make German industrial relations something of an ideal in the post-war era. The increasingly coercive nature of shop-floor relations after 1942 tells a different story, and Salter suggests that the real roots of Germany's post-war industrial democracy lay in the catastrophic conditions that Germans suffered as a result of the war and defeat caused by the Nazi regime.

This emphasis on the relatively recent origins of Germany's post-war industrial harmony is echoed in Takao Matsamura's study of industrial relations in Japan. Developing a critical analysis of another 'system' of industrial relations that is frequently held up as a model of harmonious co-operation, Matsamura underlines the relatively recent historical contexts in which contemporary Japanese industrial relations have been shaped, and the inherent inequalities that they embody. Challenging the widely held notion that the key features of contemporary Japanese industrial relations, like lifetime employment, seniority wages, mutual loyalty between workers and companies, and company-based unions, are rooted in traditional Japanese culture and institutions, Matsamura shows how these evolved in the inter-war period in Japan as a direct consequence of the 'rational, profit-maximizing behaviour of managers'.

Lifetime employment and job security were adopted by Japanese employers in key concerns like the Mistui Shipbuilding Company, the Kobe Iron and Steel Company and the Shibaura Machinery Company in the 1930s in an attempt to train and retain a skilled workforce. But, even within those companies, such practices were limited in their effect and were never extended to all workers. Moreover, the premise for the emergence of Japanese managerial strategies in the 1930s was the defeat of organized labour and trade unionism – a defeat that was the premise for the creation of company-run factory councils. After the start of the war with China in 1937, these institutions were transformed by the government's *Sanpo* administration into a means for controlling and exploiting the labour force. The conditions and wages of most Japanese workers fell disastrously, while the extensive use of captive Korean labour served to protect a small privileged minority of workers.

The features that have given post-war Japanese industrial relations the appearance of harmony and stability are therefore not only recent in origin, but are less permanent and more partial than appears at first sight. For Matsamura, the key determinants in their development have been the particular structure of Japanese labour markets, and above all the weakness of Japanese trade unionism which was unable to draw on the traditions of craft control over the processes of production that had given British unions their negotiating power in the nineteenth century.

This invites comparison with the United States, where another model of the institutionalization of industrial conflict derived from the massive defeats inflicted by the employers on unionized labour in America after World War I. In his reconstruction of the development of American managerial strategies and industrial relations from World War I to (nearly) the present, Paul Edwards also stresses the consequences of the absence of a craft union strategy in the more spontaneous approach of the Wobblies (IWW Industrial Workers of the World). But Edwards challenges the view that modern American industrial relations can be understood as a process that started with the struggles between capital and labour which resulted in the victory of the employers and the assertion of the Open (i.e. union-free) Shop after World War I and then took shape through the package of New Deal legislation (the National Industrial Recovery Act of 1933 and the Wagner/National Labor Relations Act of 1935) that gave recognition to the unions and the measures adopted by the National War Labor Board during World War II to arrive at a post-war 'system' of industrial relations based on the peaceful and institutionalized resolution of industrial conflict.

Such a view, Edwards argues, takes too little account of historical realities, exaggerates the effectiveness of post-war institutionalized bargaining mechanisms and also their permanency. Like other contributors to the volume, Edwards also argues that excessive concentration on the role of the unions has led to neglect of the more permanent struggles between employers and workers to assert control over the point of production – struggles that have not been harmonious and are by no means resolved.

From each of their chosen vantage points, the essays in this volume challenge conventional images in the history of enterprise and labour. Their objective is not to displace theory or generalization with mere empirical detail, but rather to stress the importance of modifying and rethinking general theories and interpretations in the light of new empirical research, and, above all, in relation to the essential historical contexts of time and place.

1

Entrepreneurs, Managers and Business Men in Eighteenth-century Britain

Peter Mathias

The Conceptual Debate

An initial explanation that needs to be made in any text about the operation of business in the eighteenth century concerns the word 'entrepreneur' or the more abstract term 'entrepreneurship'. It is important, not just for debates about the eighteenth century in which it has featured prominently, but equally in hypotheses about the relative decline of the British economy, in comparison with other industrialized economies, after 1870, and is much invoked in the newspapers at present. The supposed 'failure of entrepreneurship' being the explanation for the relative decline and inefficiency of the British economy compared with others in the last century is the inverse of the same debate about entrepreneurs and entrepreneurship in the eighteenth century as an explanation for the fact that the British economy was the first European economy to industrialize. Entrepreneurship, evidently located more in Britain than elsewhere, is invoked as the secret weapon that explains why the industrial revolution occurred in Britain rather than in some other countries – such as Holland – that were potentially in the same sort of economic position. Even the assertion that this was intended to explain – that an industrial revolution occurred in Britain but not elsewhere – is controversial, with the implications that the rest of north-western Europe was innocent of industrial growth. In the first instance, however, it is important to explain briefly why the words 'entrepreneur' and 'entrepreneurship' have assumed such powerful connotations and such important conceptual significance.

Essentially, two contrasting entities lie concealed in a word like 'entrepreneur'. In the first instance, it can be simply a descriptive term, another term for 'business person' and a whole series of empirical questions relates to the specifications of business in the eighteenth century under such a heading: who they were, how they were educated, how they were recruited, what they did, how they ran their businesses. Looking at entrepreneurs simply as creatures of flesh and blood, who did what they did and for the motives that they had at the time, is to use the word in a descriptive, empirical way. But, at the same time, one has to realize that much of its significance depends on the conceptual and analytical assumptions that also lie behind it. Such conceptual meaning derives, it is agreed, originally from the seventeenth-century commentator and economist, Richard Cantelon, but more particularly now from the influential thesis of Joseph Schumpeter, the Austrian and then American economist, put forward in *The Theory of Economic Development* (Cambridge, Mass. 1934). This was not widely known when originally published in German but, when translated after World War II, it became very influential.

Schumpeter's essential thesis was that the normal state of any economy was stability, that technology tended towards the stable or static (as existing technology was diffused) and that business operated in an imitative way. Decision-making in an economy in such a stable state was imitative decision-making. Managers operated in conformity with this 'stable state' economy, which did not exhibit change, innovation or progress. For Schumpeter, 'managerial' decision-making was imitative decision-making. The agent for changing an economy from this 'stable state' to being progressive, thrusting, improving, expanding was the entrepreneur. By definition, Schumpeter identified this key role as that of the innovator. This was not just a term for technological change and the invention of new machinery or new devices but had a more general meaning, too. The entrepreneur was the person who devised a new product, who saw the potential of a new market, who realized that finance could be assembled in a new way. In one way or another, either by instituting innovations that cut costs in the making of existing products, or that devised a new product, this process broke the economy out of a stable state and directed it into new paths. In a market context within a capitalist system (a basic assumption for the model), the search was for monopoly profits, when the entrepreneur, as innovator, was ahead of rivals, leading the field. In the gap between the innovation and the copying of that innovation, the entrepreneur could hope to make a fortune by virtue of being able to set prices. But the second assumption was that this took place within a competitive context and that others adopted the innovation, so that it became generalized through competitive pressures and, with this, the general economic advantages of lower costs or the availability of new products. The dynamics of innovation and competition, therefore, moved the economy on to a higher plane, but the originator of the process was the entrepreneur who, as innovator, first broke out of the 'stable state' or 'circular flow'. That at once put the entrepreneur at the centre of the process of economic growth. And it gives context to 'entrepreneurship' as the quality of being a good entrepreneur.

Thus, in the Schumpeterian model, entrepreneurship becomes a critical variable in the analysis of economic growth. It offers a new explanatory variable that set the terms of the debate. The conceptual importance is such that when the word entrepreneur is used it ought to be enclosed by quotation marks to signify that it has this particular conceptual resonance. Entrepreneurs act aggressively and creatively but, at the same time, they destroy by competition the structures that exist around them, forcing others in the same industry or engaged in the same function either to adopt the innovations themselves or go out of business. They would be driven into bankruptcy by the competitive context if they did not adopt the new cost-cutting or innovative devices. Schumpeter characterized this dynamic as 'daemonic', being creative and destructive at the same time. Subsequent commentators, such as David McClelland and Everett Hagen, sought to explore the general issue in more detail, in particular by seeking to establish the reality of motivation among entrepreneurs. McClelland focused on the need for achievement, that some people for reasons of personal psychology and the particular value systems of the group in which they found themselves had a greater need for achievement than the norm and hence became greater strivers than others. Everett Hagen put a further dimension on the debate by arguing that it was not accidental that a high proportion of the entrepreneurial roles and the enterprise functions in a society had been occupied by minority groups.

The traditional established elites in a country have often not been the main sources of recruitment for people in entrepreneurial roles in society, whether in finance or trade or subsequently industry, at least in the early stages of their institutionalization. In proportion to their numbers in the population, for example, protestant non-conformist groups, which lay outside the established Anglican church in the eighteenth century, particularly the Quakers, had a much higher proportion of enterprise in their hands than was statistically probable. They formed a very small proportion of the population but owned a significant proportion of enterprise in certain trades and industries, such as iron making, milling, brewing and banking in the eighteenth century, and chocolate making in the nineteenth. Why should this be so? One can also quote other minority groups, such as Jewish and other immigrant families in banking in the eighteenth-century. Many other examples are to be found around the world in contexts other than Europe. Everett Hagen argued that it was withdrawal of status respect from a minority group – when they felt threatened or alienated, aware of prejudice against them – that energized certain minority groups into business roles. More is said below about minority groups in business roles.

The theorizing about entrepreneurship attracted counter-theorizing, and the debate continues. The argument against the whole idea of Schumpeter and his designation of the entrepreneur as the critical factor in economic growth, the key explanatory variable, the originating cause, and 'unmoved mover' of economic growth is quite simple. The argument is that successful entrepreneurship remains a product of circumstances, a consequence of the context within which the entrepreneur finds himself or herself. The text of the opposing thesis is from Sir John Habakkuk, arguing about the causes of the relative decline of the British economy after 1870. 'Great generals', he commented, 'are not made in time of peace; great entrepreneurs are not made in non-expanding industries.' Vigour in business people thus becomes, in a causal sense, a response to opportunity – market opportunity, technological opportunity, financial opportunity and the like. In the microeconomic world of single firms it can be asserted with conviction that the better performance of one firm against another can be explained by better management or more vigorous leadership, but the performance of an industry as a whole depends upon economic competitive forces to which individual business people have to respond. Given effective competition, inefficient entrepreneurs are quickly driven out of business to bankruptcy so that competitive forces become the key to efficiency. 'We are all entrepreneurs now' is the slogan for this argument. It encapsulates the position of neo-classical economic theory, with its basic assumption of a perfectly competitive market, against which Schumpeter was always a dissident voice. In England, new life was breathed into this debate by the Conservative administration under Margaret Thatcher, who quite specifically announced that one of her principal objectives was to recreate in Britain an 'entrepreneurial culture'. The minister who most clearly articulated the public philosophy, Keith Joseph, enunciated this quite specifically and said that what principally determined the fate of England was efficient entrepreneurship and that had to be inculcated in every conceivable way*. Thus, we are living with the debate still.

---

*He was delighted with the University of Warwick because the university was a breeding ground, as he saw it, for thrusting efficient business people relating the academic world to the world of commercial success, and he did not like what was happening in the University of Oxford, which he thought was disconnected in a large measure from the 'real world'.

The Structure of Enterprise

In the eighteenth-century context, why should this be important? Why should the context of enterprise and the role of the individual business men be seen to have been so influential? In the first instance, in the context of the eighteenth-century in Britain – and broadly also for most of the nineteenth-century – the state was not important directly within the productive context of the economy. Economic growth or industrialization cannot be explained by what is happening in the public sector, despite the great importance of the role of the state in contextual ways. There were no major state industries in eighteenth-century Britain; the state operated capacity only in relation to very specialized military technology and hardware, in naval dockyards, Woolwich arsenal, some gunpowder plants, and a few similar ventures (such as the Ordnance Survey), but that was very largely disconnected from the efficiency and the path of progress for the economy as a whole. Even with military and naval supplies, most cannon and small arms, and many naval ships, were produced by private firms bidding for public contracts. So the state was not important directly in the productive context. Secondly, the state was also not important in eighteenth- and nineteenth-century England as a provider of finance for funding productive enterprise. Even for the financing of transport investment in Britain – unlike in most of western Europe and elsewhere – the state did not provide money for the construction of canals or railways or even for most roads. Such major infrastructure investment remained a private-sector operation in the capital market, raising money on terms that successfully produced a commercial rate of return for the investors. The profound limitations in the direct role of the state and the public sector in economic growth need to be stressed because, in consequence, most of the decision-making in the productive sectors of the economy – decisions about investment, innovation, adopting new technology, developing new products, prices, employment and labour conditions – were decisions of individual private businessmen. Collectively, such decisions set the national parameters of the productive context. That said, the process of economic change had a strong political dimension that cannot be ignored. The state protected the national market in agriculture and major industries; it offered great political benefits for British shipping. Colonial possessions resulted from state military action and, when acquired, the economic relationships between the colonies and the mother country were controlled with a view to benefiting the imperial power. Naval strength protected British trade. The issue is simply that, within the productive context of the economy, in Britain the state was not present in a significant way.

Within the private sector, which really conditioned what happened product-ively, most enterprise in trade and industry and the professions was in the hands of family businessmen or in small partnerships, often dominated by kinship links. Of course, this was not necessarily so and many partnerships had their principals brought into association because of the functional demands of the business. A common syndrome was that an elderly person in the sole charge of a business had a strong incentive to take a younger partner, and putative successor, with at first a small share in the partnership, to provide a bridging arrangement as the old owner gradually reduced his commitment, but maintained his income and a watching brief. In the absence of a son (or with more than one son who was destined for the business), however, partnerships often became more closely linked with kinship links in succeeding generations. The firm needs almost to be regarded as an estate in this respect so that family pressures were strong, for an heiress-daughter to marry someone who could successfully take over the business. Thus, partners often became associated later on through the marriage of their children: as their daughters or sons, nephews, nieces or cousins created a kinship consolidation with non-kin within the partnership.

Incorporated enterprise, operating through professional managers where the ownership was in the hands of shareholders not directly concerned with management, occurred only in very specialized sectors of the economy. The East India Company, a chartered monopoly company controlling the trade east of the Cape of Good Hope, was one example. High-risk overseas trade requiring high capitals invited the joint-stock company form of organization but most foreign trade was in the hands of individual merchants and small partnerships. Mining was another instance. Deep mines were extremely capital-intensive in a context of high risk – the sort of context which required incorporation, mobilizing capital from the public and trading with limitation of liability for the shareholders; or a legal form which gave these advantages without the legal status of incorporation. This was the case with many mining businesses and the ownership of ships. One or two insurance firms gained parliamentary bills to operate as companies for similar reasons of requiring large capitals and a spread of risks. But these sectors were extremely limited and far from the norm as business organizations and structures.

Managers in this period were quite unrepresentative of those groups that controlled the economic fortunes of the nation and business, if by manager is meant someone who did not own the enterprise that he controlled but was part of a formal management hierarchy, whose income as a person taking major decisions in running an enterprise did not depend directly upon profits but upon a salary (annually determined, often with recognized perquisites, rather than on a daily rate). Apart from in a few large mines, the foreign trading companies and insurance companies, the characteristic roles where salaried managers flourished, were in public-sector activities such as the customs service or the excise, the army, the navy or the church. Another reason for the relative absence of professional managers is that most business was on a small scale. It was unusual, for example, to find an industrial business that had plants in different places, or even a multiplant enterprise within a single locality. Businesses with activities going on in different places in the country were uncommon, certainly for manufacturing industry. In the early nineteenth-century, the largest mining companies sometimes had smelting interests elsewhere (as did Thomas Williams, the 'copper king' of Anglesey); Ambrose Crowley had depots in the Midlands and a base in London for the iron products he made in the north-east; some of the largest textile magnates developed several mills but, in such cases, the plants were usually not in different regions. Therefore, an identification was maintained between the ownership of a business and its management, whether the owner-manager and his foremen or the small partnership where the partners who owned the business collectively maintained the collective responsibility for running it.

One reason for such an identification was a legal one. No company could be established without a private Act of Parliament to give authority, which was almost never forthcoming for proposed companies in manufacturing trade or professional enterprise. Parliament was hostile because of the great speculation involved in the South Sea Bubble (and previous speculations before that) which prompted the 'Bubble Act' of 1719, prohibiting the existence of companies without parliamentary permission. Many commentators, supported in 1776 by the authority of Adam Smith, argued that incorporation, limitation of liability, transferable shares and a free capital market for companies in manufacturing business led to speculation and wastage of capital, to manias and stock-exchange crises. To avoid a second South Sea Bubble it was thought essential to prohibit incorporation and the company form of enterprise. It was not just legal hostility that prevented the rise of large-scale incorporated enterprise in the first phases of industrialization, however. Lawyers were as clever in the eighteenth-century as they are now and produced sophisticated legal devices that might have been able to get around the law on a large scale – such as 'cost-book companies' for mines, divisible ownership (with transferable 'shares') in ships, and hydra-headed partnerships which operated *de facto* as companies. Secondly, parliament was full of commercial representatives, with an important commercial lobby (if not an industrial lobby) in the late eighteenth and early nineteenth-centuries. If there had been massive pressure from the business community, then parliament might have been responsive. With general statutes of incorporation, which offered access to incorporation and limitation of liability in the mid-decades of the nineteenth century, there was no immediate pent-up demand from industry for incorporation.

This makes it difficult to explain the fact that enterprise was dominated by small businesses unified in ownership and managerial control, operated under the immediate eye of the entrepreneur who owned as well as ran the enterprise, simply in legal terms or in terms of parliamentary prohibition. The fact was that, in the eighteenth and the early nineteenth centuries, business operated in a context of high risk. Physical communications were very slow over long distances. A merchant could not get a message to a distant market on the other side of the Atlantic or in the Far East faster than the ship that was carrying the cargo, and it took two years to get a cargo out and returns in money from the sale of the cargo in the most distant trades. Trading with the eastern side of the Baltic or the West Indies and North America required a year, or virtually a year, to receive the order, send the cargo and get paid for the sale. Uncertainties and risk from storm, piracy or capture by privateers or hostile fleets in wartime were high in certain trades. It was very difficult to control agents at a distance: much local discretion was unavoidable because of these great difficulties in communication, and agents, if directly employed as managers, had a chronic tendency to default or to start trading with their principal's capital. Very few effective public controls existed against fraud and it was very difficult to ensure accountability in public law with companies. Legal procedures of recovering debt beyond that of simple measures to get payment for bills of exchange were very expensive and very protracted, particularly in overseas markets. As always, winning a case in the courts very often did not ensure the recovery of the lost money.

Thus, the context was of high commercial risks which invites the proposal of a sociological law: that the weaker the institutional structure, the higher the context of risk (not just in business terms but also in the political context) then the greater the importance of kinship and family links. In such circumstances 'blood was thicker than water'.

Access to Business

A context of high risk ensured a world of personal contacts, an operational face-to-face society in sociological terms. It produced a high premium on knowing directly the person with whom one was dealing. Dealing with a cousin or a friend whom you knew directly or whom your cousin knew, with a bond of personal trust, was usually a precondition for successful transactions and the best security against getting cheated. With this went a high premium, for the same reasons, on consolidating a long-term relationship, such as running a business, with a kinship link. The more cousins you had, the safer you were in a depression in getting hold of cash to tide you over a business crisis or in borrowing money to set up in business or to make a great leap forward. It is for that reason that business partnerships in the next generation were often consolidated with marriage. When one generation gave place to another, handing on the business to a son was like settling an estate for a family succession, with the added problem that successful management had to be united with the security of ownership.

If a business man had only a daughter and no son to succeed him, the wisest investment which could be made was for the daughter to marry the chief clerk (if socially eligible) or the person chosen to carry on the business in the next generation. The traditional story – or popular myth – of the successful apprentice or clerk who married his master's daughter often came true in the eighteenth-century. But, far from being the great traditional success story, it was in reality the typical eighteenth-century tragedy of a family business without a male heir to carry on the trade in the next generation. Given the facts of contemporary demography, this was a common occurrence, together with the early death of the principal. This meant that, in a context before married women's property laws, where a married woman could not own property in her own right (unless it was locked up in a family trust or in a settlement) because it was deemed legally to belong to her husband, it was sometimes even better for the successful suitor to the business to marry his master's widow than his master's daughter. The inheritance came immediately.

Apart from direct kinship succession, many recruits to a trade or industry came from neighboring functions and associated trades, often with a generational and a kinship link. A father might put his younger sons into trades that were associated with his own business. A brewer might put a son into the grain trade or the malting business. A grain merchant, who was trading round the country, might put a son into a coastal shipping business for which he was a customer. Fathers in trade would have friends in such associated businesses who could help such sons. If one son was taking over his own business, the father would not want to set up other sons in businesses directly competitive with his own. In the eighteenth century, many iron masters came from the secondary metal trades, moving back into iron manufacture from making final objects in iron: they had accumulated capital; they knew the industry; it was a closely associated business. Entrepreneurs in the glove industry often had close links with the leather trade. A flow of recruits also passed from merchanting into manufacturing. Once technology on a large scale existed, it was quite common for a merchant or 'putter-out' to invest in that technology to supply his requirements as a merchant so that his son perhaps eventually found himself not primarily a merchant but a mill owner. This happened in different branches of the textile industry and in the iron industry. Several South Wales ironworks, in fact, had been set up by merchants who had been trading in iron.

Examples of unskilled labourers themselves becoming industrialists (whether senior managers or owners) are few, with few examples even of the children of unskilled labourers becoming wealthy industrialists. The myth of 'from rags to riches in a single generation' or over two generations did not characterize the business scene. Substantial social mobility took place through the mechanism of trade and industry because these wealth-producing sectors were expanding rapidly but such social mobility did not feature prominently from the ranks of unskilled labourers just as it has been revealed that social mobility did not characterize the very peak of wealth in landed society. Most of the largest landed estates in the nineteenth century came from families who had possessed large landed estates for several generations and did not come from fortunes made in trade or even less in industry. In some businesses, like the East India trade, where rich merchants formed a charmed circle, £1000 at least was required to be taken on as a cadet apprentice with the hope of succession to a partnership. The premium for training and being introduced to the trade in a major London brewery in the 1760s would cost at least £400. Established trades, with large capitals and the prospects of a high future income, produced high barriers to entry but recruitment to trades, which were just specializing out and where the technology was such that units of production were small, made it possible for new entrants to possess very small capitals or to borrow more easily on their personal account. Here recruits could be from the humbler levels of society in a context where skills were brought to an enterprise. In the machine-making industry in the nineteenth-century, most of the famous firms in textiles were started by individuals highly skilled as mechanics, who were originally employed to make machines individually for cotton masters and then developed their own firms. Often they had started life without any significant savings and their principal asset was their skill. This could be a successful entry-point to setting up a firm at the beginning of an industry, when skilled artisans were well placed 'on the ground floor' where these functions were specializing out. By the mid-nineteenth-century, however, it would be difficult to set up a machine-making business from scratch in such circumstances: a future entrepreneur would have had to join an existing firm as an employee and then hope to make his name, accumulate some savings and then later in his career set up an independent firm.

Even though large units of production remained very unrepresentative, the beginnings of an internal ladder of promotion and access to enterprise may be seen where the capitals were large and where the organization was extensive enough to require a middle level of management. A ship's captain, for example, or a 'ship's husband' (a commercial agent operating for a merchant on board a ship accompanying the cargo) were potentially in this position. They would not have had enough money to own the ship or cargoes initially, but could hope as employees to accumulate some savings. Such functionaries could normally have a little space on the ship to trade on their own account so eventually, with enough luck, determination, and ability, they might end up by being a principal in trade. Again, a clerk in a large London brewhouse might be able to accumulate enough money to set up shop in a small way, or become a partner with others.

Functions of Management

Because of the usually small scale of enterprise and because of the links between ownership and managers, with reward coming from the profits of the enterprise rather than as a salary, leading businessmen, as owners and managers, exemplified what would now be seen as undifferentiated management: they organized all the factors of production. Many of them were not key inventors in their own right, but adapted other people's inventions or got them into practical use in a form where such innovations were profitable. Ability for technical adaptation rather than individual creative mechanical genius was the main secret of entrepreneurial success with new technology. The ability to get hold of finance – which often meant credit and therefore being of sufficient status within the community to get credit from merchants or one's family circle, or one's wife's family – was vital. Personal probity – the esteem in which a person was held in the local community or in the trade – was of the essence. In our more institutionalized epoch, it has been institutionalized as a 'credit rating'. The ability to control labour was another requirement. Different ranges and different blends of expertise were required according to different industries and trades. Where labour costs formed a high component of total costs, as they were for Wedgwood in the pottery industry, then keeping control of labour discipline in the work-force and the organizing of specialization of function in the different processes, making them answerable to higher productivity techniques, was critical. In some industries, control of technical change was critical. In all industries to know about technical change was vital – certainly to know enough to prevent the entrepreneur from being fooled or cheated by the artisans he employed.

For an established business, disaster and inefficiency could come more quickly by mistakes or difficulties in trade than in production, so that merchanting and financial skills became critical for success. Buying skills in raw materials, matching price against quality, were extremely important, as was marketing the output. The hallmark of success for early entrepreneurs lay in matching production expertise, skills in managing the production process, to skills in merchanting in buying and selling. Charles Wilson commented that 'The sense of market opportunity and the capacity to exploit it' were critical in a blend of expertise. A contemporary commentator in the eighteenth- century caught the same insight in the remark that 'the merchant stands at the head of the manufacturer . . .'.

One intriguing illustration of how organizational skills alone can build up very large firms and where organization, rather than technical change, can be identified as the critical variable is the building industry. This example, in consequence, reveals much about the nature of entrepreneurship. Archetypal large firms emerged, with typical dynastic enterprises, controlled by a family with continuity over the generations. They proved highly successful in economic and business terms but achieved success without any significant technical change at all. Technology was not a major variable in the transformation of the construction industry (for large-scale projects). In most of the industries of the Industrial Revolution, the famous entrepreneurs – Arkwright, Benjamin Gott, James Watt and their fellows – achieved fame because they made fortunes and became nationally known as individuals because they pioneered the first-generation move into massive technology. Their fortunes derived from success in translating production on to a massive scale by virtue of new technology.

In these cases, entrepreneurial success and the establishment of a family dynasty in a famous firm were integral with the successful innovation of a new technology. In the building industry, Thomas Cubitt was the most famous, but not the only, example of such a transformation. He was a major entrepreneur – a major innovator – without doubt but mechanization was not the secret of his innovations. Controlling a flow of contracts, organizing mortgage finance in a continuous sequence and employing a permanent work-force of skilled people for the first time, maintaining central work-shops, produced such an improvement in organization and in the more efficient deployment of skilled labour that he was able to dominate tendering for large-scale contracts in London and the south of England. It is a salutary example of entrepreneurial skills which can be identified as separate in large measure from riding into a fortune on the back of new technology.

Minority Groups and Entrepreneurs

The question of minority groups in enterprise roles is worth further comment, within the legal context and the context of high risk in the eighteenth-century. It is the case that certain minority groups (but not all) exemplify entrepreneurship in the Schumpeterian sense. They never dominated the British economy as a whole but they exemplified the enterprise roles in that economy and symbolized success in a kinship and motivational matrix which makes it significant to see such groups as a special phenomenon, that can reveal much about the context within which success had to be contrived in the eighteenth-century. Neither in Britain nor in the rest of Europe were minority groups totally dominant, a truth that needs to be noted, more particularly where religious ideology or theological tenets were claimed to lie at the heart of the success.

An old debate identified capitalism with Calvinism as though there was some direct theological connection between Calvinism and success in business, an assumption that has sometimes been made in the newer debate about the non-conformists in the Industrial Revolution in the eighteenth-century. One needs to remember that many of the leading merchants in Amsterdam in the seventeenth century were Roman Catholics; that much of Europe most theologically committed to strict Calvinism was entrepreneurially moribund, in agricultural communities of 'backward' peasants. The Jewish role in enterprise had been important long before the Reformation and subsequently. But an explanation is required for the prominence of the protestant non-conformists in enterprise relative to their stake in the population. For example, the smallest group of institutionally established non-conformists in Britain was the Quakers – numbering only *c*.50,000 at the end of the eighteenth-century. Yet a high proportion of the iron industry, the milling industry, and the brewing industry in London was in Quaker hands, as was perhaps 20 to 30 per cent of the transatlantic trade. Unitarians and Quakers together formed 3 to 5 per cent of the total population by the end of the eighteenth-century, and were much less significant in demographic than in enterprise terms. The largest non-conformist sect in England at this period was the Methodists (larger than all the others collectively) but scarcely a Methodist is identifiable among individually cited entrepreneurs in the eighteenth-century. No single Bristol merchant in the eighteenth century was known to have been a Methodist. As a sect, the Baptists also seemed to have low entrepreneurial potential. In the index of the famous little text book *The Industrial Revolution* (1948) by T. S. Ashton, 41 per cent of the English businessmen cited, and 49 per cent including Scotland, were non-conformists rather than Anglicans. The smallest sect, the Quakers evidently enjoyed the largest entrepreneurial commitment. Unitarians in Manchester comprised another major entrepreneurial group as industrialists more recently in the cotton industry; in Liverpool the leading sectarian merchants were also Unitarians. In the second half of the eighteenth-century, half the merchants in the West Indies and American trade in Bristol were Presbyterian. Thus, even if most merchants remained Anglicans, the minority groups had become of major importance.

No single explanation for this phenomenon is convincing. In certain instances the minorities were immigrants, and the international transfers of technology in the sixteenth, seventeenth and eighteenth-centuries usually involved the physical immigration of skilled artisans from overseas. The silk industry in London, for example, was successfully indigenized through the manual skills and dexterity of mainly Huguenot French immigrants. In the sixteenth century the same was true of most new mining technology, which came from German immigrants, while in the brewing industry, those who knew about hops and the new techniques of brewing beer (rather than ale) were continental immigrants from Flanders. Immigrants were also prominent in transfers of capital and finance in the Middle Ages with Jews and Italian bankers conducting international loan business in England. In the seventeenth century, Dutch and Portuguese Jewish immigrant bankers became prominent, with a new wave of German and Jewish immigrant bankers from the continent during the Napoleonic wars. To a certain extent, therefore, minority groups were associated with immigrants and that was associated with technical skills and technical requirements. But by itself immigration is far from complete as an explanation. Most minority groups were indigenous. All dissident religious sects (which included Roman Catholics as well as Protestant non-conformists and Jews) were formally excluded by law from holding civil or military office at national or local level in seventeenth- and eighteenth-century England. In the seventeenth century, Jews were not allowed in the retail trade. Non-Anglicans were excluded from Oxford and Cambridge, the only two universities existing in England, but were not prevented from attending universities in Scotland.

Self-exclusion or informal discrimination reinforced such legal prohibitions. Jews could not work for Christian employers, which encouraged them towards self-employed roles. Quakers would not pay tithes, as taxes supporting the Anglican Church, and would not own land that had the obligation of paying tithes. The formal exclusion from the social status given by civil office – as Members of Parliament, justices of the peace, lords lieutenant or sheriffs of counties, Members of Boards of Guardians of the Poor – brought with it a certain alienation by such sectarians from holding wealth in the form of fixed assets, particularly land. They could not participate in the normal status occupations of landed society, not being full members of this traditional elite. When wealth was being initially created in the seventeenth century, in a context of strong social alienation or even potential physical hostility in troubled times, it could be dangerous to hold wealth primarily in the form of fixed assets such as land. Mobile forms of wealth were more prudent, and it was better to be committed to the careers and the economic roles that went with that because, for a sectarian, wealth becomes the basis of independence. Wealth provides the security and the cohesion for a religious sect and for a minority group. The chapel or the meeting-house has to be owned privately and paid for by the group. Financial buttressing was not provided by officially endowed support, or long-standing assets (normally held in land). Quakers and Jews did not receive payments in public money if they became paupers. It was a point of honour that members of the community be self-sustaining: dependency might create incentives for receiving Anglican charity and thus defecting. Social consolidation in support of the sectarian way of life developed round the chapel, the meeting-house and the synagogue. Sectarian groups turned in upon themselves to consolidate as communities.

The choice of marriage partner tended to be determined by membership of the sect, not necessarily the local branch, to co-religionists. Sometimes, this was formalized through a separate language, as with the Huguenots or other immigrant groups, or by a 'ghetto' style of life in certain particulars. A formal ghetto was proposed for the Jews in London in the 1680s but never took place. Minority groups were not normally physically segregated in their place of settlement. But a sort of invisible ghetto surrounded the sectarians who stayed faithful to their religion, which remained the organizing instrument or agency, the instrument of cohesion for the group. International connections in finance and in trade offered very important advantages for minority groups established in these roles. The Jews had such long-standing links world wide from before the Reformation and operated their international connections no matter what the politics or religion of the different countries were. This was of major importance in finance because the main opportunities for making a fortune in trading in money were international, arising from transfers between governments and in foreign trade, or through the movements of money and credit associated with war, and debt arising from war and money dealings. Financial dealings were also the area where competence, trust, discretion and kinship premiums were at their highest. It was also an expanding sector as states mobilized resources on an increasing scale for the demands of war and empire.

'Networking', as we would now call it, has recently been identified as an effective technique for ensuring the passage of information and rapid communication, with ability to remain established on the frontiers of knowledge. Nothing could be more effective in networking than these international minority groups in the eighteenth century. The network – the wider group in effective communication – will always be successful compared with the solitary individual who is at arm's-length relationships with suppliers, with his banker, or even his customers. Simply being a member of the Anglican Church is not to imply the absence of a kinship network, that such persons had to operate in an individualistic way against all the other members of the Anglican Church: that is too simplistic an assumption on the

Anglican side. A complex overlapping of groupings existed, with competition between them: the relationship was not just a question of individual or small nuclear families operating against wide kinship groups consolidated with a religious bond of confidence and trust. Such relationships have to be explored empirically. The Quaker communities consolidated over far-flung trading regions, however, and formed ready made 'networks' of great efficiency.

Through their economic roles, the values of minority groups become endowed with ideology, values and motivations. The earlier debate about why Calvinism was associated with capitalism tried to fix the explanation in terms of formal theology, in terms of a person's calling justifying his existence before God in the role in this life to which he and his family had been called. A debate was cast in terms of individual religious consciousness and formal theology. Diversity of experience within Europe suggests that linkages were less direct in theological orientation, while outside the European context, quite apart from the Jewish instance, one finds minority groups identified by race and religion very often established in finance, enterprise and trading roles. The Chinese in south-east Asia, Armenians in the Near East, the Indians in East Africa, Parsees and Gujeratis in India, are instances. Equivalent social values in relation to business identified these groups. Demonstrably the same kind of enterprise roles can be associated with minority groups where religion is a cohesive force, and the 'carrier' of motivational norms and values, an identifying agency for the group but where the content of the theology, whether Buddhism or Hinduism, was totally different from any Christian theology in western Europe. This suggests that the actual theology of these minority groups was not a determinant issue but that one has to look at the sociology of religion, the social consequences of religious sectarianism, in the context of high risk and a weak institutional structure, when enterprise was a function of the private sector in the process of economic growth. Within their economic roles, the social virtues appropriate to economic and business success – sobriety, hard work, accumulation, honesty in dealing, a doctrine of calling – consolidated as motivational structures appropriate to success and the perpetuation of success. They had become associated with the practice of particular religious cults but not necessarily as a consequence of their theology.

The actual genealogical success of many of the Quakers, and Jewish and non-conformist groups itself proved a potent advantage in business. The families did not die out so frequently in the direct male line or in the wider line of collateral descendants. The significance of what was implied by 'family', if one belonged to a Quaker clan, extended to second or third cousins who remained consciously within the wider kinship group. In those Anglican nuclear families that have been documented in business, there seems to have been a propensity to a higher casualty rate simply through the failure of succession which caused business to be transferred to new owners or simply to die out with the family's genealogy. As has been argued, business tended to be helped by a wide supportive kinship group. A large family clan could rally to the partners in difficult times; cousins, who were trading allies in related functions (as customers, suppliers, or bankers) within the wider bond of trust nurtured in a sectarian group, could be mutually supportive. As mentioned above, 'networking' was built into this context.

In addition, an extensive kinship group gave partners the opportunity of choosing intelligent and committed members, rather than the stupid ones, for the succession. One of the common crises of the family firm in a small nuclear family lay in the fate of having only one male heir who was not highly motivated towards the business. In Anglican families, also, wealth (and an education among the cadets of wealthy landed families) brought greater temptations to the pursuit of non-business leisure activities than for strict Quaker or Jewish families in business. The work ethic was never a patrician or aristocratic credo and did not characterize the motivations of the landed gentry. Quaker and Jewish partnerships were ruthless in choosing younger sons or nephews or cousins within the kinship group for the succession where eldest sons had not impressed. In larger partnerships the 'non-managing' partners became a form of 'shareholders' interest', anxious to share the flow of wealth but also to maintain the profitability of the business.

Within sectarian groups, the 'marriage market' seemed to operate more efficiently, with a higher propensity for women to get married than in the population as a whole. Apart from fertility within a single marriage, members of such groups showed a propensity to take second partners when a man was widowed or a woman lost her husband by death. Given the contemporary 'life-table' context, with a high incidence of early death compared with later times, such 'contrapuntal' marriage patterns led to widely extending cousinhoods, as the briefest perusals of the genealogies for such families as Barclay, Fox, Gurney, Bevan, Hanbury or Rothschild will reveal. For those reaching a position of consolidated wealth in business there were particularly strong incentives to marry and remarry.

Such genealogical success had a personal dimension to the equation of fertility and mortality. Sufficient income for good nutrition, a healthy standard of living and good housing comprised one parameter. But, when families lived restrained and reputable lives, they did not become exposed to those surfeits of diet, pleasure and disease which were likely to ruin their physical condition or prejudice their virility and ability to have children. The habits of good living within strict and rather simple regimes, for which the Quakers and other religious minority groups were noted, were themselves highly favourable genealogically to large families.

With great wealth came a tendency to 'fall into the establishment' as it was called, with a consequent subversion of at least the stricter tenets of the earlier lifestyle. Such mutations often took place with intergenerational change. The family head who had made great wealth, whether or not a sectarian, was tempted to buy a landed estate: country-house living was one of the nicest forms of life in eighteenth-century England. The more a family was drawn into landed society, the more it was exposed to the values of a landed society, and the work ethic was not part of the traditional value systems of the aristocracy. The aristocracy (like the poor) had a leisure ethic rather than a work ethic which flourished among the 'middling orders' of society, neither at the very top nor at the very bottom. The poor identified with the aristocracy in a leisure ethic, both being passionately interested in horseracing, dogs and gambling. The bourgeois and business groups looked to a different work ethic, and a different set of values. Hence, when great wealth began to be associated with the way of life of the traditional elite, the traditional orientation towards the bourgeois virtues was put at risk. If the man who had made a fortune wanted to identify himself and his family with his betters, he would probably send his son to a major private school. The boy would grow up with the children of the older elite, of peers and landed families. If a public school was followed by Oxford or Cambridge, the social values associated with that form of education made it much less likely that the recipient would want to devote his life to hard work in business.

The attributes of motivation to business, the inculcation of the 'business virtues', the cohesive importance of kinship and religion – stressed in this discussion of minority groups – were not absent in Anglican families in enterprise. The excellent documention available for Quakers in particular (deriving from their own assiduous correspondence, diaries and genealogical concerns) has exposed the interrelationships more clearly than in the business community as a whole. They were, however, pervasive in the climate of enterprise more generally in this period.

Education

Education remains an important dimension in the study of entrepreneurs in the eighteenth-century – as in any other period. What education did business leaders themselves experience? what educational facilities did they themselves promote either as patrons or locally in relation to training their own labour force in localities where they were the main employers, creating an identification between the single employer and the single firm and the recruitment of labour? More generally, in the national context, how did education develop in response to needs emerging from the business community? In the wider sense, education has always to be seen, not just as instruction in basic skills or forms of expertise – although that was obviously an important part of its function – but as critically important for imparting values and motivations, promoting aspirations, consolidating, enhancing and seeking to perpetuate the social, cultural and religious values of the social groups sponsoring the instruction and supplying the pupils. This was necessarily the case in the absence of a state-funded national system.

Because the public schools and the two ancient universities were the preserve of the traditional elites, minority groups set up their own educational institutions at all levels, with private tutors in the family, subsequently schools when communities became above a certain size, and 'dissenting academies' as they were known. Such schools were controlled by the churches and by the sects where the young would not be at risk from having their values subverted from the true faith and the true values. Schools actively supported the mission of the religions. Beyond their religious orientation, however, educational institutions sponsored by the minority groups became important schools for inculcating the business virtues. Because these minority groups became associated with certain roles, and sought to prepare their sons for the succession to business, they were taught simple mathematics and bookkeeping, and often modern languages rather than the classical languages. Teaching skills that were going to be useful for them in later life in their economic and business roles co-existed with the fundamental purpose for the existence of those educational institutions which was to perpetuate the faith. The context of teaching in the 'dissenting academies' was significantly different from the syllabuses of the long-standing grammar schools (centred on the classics) and the old public schools, like Eton and Winchester, and also from the syllabuses which existed in Oxford and Cambridge, the former being dominated by classics and the latter, by the end of the century, by simple mathematics for the ordinary degree. In a count of the businessmen who feature in the *National Dictionary of Biography*, over half of them were identified as having attended traditional grammar schools.

Where new schools were founded in the eighteenth century under the patronage of businessmen not associated with their work-force, the 'grammar-type' of education was often oriented towards a 'modern syllabus' with mathematics, modern languages and bookkeeping. Some such schools had such an intention specified in their titles: Sir Joseph William's mathematical school in Rochester is an example. Comparable schools were established by Liverpool and Bristol merchants. 'Mathematical schools' in main port-cities taught in particular techniques of navigation (which involved the use of astronomical tables) where future careers would be at sea. The new patronage of educational establishments in the eighteenth century was clearly responding to practical needs. Scottish schools and universities (which did not deny access to sectarians) also had practical syllabuses responding to demand, because professors and tutors received most of their income from fees paid for attendance at lectures. It was not uncommon also at university level for British non-conformists to go to Leyden and one or two other Dutch universities that were safely Protestant and acceptable. For a young man destined for a business career, formal schooling was often followed by residence with the family of a fellow sectarian, often overseas, to learn the business and to be part of a household identified with the same values. Close links existed, for example, between Quaker merchant families in London, Bristol, Falmouth, Liverpool and those in Baltimore, Philadelphia or Boston. Formal schooling has to be seen in association with other forms of training, the whole context, whether formal or informal, being within the same value system.

The sort of schools which industrialists set up to train their work-forces had different objectives. In smaller localities, in the early days of large mills often sited for water power, where a single firm dominated employment in the locality, the man who owned the business had incentives to become the 'social engineer' of the community, to become a landlord, because of the need to house the work-force, and to provide other social facilities, including a school. The instruction provided was usually narrowly limited to teaching basic reading and writing skills, associated with what we would now call the encouragement of social controls, inculcating the habits of obedience, honesty and the other qualities (particularly sobriety) deemed to be useful for an employer. These were normally very basic forms of instruction. The same was true of the part-time Sunday schools, which were set up on an extensive scale under local patronage where, apart from Bible study, the aim was to enable people to read and write – but principally to read so as to have access to the Bible. This was accompanied by strong emphasis on the merits of the desirable bourgeois virtues of hard work and sobriety.

Formal education provision specifically for business, above the level of training for clerks and those who needed to know basic bookkeeping, was almost absent. Indeed, this remained the case until the twentieth century. During the first century of the evolution of an industrial economy, a similar dearth of provision applied to formal education in technical fields, such as the teaching of science relevant to progress and efficiency in the nascent chemical industry, or in engineering. Some linkages were provided through private initiatives or through Scottish universities (particularly the University of Edinburgh). But compared with the widespread teaching of chemistry at university level in Germany, or the Ecole Polytechnique in Paris (established during the Napoleonic wars), and other well-funded state institutions, Britain was bereft of education in science and technology oriented to enterprise.

The fact that management in England was not regarded as a specialized skill, and did not require formal expertise for success in the early phases of industrialization, produced a myth about the 'practical man' that was supposedly one of the admirable features of English success in business. By the mid-nineteenth century, it was widely assumed in the British business community that investment in formal training or technical education had low priority. There was no need to employ professionally trained metallurgists in the iron industry; in the chemical industry, skills could be learned on the job, without employing staff professionally qualified as university chemists. Already this was in sharp contrast to the German and the French tradition. The glorification in England of the practical man, carrying with it no consciousness of need for professional training and scientific education in the application of science to industry, became one of the profound weaknesses in the British economy in the second half of the nineteenth century and the twentieth century, as the dynamics of innovation changed. Such managerial attitudes in Britain were a hangover from the first century of industrialization where such linkages had not been a precondition for industrial success.

2

Labour and the Process of Industrialization in the First Phases of British Industrialization

Peter Mathias

Labour and the Process of Industrialization

In this chapter the role of labour as a productive factor in the economy will be the central theme. The history of labour embraces many wider issues – wages and the standard of living, social policy and social justice, labour organization – and all these relationships impinge directly on the process of growth in different ways. But the central concern for understanding processes of economic change must still be with the development of the labour market itself – with labour as a factor of production.

In discussing labour in the eighteenth-century economy many difficulties are imposed on the historian seeking to make national generalizations. It is more difficult to draw reliable national conclusions about the range of issues and relationships concerning labour than about anything else except, possibly, for debates about social attitudes. Regional variations abound; a series of 'micro' or regional economies often determined these relationships rather than a single national economy. Because of the great structural changes under way in the economy during the eighteenth century, the fortunes of different economic sectors, many very localized or regional, showed great contrasts. Large occupational groups, such as the hand spinners or the outwork bleachers, were having their positions undercut by technological change in the closing decades of the century. Tides of local migration, or the incursions of the Irish, were beginning to affect other occupational groups and regions.

At the same time, technical change was also creating demands for other skills much faster than supply was responding and inducing new occupational groups into existence. As the economy was becoming larger and more complex, so the occupational structure and society at large were growing more differentiated.

The developing relationships between handicraft and machine technology changed over time – and they were neither simple nor moving in a single direction. Where factory production was becoming directly competitive, the much higher productivity of powered machinery drove down prices to the point where handicraft artisans were reduced to penury, and a refusal to leave the trade produced a long-drawn-out social tragedy. This was so with the great army of hand-loom weavers in the generation after 1820, when steam was spreading across the weaving side of the textile industry, but, in the last quarter of the eighteenth century, the relationship was very different. In the cotton industry, the mechanization of spinning after Arkwright's successful mill of 1769, in the absence of power-weaving, created an enormous demand for hand-loom weavers. Because of the great gap in productivity between the spinning mills and the hand-loom the number of weavers grew at a faster pace and to a larger total than the spinners working the water frame and the mules. This was a symbiosis between new powered and old handicraft skills, between modern and medieval. It was more characteristic of these relationships in the growth of industry in eighteenth-century England than confrontation.

The primary side of the iron industry became characterized by large blast-furnaces and rolling mills serving a secondary metal-fabricating industry where the small workshops of the Black Country and outwork handicraft nailing predominated. Steam pumps in the mines of Cornwall and the north-east coast enabled ores and coal to be won at ever greater depths by pick-and-shovel labour. 'Domestic' industrial employment and outwork grew at a faster pace than 'large-plant' dramatic technology in the Industrial Revolution, despite the concentration of historians on the latter developments. And, paradoxically, in the capital goods industries which supplied the plant and equipment for the mass-output mines – the nascent engineering industries – the individual skilled artisan was the critical agent of economic progress. In the machine-tool workshops of Joseph Bramah and Henry Maudslay in London, the engine-making business of Boulton and Watt at Soho, and in the spawning workshops of the textile machine-makers, the steam-engine makers and the mechanical engineering industry in general, the Industrial Revolution gave birth to the triumphant reign of the skilled artisan. Looking ahead, there was to be a similar symbiotic relationship between the steam engine and the horse in nineteenth-century Britain. The railways were the greatest creators of demand for horses that had ever been known. Victorian England – for local journeys – was a horse-drawn society.

In addition to regional contrasts, commodity prices, particularly those of bulk produce, differed widely because transport costs, though falling, were still high and variable in different areas. Cyclical fluctuations from foreign trade, the investment cycle or the harvest cycle affected growing, but changing, proportions of the labour force because of the cumulative industrial changes of the period, the marginal position of the country over food supplies, and the rising stake of foreign trade in the national income. Evidence, therefore, becomes crucially determined for its significance by *time* (to which year or to which season cyclical pattern it relates) as well as by *context* (to which region and to which occupational group it relates). Structural change, and much 'localization' of such changes, probably mean that national averages and national aggregates during the first century of industrialization conceal more than in either earlier or later periods. One has neither the greater uniformity given in earlier centuries by a much more static, structurally homogeneous, more dominantly agricultural economy, nor that given nationally in later times by greater institutional and economic homogeneity – with nationally organized trades unions conducting national bargaining procedures, with fairly uniform national prices and wages, skill for skill and grade for grade.

Quantification raises a particular difficulty. Many of the issues can be resolved in an intellectually satisfying way only by quantifying them. What proportion of the labour force is benefiting, and what proportion suffering from wage, unemployment, price trends? What are the unemployment rates? And so on. As yet no reliable series exist. Employment patterns are known only in the broadest terms; changes in the volume of employment, from underemployment and unemployment of all kinds, and overtime earnings are impressionistic only; one cannot quantify payments in kind, or even their trend. Daily or weekly wage rates only are known, rather than individual earnings or, even more relevantly, family earnings per year. Price series tend to be based on the wholesale, long-term, contract prices of institutional purchasing mainly in the south of England rather than on local, retail prices in different regions. Cost-of-living index calculations are bedevilled by variations in prices as well as in the 'basket of goods', with marked regional variations in diet, rent, fuel costs and the like, and also with changes in the exact content and quality of goods in the 'basket' over time.

I confess that I do not see answers to many of these inadequacies apart from building up a series of micro-studies of the relevant groupings – by industry, locality or occupational group – and hoping in time to establish a pattern or representative samples from which better-grounded generalizations may at last be drawn. Because of all these limitations very generalized comments only can be made.

Looking at the role of labour in the process of British industrialization at the end of the eighteenth century, the most important conclusion must be – despite all qualifications about inefficiency in the deployment, the attitudes and the utilization of labour – that labour supplies showed great elasticity, that constraint came more from the problem of skills, or of inefficient utilization, than from any aggregate labour shortage *per se*.

The extent of the responsiveness (or 'slackness') in the peace-time labour market is evidenced by reactions to the great demands for labour imposed by the armed forces during the Napoleonic Wars. It seems that 400,000 to 500,000 men were drawn into the armed services relatively quickly, and many thousands more not in uniform were working in directly supporting occupations. The Navy had 10,000 to 20,000 men on strength up to 1792. By 1795 there were 100,000 men on the muster rolls and, by 1800, 130,000. The merchant-shipping fleets were employing 100,000 to 110,000 seamen in the 1790s. Thus, requirements for seamen more than doubled. The 1790s were also years of increasing food prices – with new famine conditions in 1744–5 and 1799–1800. Money wage rates in agriculture advanced by 50 per cent between 1793 and 1800; those of London artisans by 15 per cent; and real wages fell. Thus, wage rates were moved by 'cost push' as well as 'demand pull': it was not just the supply situation which forced up rates. In the labour market for skilled seamen – the epicentre of the manpower crisis focused on the Newcastle-to-London coal-run – there was greater reaction. Wages per voyage were £3.0 to £3.13s. in peace time in the early 1790s. From 1794 to 1798 they were £5 per voyage and built up to £11.11s. per voyage in April 1800.

The broad facts of population increase, emphasized in the areas where employment needs were expanding fastest, and of local mobility, lay behind this responsiveness. The main evidence for elasticity in labour supplies is in the relatively slight movements in wage rates – as distinct from earnings – over long periods of 20 years or more, grade for grade, when translated against the considerable changes in progress in the economy during these same decades. It is not a question of wage rates being unresponsive in the longer term. Wage rates doubled in Lancashire in the course of the second half of the century as this industrializing region, with some others in the Midlands and North, became high-wage areas on a level with London, from being low-wage areas in the first decades of the century – lower than agricultural countries in the south and west. The trend of basic wage rates, however, was to move from one plateau to another rather than to vary from year to year. The 1770s had seen wage rates rise to a new plateau (doubtless also encouraged by the demands of the forces in the American War of Independence in taking men off the labour markets). From 1780 to 1795 internal demand was being extended more by population increase, by increases in earnings from a rising volume of employment, and by a relative change in the structure of employment towards high-wage sectors and high-wage regions, than by rising wage rates within each sector.

A rise in wage costs (as distinct from wage rates) did not curb the process of growth in industrializing regions – more particularly in a context of rapid technical change in growth sectors, such as cotton and iron, which brought falling real costs per unit of output or per man of the labour force through higher productivity of labour, and probably higher profits to allow for higher productivity of labour, and probably higher profits to allow for higher investment and more technical change. Clearly, this is a 'happy circle' with higher wage rates not leading to higher wage costs. Export-oriented industries were not inhibited by labour shortages increasing wage costs, and hence prices in export markets. Rather, there is the clear recognition by commentators that technical change and higher productivity of labour – and improvements in the quality of labour in Britain – were at last making a high-wage economy (for example, in comparison with continental wage levels, in France, Italy and elsewhere) compatible with low export prices; thus allowing for the first time compatibility in the drive for exports and an extending home demand. Previously the whole weight of public policy, traditional attitudes and the broad facts of the context conspired to argue for *low* wages to allow *low* prices in export markets. In handicraft industries, wage costs (with raw material costs) were the highest constituent of total costs and, in circumstances of broad stability in techniques – or a very slowly rising level of techniques – they tended to be an inflexible proportion of total costs.

Evidence exists of greater labour mobility after 1780. Local variations in wages were being reduced, whether the town/country differential or the north/south differential. At the same time, and connected with this trend, local migration flows were increasing with urbanization. Less than half the inhabitants of large towns counted in the 1811 census had been born there. This mobility created an increasing impact on wage levels in the 'exit' areas: with greater mobility of labour as a factor of production came a greater equalization of its price in different areas, grade for grade and skill for skill. Major regional variations remained for much of the nineteenth century, however, in agriculture and in industry.

This process of mobilization of labour, of determining wage levels, was influenced only marginally by public policy. By the end of the century, only the debris of the old system of price and wage fixing by the Justices survived, in marginal pockets, such as the Spitalfields weavers or the coal 'whippers' on the Thames. The disappearance from the statute book of these legal restrictions and others enshrined in the Elizabethan Statute of Apprentices was paradoxically encouraged by the efforts of local trade societies to invoke these legal interferences with the market in favour of labour during the years of great dearth in 1794–5 and 1799–1800. Even the old medieval laws against 'forestalling, regrating and engrossing' were being dusted off again, with local magistrates often showing great sympathy for the poor in these symbolic ways. They had originally been used, of course, principally in an attempt to keep wages down: when invoked to pull wages up, Parliament quickly took a different view of their utility.

The Settlement Laws, under which poor-relief qualifications applied only within the parish of a family's birth, do not seem to have acted as a serious brake against mobility. They may indeed have prejudiced settlement in a neighbouring agricultural parish, and the records of the local Guardians of the Poor are studded with individual instances of removal and the fetching back of those denied a settlement elsewhere, but this may have induced would-be migrants to press on to a non-agricultural context, to the nearest town, or part, or mining area or to industrial employment, rather than to have inhibited mobility in the first place. Judged by results, the evidence of mobility is inescapable. The differential in wage rates and the differential in the offer of work were the operational factors. The same may be said about the Speenhamland system of supplementing wages by poor relief, which spread into some of the agricultural countries in the south, from Berkshire, after 1795, in response to the short-term crisis of famine prices. The national influence of this was restricted initially – but it subsequently acted as a certain deterrent to labour mobility in the rural areas where it survived as a long-term measure, rather than a short-term emergency response to high food prices in 1794–6.

Something should be said here also about labour attitudes affecting labour supplies – in conceptual terms the 'backward-sloping supply curve' for labour where the response to higher money wages was to work less. Much has been made of this by moralistic eighteenth-century commentators, and some present-day observers, noticing the more immediate impact of higher money wages in some very poor countries in the developing world. It is very doubtful how widespread this response was in late eighteenth-century England, at least as a long-term characteristic of market behaviour. Such a motivational structure was more a characteristic of a static, subsistence economy, where consumption margins were very limited and patterns of consumption highly conventional at a basic level, where a distributive system was vestigial and the range of consumer products very small. Such attitudes, moreover, were encouraged by a context where 'disposable' income above bare subsistence needs remained erratic, so that it could be socially dangerous to develop habits of regular higher consumption and greater regular commitments in purchasing – in short it could be a rational, defensive mechanism. Arthur Young and Malthus, among others, certainly assumed that high wages reduced the offer of work by the poor because of 'leisure-preference'. After carefully considering the issue, Adam Smith rejected 'leisure-preference' as a national generalization although he acknowledged that it might exist to some degree in local circumstances. This was likely to appear in the short run – for example, after a bonanza harvest – before the taste for wider consumption patterns caught up with the anticipation of continuing higher money income. Such attitudes existed more widely among the pockets of most depressed casual labourers in the docks, the most depressed 'poor relief' agricultural families, the 'voluntarily unemployed' or 'semi-employed', among some of the Irish and mining communities and long survived as such.

Inherited traditional patterns of consumption may well have influenced the pattern of spending more than leisure-preference as such; in particular, beyond a fairly restricted range of consumer spending, surplus cash was poured away into liquor. When the higher money wages of urban, industrial and mining employment were translated against traditional spending patterns, then social chaos could result in the short term. The isolated character of many mining communities with limited retailing facilities, encouraged this response, particularly after paydays, and in good times when piece-rates were high and 'bull-weeks' were worked. In the new context of life and work, the money wage was the sole defence against destitution – the sole means for all retail purchasing, weekly rent payments, and the sole safeguard in case of dependency for any cause, accident, sickness, old age, trade depression or any other interruption of work. Money, in terms of cash, did not tend to have this same unique importance in the older context of rural putting-out industry or agriculture or living-in servants with greater chances of some buttressing against the cash nexus–some payments in kind, a garden, perhaps a holding big enough for a pig or a cow, possibly a rent-free cottage. In the more starkly proletarian context, with a purely cash and debt nexus, affecting a rising proportion of families, much greater social sanctions were needed against squandering cash incomes in socially irresponsible ways. Quite new norms of self-discipline in the context of living were required, as they were needed to an increasing extent in the new context of work.

If one looks at the modern 'norm' of employment, some of the inefficiencies in the deployment of labour in the eighteenth century become at once apparent. The criteria would include: regularity of work, regularity of payment, weekly payments in cash (individually, in coin of the realm), an individual contract with an employer, a concept of 'unemployment', or a *rate* of unemployment (which is conceptually meaningful only in relation to a concept of full employment). Such clear-cut differentiation was certainly not characteristic of the eighteenth century and, even without a 'backward-sloping supply curve for labour', the great inefficiency in the deployment of labour within the eighteenth-century context points the contrast with these modern norms. The chapter on labour in T. S. Ashton's *Economic History of the Eighteenth Century* gives an eloquent review of these themes.

Most people knew underemployment and intermittent earnings. Even though greater trend regularity developed through the structural changes in industry, agriculture and the services sector in the century, this was interrupted by the greater impact of short-term fluctuations. Seasonal unemployment, periods of idleness in storm, flood, drought or frost, affected large occupational groups. Malting and brewing were seasonal (brewing unusually so in that production was usually stopped during the summer rather than the winter). Much construction work was at a low ebb during the winter; most shipping did not operate during the worst winter months (this had changed on the Newcastle to London coal run by the 1790s), with much less activity in the ports; little fishing was done; there was not much which could be done on the land in arable farming in the wet months from November to March. 'Single-role' employment was scarcely the norm in many areas, in part because of such discontinuities; there was much casual labour in the countryside and in the towns, much extra temporary work at harvest time, both in the villages and with urban people going into the hop-gardens and fruit farms, while seasonal migrants from Ireland also followed the harvest in East Anglian cereal areas. 'Putting-out' work was diffused through agricultural areas, particularly in non-cereal regions. Even the factory owners could not hold their labour force together at harvest time.

The family context of self-imposed work discipline in the domestic trades encouraged the inefficient, less specialized, deployment of labour. Exaggerated rhythms of intense work followed by periods of idleness over the course of a week, with a long weekly tramp to the putter-out's warehouse, did the same. The great problems of creating work discipline in the new industrial context, when co-ordination of work rhythm and regularity was demanded in factory employment, produced formidable sanctions imposed against drunkenness, indiscipline, labour turnover and the like. Such sanctions – against drunkenness, in particular – were self-imposed within the work group in such cases as printing or mining where group earnings could be threatened by indiscipline, and not just imposed upon workers by ruthless bosses. Equally with pay: the infrequency of payments, irregularity of reward, payment in truck or claims on the 'tommy-shop' of the employer, group-payment in large denomination coin or paper prevented clear-cut transactions, encouraged debt and credit and thoroughly merged the pay and the loan functions. Payment in kind, assumed perquisites and straight embezzlement of materials owned by the employer did not have sharp frontiers. Clear-cut differentiation of roles, had circumstances allowed, would have enabled greater discrimination and the more efficient deployment of labour. It would also have offered the workers as well as the employer, greater protection against being cheated, and made possible public regulation in their defence more feasible.

The differentiation of employer-employee roles was not clear-cut – even within the cotton factories. Employers offered 'family employment' in the early years, with subordinate roles for wives and children. The 'putting-out' system construed this in an explicit way with the employer removed from direct responsibility for work intensity, hours, conditions, place of work or wages. All payment was by the piece or by the stint. Even in large-plant units much subcontracting took place. Mine owners leased concessions to 'butty masters' who then took on groups of workers; mill owners took on families; skilled cotton spinners' societies determined their own recruiting rules; in agriculture there was 'gang work' at harvest time. In all such modes of labour organization, payment passed from the employer to the foreman, or gang leader, or parent, who then subdivided according to convention or agreed rules which were not predetermined by the employer.

The offer of labour, particularly of women's and children's labour, raises special issues. With much underemployment on the land, in agriculture, and low real income (despite improvement in the course of the century), very great pressure existed for families to supplement earnings wherever possible, and for such unskilled supplementary earnings by women and children to be rewarded even more marginally than men's wages in agriculture. The problem pressing on the poor in such a context was felt to be the *shortage* of women's and children's labour. The age-structure of the population added to the burden. As population rose, principally by an increase in marriages, fertility and the number of births, so the proportion of dependants in the population increased; and the burden of young children for poor families. The proportion of those aged below 15 and above 60 in relation to those in the working age-group, 15–60 was 82 per cent in 1700–50, and rose to 94 per cent in 1800, and to 100 per cent in 1826. Expressed as a percentage of the whole population, those in the non-working age-groups – young and old – rose from 45 percent in 1700 to 48 per cent in 1800 and to 50 percent in 1826. Thus, at the same time as wage rates and the disposable national income were low, a high proportion of dependants existed in the population. A large family, with its head an unskilled labourer facing erratic employment, could very commonly stave off want only by child labour and poor relief. A rising population, particularly if the mechanism was an increased birth rate and an increased survival rate for babies and young children, thus sharply increased the inducements for children's and women's labour – and a long tradition of philanthropists could see only virtue in this, which removed moral sanctions against the practice and the prospect of legislation. Judged against other societies, perhaps in retrospect the unusual thing is that the women's role in agriculture was so limited in England.

Children's and women's labour are one example of the generalization that many work practices and conditions of employment spreading through the rising industrial sector were straight transfers from a 'pre-industrial' context and a 'pre-industrial' tradition. The opportunities for such sustained, 'externally' directed, large-group labour for women and children scarcely existed in the 'pre-industrial' context, in contrast to the new spinning mills and mines, but no social, moral or any other kind of sanctions existed against it. The 12-hour shifts, for example, existed in the first large-scale silk-throwing mill set up by Thomas Lombe in Derby in 1718; and the worst examples of long hours, evil conditions, harshness of treatment and miserliness of reward in the new context were matched by the old-style workshop and putting-out trades (where they were to survive much longer than in the new-style factories).

Family labour was another bridge between the old and new contexts of employment. The concept of individual employer/employee contractual relationships proved unreal in many contexts. It existed in law but the social reality was often very different. Family units entered mine and textile factories much as in the old 'household' economy, with children working for their mothers or fathers, 'piecing', tying threads, and doing other subordinate jobs. The adult migrant came to mills – with his family. In 1801–2, at Robert Peel's mill at Bury, 95 out of 136 employees belonged to 26 families. Relatively few of this labour force were skilled adult males. This tendency was enhanced, of course, as industrial communities grew up as small rural entities based on a single mill on sites determined by the availability of water power. When mills grew in number and the small communities expanded into fast-growing industrial towns, the kinship links within individual mills would not be as prominent.

Colliery 'butty' masters contracted with families as did mill owners. It resembled more leasing a concession than direct individual employment. This 'family' earning and subcontracting tradition in the mill and the mine reinforced the child-labour tradition. In such a context, children worked of necessity the same hours as their parents. At the end of this period came the first wave of protest: not from workers, but from 'external' critics: humanitarians, doctors, Tory radicals. The response to this, Peel's Factory Act of 1802, applied only to pauper apprentices in the textile mills outside the kinship system, upon whom family discipline could not be imposed. The fact that discipline was imposed largely still within kinship groups made the harshness of new regimes in the mills socially tolerable and, at the same time, extremely resistant to external legal interference.

Trade societies also tried to consolidate the kinship system in spinning mills. Only children, or relatives or nominees of the adult skilled spinners, could be accepted for training as skilled spinners: they operated very much of a local 'franchise' within broad parameters determined by the owner. This strangely resembled the conventions in the servant hierarchy in the large houses, where the housekeeper or the butler effectively 'hired' and 'fired' the subordinate kitchen or house-maintenance staff (not so much the personal servants of the family) rather than the owner. Usually mill owners were not themselves directly responsible for hiring their work-force, which gave great authority to the foreman or overseer (particularly for the unskilled workers).

Combinations and Collective Action

By the end of the eighteenth century, local combinations were universal in skilled trades, both long-standing traditional occupations and the new skills evolving in the industrial revolution, wherever the unit of employment was a group affair. Local combinations of a new sort, unconnected with the heritage of medieval guilds in long-established city industries, appeared among skilled workers in the textile trades in the early eighteenth century. They were virtually confined to skilled adult males. Shipwrights in dockyards, printers, compositors, papermakers, millwrights, skilled workers in textile trades such as wool-combers, hatters and tailors, all had their societies. Spinning societies appeared in the cotton mills as early as the 1780s, within a decade of Arkwright's innovations. All these were confined to the 'aristocracy of labour'. The rudimentary 'tramping-artisan' system for the skilled printers at the end of the century on their way looking for work between the 'chapels' of different towns, implied quite widespread local societies. An investigation in 1806 into the woollen industry revealed universal, open organization, regular correspondence between different regions, a paid secretary, concerted petitioning to Westminster and concerted action against recalcitrant employers not willing to pay the going rate.

These groups remained responsible bodies on the whole, not being much seduced by visionary hotheads. They sought direct, limited, practical ends, and were aimed as much to defend their position against incursions from below as against pressure from employers above. They enjoyed status, savings and bargaining power at the local level in the short run. They sought to enforce apprenticeship restrictions, exclude 'foreigners' from the trade, restrict the numbers of apprentices and set limits to those who were to become apprentices, often refusing entrance on principle to Irishmen. Their entrance fees were quite high – 10s.6d. for some Lancashire skilled spinners' societies – which represented half a week's earnings. The weaknesses of these societies were apparent. Only a small percentage of many of these artisans worked in organized groups, in comparison with the large population of the self-employed (in the case of such tradesmen as carpenters, tailors, millwrights). No control over access could exist in such circumstances. With printers, compositors and papermakers the case was different. But still, in the long run, they had only very limited powers, and as effective bargaining forces at the local level, they tended to be the temporary flowers of the good employment position at the top of the boom period of a trade cycle, which withered at the touch of a trade depression. Technological change also undercut many strongly entrenched positions, such as that of the printers in the face of steam-driven rotary presses. It remains doubtful whether these organizations had any effect on the long-run level of wages.

Collective reaction to technical change in an attempt to destroy it – Luddism – was a much less characteristic form of protest in the eighteenth century than food riots and, as with agrarian violence, it was principally confined to the short run, often being integrated with a response to bad years of employment and high food prices. As with food riots, such violence tended to be local, spreading quickly along certain routes but not being a generally diffused phenomenon, and limited to individual years or two years together rather than proving endemic over time. Yet many instances occurred at such times – in 1766, 1794–5, 1799–1800, 1812, 1816.

The main objective was to improve wages in handicraft industries. Although pressures built up from particular technological competition, the timing of acute distress was usually occasioned by trade conditions in the short run. Luddism did not characterize workers' response to technological change as a whole: aspects of the context *other* than the technology in question are critical for understanding outbreaks of violence expressed against new technology. When new technology was associated with the spread of a new industry and new employment, in the absence of already established industry, little opposition was encountered from workers in such localities (rural landlords and farmers were sometimes not so enthusiastic about competitive employment opportunities spreading through their localities). But where particular advances in technology were perceived as threatening the family-based economy or particularly entrenched handicraft skills, then discontents could be easily focused. The handicraft cloth 'croppers' identified shearing frames and 'gig' mills as their enemy; artisans operating the old narrow stocking frames in Nottinghamshire attacked the new 'cut-up' stocking frames. Even these outbreaks were confined to certain localities however, while just a few miles away other localities or individual mills remained untouched. Given the 'patchy' incidence of Luddism spatially and over time, it is doubtful how great were the general constraints it imposed upon the diffusion of new technology. And technology which was seen as a threat today then became defended as traditional tomorrow.

In certain respects, Luddism should be seen as a particular manifestation of a wider tradition of 'collective bargaining by riot'. In extreme conditions of the market, especially with famine prices of food, medieval regulations against the free operation of market forces were invoked by workers as well as by magistrates, in the effort to limit price rises. In reality, however, such attempts to intimidate all those in the market chain, such as shop keepers, grain merchants and millers, would have the result of keeping supplies from flowing through to the shops and markets and thus intensify the scarcities. Attempts to destroy toll-houses along turnpike roads (which featured in the Rebecca riots in Wales in 1838, and in local outbreaks of violence long before) had a similar objective. While reducing food prices in towns, improved, lower-cost transport did tend to equalize food prices over the catchment area of the market, which meant the possibility of increasing prices in the rural localities of supply. But, again, the more general effects of cutting transport links would have been disastrous for the poor (in supplies of food and fuel) in the wider context.

Where the legal position in common law remained in doubt, in the absence of specific determination of the general issues by statute, attempts were made to breathe new life into the ancient prohibitions against 'forestalling, regrating and engrossing', particularly during the years of high food prices during the French Wars. Any intermediaries in the chain of commercial dealings between farmer and retailer (particularly where stocks were being held) were targets for such changes. In addition, where the position of traditional artisans was perceived to be at risk, apprenticeship regulations, rules setting the maximum number of journeymen per master, and controls imposed in the interest of preserving the quality of goods through the guilds were dusted off. Even Tudor wage regulations, originally deployed in the interests of employers to keep wages down, were reactivated to protect employers against inflation, together with demands that the 'just price' be re-instituted to control market forces. Thus, in troubled times until the nineteenth century, the distant trumpets of medieval and Tudor corporatism were heard again – but the walls of market capitalism were never breached.

Apart from occasionally seeking to test free-market assumptions in the courts, the search for norms against which to challenge the verdict of the market-place was justified by the concept of what was 'fair' or 'unfair'. In this sense, a 'moral economy', in the words of Edward Thompson, was certainly invoked – characterized by the demand for 'fairness'. The exact derivatives of such a concept were relative rather than absolute, regional or local rather than national, being much determined by the circumstances of the specific local context, but nonetheless it had widely accepted constituents. 'Fairness' constituted levels of expectation drawn from precedents, the experience of past times refracted through memories and the assurances of older persons about how things 'always used to be'. The subjective interpretations of traditional standards were prominent in such assertions, as the past was invoked as a means of justifying protests against the present. A return to accustomed expectations was a more prominent objective than the anticipation of a Utopian future.

Relativities with neighbouring groups and occupations provided other bases for desired norms. In retrospect, demands can be seen more as moderate than as extreme. 'Fairness', as a concept, needed then, as now, to carry public opinion in support if it was to establish credibility and provide a norm for the legitimation of demands – and the wider the public whose sympathy was sought, the less extreme needed to be the claims. Capturing the middle ground upon which to establish a convincing claim of 'being fair' is still, in our day, a prime concern where public opinion is influential in political or labour disputes. Thus, moderation in claims became a necessary condition for bidding for and maintaining support in adversity among related occupations and local groups, where the legal, economic and political context was hostile. Claims were often formulated in relation to 'the custom of the trade', apart from local memories, with much industry being very localized for exact comparability. Moderation also characterized the consequences of illegal actions: when grain supplies were seized by local mobs in food riots, the response was often to sell parcels at the 'fair' or 'traditional' price rather than outright looting.

Such manifestations of social violence and public disorder in the eighteenth-century were not so much characterized by opposition to 'capitalist' relationships *per se* in the economy. These had existed in the outwork industries for several generations, without benefit of machine technology, as well as in capital-intensive economic activities such as iron, glass, or main sections of the mining industry. The same was true of agriculture and shipping. In all these fields an 'industrial proletariat' long predated the factory system: workers without the ownership of the means of production (save only for simple tools) were employed in the main for money wages (doubtless supplemented by perquisites). Nor was social protest simply against technological change – as we have seen, this response was erratic in its incidence, and the new technology introduced amid opposition in certain circumstances became exactly that which was defended by established working-class interests at a later date. Violence and law breaking were much more responses to the short-run phenomena: short harvests and increases in the price of bread, surges in unemployment and short time. The context of work was more important even in explaining Luddism than the technology of work, which provided a focusing agent for protest. A much greater incidence of turbulence, social protest and violence characterized earlier centuries and continental contexts where capitalistic structures and market relationships were much less in evidence. In economic terms, judging results against objectives, attempts to hold back the tide of change were not effective and remained, in the main, backward looking.

3

Women and Work in Britain, *c*.1870–World War I

Pat Thane

This chapter is centrally concerned with the activity of women in the paid labour market. We must also, however, be aware of the importance of unpaid female labour as inputs into the economy in the household, in agriculture and in a variety of family businesses, difficult though these are to quantify.

There are indeed serious obstacles to quantifying paid female work. The decennial censuses, which are a major source for quantifying occupational status, substantially under-recorded part-time, casual and seasonal work, in which many, especially married, women were engaged, just as they underrecorded the work of women who were occupied alongside their husbands in shops, small businesses or farms. Nor are they wholly reliable guides to full-time paid employment, even in factories. The census is an extremely valuable source, but only if used with close attention to what was actually being recorded and to possible omissions.[1] It is important to distinguish between the information it can and cannot accurately provide. It can, for example, probably give an accurate guide to the numbers of full-time female schoolteachers, married and unmarried, because members of such an occupational group were likely to record themselves and to be recorded accurately, being educated, generally full-time workers and with little ambiguity about their occupational status. It was, as we shall see, a poor guide to the much larger category of domestic servants. An entirely accurate picture of Victorian female paid labour may be one of the important sets of historical data that we shall never possess; though local, including business, records may enable us to build up a reasonably accurate picture for specific firms, occupations or districts.

There is no reason to doubt, however, that the largest female paid occupation – indeed, the largest single occupational group, male or female – was domestic service. But there is serious reason to doubt certain widely held assumptions relating to it, in particular that the British employed significantly more servants in this period than their European neighbours, and that the number of servants was falling by the end of the century. In the 1871 census the number of paid domestics in Britain may have been inflated by as much as one-third, due to the enumerators' practice of categorizing as 'house-keeper' or 'servant working at home' women living at home and participating in the household labour who were most unlikely to have been paid for their labour or to have performed paid domestic service in any other household at any time. The Registrar General's office was aware of this problem and sought, census by census, to make a more careful distinction between paid and unpaid labour. Hence what has appeared as a late-century decline in the servant population may be, rather, the census achieving greater precision.

This suggests that there is also little substance in another well-established assumption: that servants were not merely useful, but also an item of conspicuous consumption, an indicator of status, possession or non-posses-sion of a servant indicating the barrier between working and middle class, of whom households bought as many as they could afford. Recent evidence suggests that servant-keeping was often determined by need and is not a secure indicator of status. Relatively wealthy families containing enough fit grown females to perform household tasks did not always employ living-in servants (though they may have employed non-resident daily or other 'help', undetectable in census records) Relatively poor artisan families, containing children or other dependants and no adult female other than the mother, could, and did, employ workhouse girls for little more than their board.

Most servants worked as the sole general servant in a not very wealthy household, hence the harshness of their working lives. It was certainly an unpopular occupation from which women escaped at the first opportunity to any acceptable alternative, especially if they were town dwellers. Unmar-ried women of rural origin were most likely to become servants, probably because they lacked the skills or the contacts which might give them access to alternative urban occupations.[2] Jobs in the cotton textile factories, for example, were often obtained through family and neighbourhood contacts. Lack of freedom and companionship, or petty mistreatment by employers in the immensely variable environments in which servants worked, could drive them to leave even for relatively worse-paid jobs. And many women hated the subservience required. 'I couldn't bow and scrape' was one reason for leaving.[3] Hannah Mitchell, a country girl, left her post in service in the town, aged 16, to earn less, an inadequate 8s per week in a dressmaking shop, because it gave her more control over her own life, the opportunity to make friends and her Sundays free for reading – changes which, despite a period of near-starvation, she never regretted.[4]

The serious deficiencies in data concerning women's activity in the paid labour market have consequences for estimates of productivity in the economy as a whole. These include overestimates of labour inputs into segments of the service sector, such as domestic service, and underestimates of others, such as part-time laundry work. More importantly, the female input into agriculture has been underestimated as has that into a range of consumer goods industries which were expanding rapidly in the later nineteenth and early twentieth centuries. The garment industry, for example, was heavily dependent upon female 'sweated' labour, working either seasonally or hidden as outworkers in their own homes.

But, so far as it can been estimated, what paid work did women do? Women's paid employment has historically appeared to be at higher levels in Britain than elsewhere in western Europe. In this period, however, this may be a statistical reflection of the higher and earlier level of urbanization reached in Britain by the 1870s compared with her European neighbours, and the near absence of a peasant farming sector to which women were often statistically unnoticed contributors in other countries.

Despite the problems of precise quantification, domestic service, as already suggested, was the largest female paid occupation. The next largest was textiles, followed by the clothing industry which expanded factory and workshop production in this period. This was followed by agriculture and then by a host of minor trades, among which the pottery industry was prominent in the employment of females. Women were indeed employed in a wide variety of manual occupations.

From the 1870s 'white-collar', tertiary-sector employment expanded significantly, notably at the lower levels, with the growing scale of business and the consequent need for larger clerical and administrative staffs and the growth in local and central government. This was accompanied by changes in office technology and the creation of new skilled occupations, as typists, telephonists, telegraphists, for example. The education and health services also expanded, with the growth of state and private provision. All demanded labour power possessing a certain level of education which was not available in sufficient quantities exclusively among males. Hence, increasing numbers of women were recruited into respectable, but low-level, occupations, often at levels below their educational attainment and with minimal opportunities for career advancement because it was the only source of socially acceptable independent occupation open to them. The expansion of retailing and the emergence of the large department store in towns and cities provided another new source of respectable, and closely regulated, employment.[5]

Much more gradually, women acquired, against strong opposition, access to higher levels of training and education and to higher-status occupations. Certain sectors of the higher civil service opened up to them from the mid-1890s (they could, for example, become lady factory inspectors, inspecting only female working conditions) and they had to resign civil service posts on marriage. In the early 1870s, the medical register was opened to them, though there were still only 212 female doctors by 1901. They made their way fastest in occupational sectors not occupied by men (such as nursing) or for which males with appropriate skills were in short supply (as with clerical and secretarial work.)

Why did women, especially married women with children, work for payment? The answer is complex and varied with class, region, custom and individual and family preference. In the late-Victorian middle class increasing numbers of young women sought independence and escape from social norms that prescribed domesticity as their sole role.[6] Also, females outnumbered males in the population. In 1871 there were 11,653,100 females in England and Wales and 11,058,900 males; in 1911 18,624,900 to 17,445,600. In consequence, significant numbers of women could not expect to marry, the more so due to the higher propensity of middle- and upper-class men to remain bachelors than has been the case since World War I. Women who faced, or chose, the possibility that they would not marry did not wish to remain idle and dependent, nor could many middle-class families afford to keep them so, though others strenuously opposed their daughters entering independent employment. It should not be assumed that opposition to female careers was universal in the later Victorian middle class. It was stated in a leader in the respectable, if liberal-minded, *Daily Telegraph* in 1888:

> The idea that a woman is born either to lounge through life as a lady or to drudge through it as a poor man's wife with, in both cases, narrowed domestic interest is a superstition having its origins in the east. Women have souls and aspirations of their own and if ... they possess personal talents or tastes we see nothing to object to in their entry into a fair and free labour market.[8]

The *Telegraph* was then an expanding middle-class newspaper, anxious to satisfy its growing market, and it is unlikely that it would have expressed such views in a leader had they not been appealing to a significant sector of its readership (including the female readership for which newspapers were at this time competing). Indeed, for two weeks following the publication of the leader, letters poured in response expressing almost every imaginable view. Surprisingly typical was that of a London 'City merchant' who claimed to have employed women in his office for years. He wrote:

... if the movement of women working for themselves goes forward, as all true men wish, thousands of women will be far too enlightened and circumstances will not make it necessary for them to rush into ties of matrimony without due consideration ... let mothers bring up their daughters to think that it is lowering to their womanhood to look upon matrimony as the 'one thing needful', that if they have not a dependency they must work ... are there no fathers who repent the day they saw their daughters marry? And how often do we not hear married women advise their sisters to 'keep as they are'? If a woman can marry a worthy man, by all means let her do so, but with a profession or trade behind her she can look before she leaps.[9]

Middle- and upper-class women would very rarely work for payment after marriage and, as already suggested, in certain occupations such as the civil service and teaching, they were prohibited from doing so.

Most working-class and lower-middle-class women worked before marriage and very many working-class women did so at least intermittently thereafter. It is reasonable to assume that many of them did so due to material necessity, because husbands were dead, deserted, and / or underemployed, disabled or low paid. But definitions of necessity above the level of starvation were variable, and patterns of married women's work were also influenced by the local economy, local custom, the family life-cycle, domestic routine, by the husband's attitude and occupation and by the individual responses and experiences of women. As one woman told the social investigator Clementina Black in 1904: 'A shilling of your own is worth two that *he* gives you'.[10] Black convincingly described the process whereby for some women working, which began as necessity, became over time habit and a source of comfort, companionship and independence even when the husband's earnings improved. Also some women might continue to work to save to educate their children, to get a better house or for other goals.

In the Potteries married women who did not contribute to the family income were regarded as 'lazy' and 'The figure of the totally dependent woman is not easily discovered'. The rhythm of work on the potbanks, with frequent breaks in production, the tradition of self-imposed work routines and the close proximity of home and work eased the integration of domestic and paid labour, as did a certain local acceptance of role sharing between the sexes in the home.[11]

In the Leicester hosiery industry it was taken for granted that married women would work.[12] In Preston, a town with exceptionally stable work opportunities for women in weaving, in 1881 the wives of relatively well-paid skilled and supervisory workers worked in significant numbers though it cannot have been necessary to keep their families from starvation. Indeed, the wives of lower-paid, irregularly employed men in Preston were less likely to be recorded in the census as being in employment. They may well, however, have engaged in the low-paid, casual labour which was least likely to appear in the census.[13]

The irregularity of work and pay that was inadequate for full support of a family experienced by many, perhaps most manual workers, even in skilled jobs, in the period explains why many women worked at least at certain points in their marriage. Timing was also influenced by the age of their children. The norm was the reverse of today: women were more likely to work when children were young and demands upon the family resources greatest, giving up, often with relief when the children were old enough to earn; though they had sometimes to return to the labour market at a later age, when the children left home and the husband, if still alive, was experiencing declining earning power. Faced with the grimness of the double burden in late-Victorian conditions, women often saw giving up paid work, rather than entry to it, as liberation.

The acquisition of additional household resouces, by one means or another, by the wife, was for many women an extension of the role of household manager and inseparable from it; their paid and unpaid work roles were complementary rather than opposed. The former might include taking in lodgers,[14] or laundry, or running a small shop from the home as well as 'going out to work'. It appeared to contemporaries that, by the end of the century, fewer married women were in paid work, but the precise extent and distribution of this decline are unclear. It is certainly arguable that, in households which could acquire sufficient to meet their immediate needs from other sources, unless the wife was in the rare situation of being able to earn substantially, it made more sense for her to devote herself to managing the household. She might better maximize the living standards of the family through careful management, including shrewd shopping, skill with the needle and judicious use of the pawnbroker.[15] Her skill in extracting maximum value from the household resources—her role as 'chancellor of the domestic exchequer', as contemporaries often described it – was a vital determinant of its standard of living and of its outward respectability and status.

The type of paid work available to women was generally, though not invariably, strictly demarcated from that open to men. There were shifts in the lines of demarcation over time, however, and the determinants of the gender division of labour were complex. Technological change, in the direction of increased automation of work processes, was sometimes accompanied by the replacement of male with cheaper female labour. Examples of this do not seem to have been frequent but nor have they been exhaustively researched. It was not necessarily in the employer's interest to do so if, for example, it might lead to higher labour turnover due to the tendency of women to leave upon marriage; to loss of the benefit of an experienced, long-staying work-force; or to serious conflict with male workers threatened with displacement or because men were actually more productive because of greater age and experience on the job. A complex of all of these influences appears to have kept women out of cotton spinning in Lancashire, despite considerable technological change.[16] A similar picture appears in the factory hosiery industry.[17] In Glasgow cotton spinning, however, another major centre, after the failure of a strike in 1837, employers did drive men out of the occupation which became thereafter a female preserve. This seems to have been possible partly because of the growing availability of alternative employment for men in the region, in mining, metal-working and building, which diminished their resistance to displacement from spinning. Up to that point men had been largely engaged in Glasgow cotton-spinning, even though it was lower paid than in Lancashire and lacked the supervisory powers that gave Lancashire spinners some of their status. Also Glasgow employers were under greater competitive pressure to keep wages lower than in the more successful Lancashire industry. In terms of technological change, there appears to have been little difference between the regions, though the finer Scottish spinning placed a greater premium upon skill than upon physical strength; skill which was not, however, rewarded by higher pay than in the region where less skill was required.[18]

In other cases, employers used an unsuccessful male strike to replace male with female workers, as in the Edinburgh printing industry in 1872. Thereafter there was an unusually high proportion of women in the Edinburgh printing industry: but this did not occur in other printing centres.[19] Opportunities directly to replace male with female labour were highly contingent upon, among other things, the nature of the occupation, the condition of the labour market and of industrial relations within the industry. Certainly the framework often employed in discussion of gender divisions in the labour market, which assumes a steady 'de-skilling' of the labour force through the nineteenth-century and the relatively easy substitution of female for male labour, conflicts with evidence currently available (limited though that is). More useful would be a framework adjusted to the complex ways in which skills were transformed and new ones created, and upon the processes that determined which new occupations and skills were assigned to either sex. We have already seen how newly developed office skills, manipulating new forms of technology, became a female domain in the later nineteenth-century, in a situation of shortage of suitably educated men and in which the work could be so structured as to limit the potential for advancement.

In general, it is clear that females experienced an inferior position in the labour market compared with males. It is important to focus upon the means by which that inferior position was constructed and sustained, and much more research is needed before the picture can become clear. The female experience was not invariably inferior, however. It is also important to emphasize the variety of women's work experiences. The historiography in general offers a picture of women's paid work, certainly from the 1870s, as almost universally of lower status and skill than that of men, and paid at significantly lower rates. More striking, on closer inspection, is the *variety* of levels of skill and pay at which women worked. Within the important sector of cotton textiles alone, the tasks performed by women, the proportion of them working and their pay levels varied not only between spinning and weaving, the two main divisions of the trade, but between different towns specializing in either branch. Local variations appear to have been still greater in Yorkshire wool textiles (where married women were less likely to be employed than in cotton), and were also significant in Yorkshire clothing manufacture, as were local variations in the definition of tasks assigned to males or females.[20]

In the cotton-weaving towns of Blackburn, Burnley and Preston, where both men and women worked on the looms and where women could earn a good, regular wage, married women were highly likely to work, though most did so in Preston which had poorer work opportunities for males than the other towns. Women weavers in Preston earned more than in Wigan, where they also predominated in the weaving work-force but where men had good work opportunities in the mines. In wool-weaving Bradford, where women weavers predominated, they earned less than in the mixed weaving community of Huddersfield. In the cotton-spinning towns of Bolton and Rochdale, and in wool manufacture generally, married women were less likely to work, though most unmarried women in these towns would spend some time in the mill.[21]

At the local level a highly complex picture of women's work and earnings emerges. In general, especially in rural areas, women's wages were highest where men's were also highest. In 1906, female agricultural workers in Lancashire could earn up to 20s. a week compared with 9–12s in Wiltshire and Berkshire.[22] The widest range of earnings for women was to be found in the variety of trades in the East End of London though, outside the East End, women's wages in London were the highest in Britain.[23] London shop assistants could earn 10–25 per cent above provincial rates; and women in the London printing trade in 1916 earned almost 70 per cent above those in small East Anglian towns and more than half as much again as those in larger towns such as Norwich, Ioswich, Colchester and Cambridge[24] (though the war period may have widened such differentials). The Trade Boards Act, 1909, set minimum rates for the first time in a number of low-paid, 'sweated' industries, most of them predominantly female, and in which conditions had long given cause for public concern. These were tailoring, chain-making, box-making, and the lace-finishing trades. The Act became operative in 1913. In tailoring and box-making it had little effect in the north, but raised wages in the low-wage sectors of the south; otherwise its effects have been little investigated.[25]

Women's earnings were consistently highest in cotton weaving, and women were a majority of the weavers, though weaving supervisors (overlookers) were generally promoted from among the minority of male weavers (especially in Scotland). Male and female weavers were generally on the same piece-rates (the predominant system of payment) though males generally took home higher pay each week (*c.*29s. in the 1900s compared with 25s. for females). The reasons are complicated. Men were more likely to operate more looms than women (six rather than four) and to be engaged in heavier weaving, which earned more. This might come about because of their generally greater strength, or because male overlookers put more profitable work the way of men. Men also tended to work longer hours, due partly to legislative restrictions upon female hours. Also, male weavers were likely to be older (up to age 55 and beyond), while most female weavers were under 25. Weaving was a skilled job because looms were not automatic and required familiarity and constant attention to secure smooth production. Longer serving workers, male or female, became more skilled, more productive and practiced at repairing their machines, hence avoiding loss of time and money while waiting for the overlooker to make the repairs (a normal part of his responsibilities). Such realities account for part, though not all, of the disparities between aggregate male and female earnings. In general, men did better, but not always due to discrimination against women or to ideological assumptions about their needs and roles, powerful though these were. Some female weavers earned more than males in the same occupation and many of them earned more than males in other occupations.[26] Nor did employers always seek to employ women at the lowest possible pay levels. In 1915 a Leeds tailoring employer commented: 'Badly paid labour is the dearest you can employ . . . we must have the best labour on the market and to get it we must pay the best price.'[27] Though their definition of the 'best' pay for a female might fall below the level applied to a male worker.

In another important source of female employment, the potteries, women's jobs were largely lower paid, less skilled and involved less exercise of authority or control than did men's. The employers used women as cheap labour during the trading crises of the 1880s and 1890s. Yet women worked in every department and throughout the main skill divisions of the potteries. Women's skill at decorating in particular had long been highly valued and more highly paid than a high proportion of male work in the industry. As in weaving, a comparison of *aggregate* male and female earnings puts men well ahead, but such comparisons obscure variations in female earnings and, again, the fact that females were generally markedly younger than males. When such variables are allowed for, the disparity between the experiences of males and females of equivalent age and experience is less stark.

Most manufacturing industries contained gender-segregated hierarchies of skill and pay that offered men the most favourable prospects, but they were hierarchies rather than gender-determined strata: in all industries where both were employed, some women earned more than some men. A simple stratified conception of the labour market, or crude dual labour market theories, are not entirely helpful in attempting to analyse the construction of the sex division of the paid labour market. Men were often to be found in the secondary labour market, though to a lesser extent than women and there was a large male casual labour sector.

Comparison of male and female earnings is, indeed, highly complicated. *Any* statements about earnings for this period should be treated with caution because the available data is, at best, patchy. This is partly because actual earnings can be difficult to establish. Many workers were paid on piece-rates, with results that varied among individuals and from week to week but, in some occupations (such as in the potteries), there were complicated group rates; and bonuses and fines could crucially affect take-home pay.[28] In the Leeds clothing industry, female workers were apparently more liable to fines than males. Also it is difficult, when comparing male and female earnings, to compare like with like because they rarely performed precisely comparable tasks. Where they did so, women did not always come off worse. In printing, the slowness of the more complex tasks undertaken by highly skilled men (one-off layouts or printing a foreign language) could bring them lower earnings than less experienced women on more routine typesetting operations.

Women's earnings prospects were not good but nor were those of many men, and little purpose is served by making women's experiences appear relatively even worse than they were. The important problem is to establish the actual levels of earnings and the means by which they were constructed. Male workers justified, and sometimes demanded, their relatively higher pay levels on the grounds of their family responsibilities. In practice, few of them, even in the early years of the twentieth century, regularly earned at high-enough levels to support a family at more than minimal levels, and many women workers were either the single or the main breadwinner in a household in which a husband was dead, deserted, disabled, sick or unemployed: or they were responsible for the support of parents or other relatives. In the textile town of Dundee, for example, notably large numbers of households were headed by a female and she was the chief breadwinner. Men in Dundee were nicknamed 'kettleboilers' because many men remained at home while the women of the household went out to work in a town offering relatively little male work.[29] Paying males at levels sufficient to support a household remained a stronger aim of the trade union than justice for women with similar needs, however. Nevertheless, the relatively weak trade-union movement of this period bore less responsibility for the limitations of female pay and opportunities than do the strategies and decisions of employers.

Nor were the disparities between male and female earnings always as acute as they appear on the surface. Even in domestic service, which is generally regarded as a seriously low-paid occupation, it has been estimated that, when the earnings of living-in servants are adjusted to include the value of board and lodgings, general servants are shown to have had real earnings at around the industrial average (£25–£30 per annum for the period of the 1870s, 1880s and 1890s) and the skilled elite of cooks to be earning the good wage of £35–£40 per annum.[30] This did not necessarily make domestic service any the more attractive, and lower-paid work in other settings was not relentlessly grim. The account of Hannah Mitchell testifies to the supportive and enjoyable atmosphere of the miserably paid dress-making workshops to which she escaped from domestic service.

Women's hours and conditions of work had been protected by law since the earlier nineteenth century. From 1844 female textile workers had their working day reduced to 12 hours and were excluded from night work. In 1847 their working day was further reduced to 10 (raised again to $10\frac{1}{2}$ in 1850). A series of Acts in 1853, 1860, 1864, 1867, 1878, 1891 and 1895 extended this protection to women in other industries, including pottery, china, glass, paper, tobacco. The 1867 Act defined a factory as an establishment employing 50 or more workers. The 1891 and 1895 Acts attempted to control conditions in small workshops, but they were extremely difficult to implement. In 1893 the first female factory inspectors were appointed, to supervise the conditions of women workers. The 1906 and 1913 Shop Acts laid down maximum hours for shopworkers; they were extended to cover laundry workers in 1907. The Trade Boards Act, 1909, established wages boards on which employers and employees were to be represented, to settle the hours of work and rates of pay in four trades; in 1913 six more trades were added. There were no controls over women's employment in their own or other people's homes. From the end of the nineteenth century, some feminists protested against such legislation as discriminatory, patronizing and limiting women's opportunities for pay and advancement; they received no support from working women.

Women's opportunities for promotion to supervisory positions were decidedly inferior to those of men. In the Leeds factory clothing industry women were supervisors in departments employing only women; men always supervised mixed or all-male departments. In Scottish cotton spinning all overseers were male even after the work-force had become entirely female; and in Lancashire weaving overseers were normally male despite the large female presence in the work-force.

In general, women's work opportunities were certainly limited and subordinate compared with those of most men. But by no means all of them endured subordination passively. There has been much stress placed upon women's inactivity in trades unions, and the hostility of male trades unionists to them. Women's assumed lack of industrial militancy is attributed to innate passivity, lack of commitment to the job, male opposition, lack of time due to domestic commitments and lack of money to pay dues. Yet female trades-union membership rates were not lower than among men in comparable occupations; men in low-paid, unskilled and casual occupations were similarly absent from unions though, of course, fewer of them were in such occupations. Levels of female unionization were high in Britain compared with other countries and followed a similar pattern of growth to male membership. It can reasonably be asked whether the reasons why the great majority of female workers were not in unions differed from the reasons why the great majority of males were not. There were about 10,600 female trade unionists in 1876, 117,888 in 1896 (102,847 of them in cotton-textile unions) by which time women were 7.8 per cent of all trade unionists. No more than 10 per cent of female full-time paid workers were unionized by 1914. The speed with which female membership increased at certain times (for example, the increase in the potteries from 2,000 to 23,000 between 1914 and 1918) casts doubt on most general explanations of female reluctance to unionize.

Also, failure to join a union should not be taken to mean that women did not stand up for their rights or protest against grievances. Levels of activism are necessarily hard to measure. Women were certainly active in major strikes. The well-known action at Bryant and May in 1888 was only temporarily successful in improving conditions and did not lead to the formation of a permanent union (it was very weak in the 1890s and died after an unsuccessful strike in 1902). In the following year there were strikes of female blanker-weavers in Yorkshire, cigar-makers in Nottingham, cotton and jute workers in Dundee and mill girls in Kilmarnock. Women (not necessarily unionized) initiated the long and unsuccessful Manningham mills strike in Bradford in 1892, which led to the formation of the Independent Labour Party. Evidence for the inter-war years suggests that female involvement in strikes could indeed be in excess of their proportionate involvement in industry.[31]

Women appear to have been more active in strikes than in unions, though precisely because many their actions were spontaneous and lacked organized backing they were often unrecorded. The official statistics reveal 82 strikes of women in the Dundee jute industry between 1889 and 1906, the vast majority initiated by women and involving only women. They mostly involved between 14 and 500 workers although, on at least five occasions, most of the mills in the town were out, involving 20-30,000 workers, mostly female. The strikers were normally demanding higher pay. The strikes were short, frowned upon by the male-dominated unions, and were effective.[32] Almost certainly many similar strikes were unrecorded. Male unionists also disapproved of the indecorous behaviour of the female strikers of Dundee:

> Those on strike paraded the streets yesterday in grotesque processions bearing emblems of their trade suspended from poles, such as mats, jute, etc. They also indulged in shouting and singing, the latter being a peculiar sort of march, the words of which were principally intended to convey the information that they were somebody or other's 'band'. Besides this, they held threatening demonstrations in front of the works where nobody had turned out. Between 2 and 3 o'clock large droves of them marched to the Cowgate, and here they held an indignation meeting in the midst of the merchants who were assembled there in large numbers, it being market day.

It was commonplace for the strikers to dress up in comic fashion as they paraded through the streets, often in a manner mocking male authority, wearing male hats, including policemen's helmets.[33] Such spontaneous strikes, outside union control, were not a demonstration of the incapacity of women to organize. Rather they were an effective response to their position in the labour market. There was generally a shortage of labour in Dundee in this period, and their scarcity was the only form of bargaining power possessed by these low-paid, unskilled women. In this situation a short strike could be effective and did not require the union support necessitated by a long strike. Also such action was an assertion of independence by the women against male employers and male trade unionists who conspicuously failed to support them or to act against their grievances; the women felt that they had little gain from membership of such unions; and many of them did not remain in the work-force for long enough to gain from union welfare benefits. Most of the Dundee work-force was young. This partly accounts for the carnival nature of the strikes; they were an extension of the normal boisterous street behaviour of the girls.[34]

Henry Broadhurst's statement to the 1877 conference of the TUC is frequently quoted as typical of the attitudes of male trade unionists:

> They had the future of their country and children to consider and it was their duty as men and husbands to use their utmost efforts to bring about a condition of things where their wives should be in their proper sphere at home, seeing after their house and family, instead of being dragged into the competition for livelihood against the great and strong men of the world.

Read in the context in which it was delivered, in one of a series of debates on factory legislation, in which the Women's Trade Union League challenged legislative controls on the hours and type of work available to women (they argued that women would be better protected by the appointment of female factory inspectors) it is clear that the women had explicit male support, and that the virulent tone of Broadhurst's frequently reiterated antagonism was a typical. Year after year he failed to get majority support for his opposition to female factory inspectors, and the women found firm male defenders.[35]

Male trade-union attitudes to women appear to have been variable and contingent upon personal and trade circumstances. Many male unionists feared female competition in an overstocked labour market, even though men and women rarely competed for the same jobs. Many believed firmly that a woman's place was in the home. Many, too, had good reason to wish to relieve wives of the double burden of work in and outside the home in the conditions of the time, while recognizing the need for their incomes and those of their unmarried daughters. Of course, they fought at least as hard to exclude other male workers who threatened to compete with them. Women workers had good reason to see little potential benefit to themselves from joining an established male union.

They did, however, support strikes by male trade unionists. Wives and Labour Party women were active fund-raisers and campaigners for the miners and other workers in the strike wave of the years before 1914.[36] In return, the TUC annual conference voted to support Votes for Women in 1913.

But strikes are an extreme and infrequent form of protest. Women, like men, responded to unfavourable working conditions in a variety of ways. Despite their reputation for docility, 'it was rare for a working class child to grow up cowed and spiritless. If and when the need arose authority . . . would be challenged', as much among females as among males.[37] Women improved their position and resisted or evaded authority, like men, by negotiating and complaining, individually or collectively, by being awkward and by changing jobs, as Hannah Mitchell did until, at the time of her marriage in 1895 (when she gave up paid work), she was earning 25s. a week. Similarly, female clerical workers, though unionized, improved their positions through negotiation and frequent job changes in a favourable market.[38]

Union membership, like work itself, was often determined for men and women by the attitudes of Kin. Some women did not join a union because their menfolk forbade it (apparently a custom of weavers' overlookers in Preston): others were ordered to join by fathers or mothers. Sometimes husbands and wives joined or left the union together; or mothers ordered sons to join; or a husband's dues were paid by the wife when the household budget allowed.[39] Some women, who joined the union because they were expected or pressured to do so, never thought of turning to it for help over shop-floor problems, which perhaps also applied to many men.

An important difference between male and female trade-union movements was that the organizations formed to promote female unionism (the Women's Trade Union League founded 1874; the Women's Trade Union Association, founded 1889, later the Women's Industrial Council) and some of their unions were led by middle-class women (such as Mary Macarthur, leader of the WTUL) who had no experience of manual work. This did not necessarily mean that they misunderstood working women's needs, but there were on occasion divergences between them and working women, arising in particular from their tendency to give greater priority to solidarity among women than among workers. They did not always understand or encourage the sympathy of female workers for the grievances of male co-workers. In 1910, female compositors in Edinburgh struck alongside the men for higher pay for all, despite feminist pressure to use the opportunity to see the male strike defeated to enable more women to replace them in the trade. In the 1900s Mary Macarthur differed from the ex-mill girl Julia Varley (an official of the wool textile workers union in 1895 and a member of Bradford trades council at the age of 14; later the first female official of the Workers' Union and responsible for substantially increasing its female membership) over whether women should be organized separately from, or together with, men. Varley's use of the latter strategy proved the more effective.[40]

Levels of female unionization rose in World War I, but women's levels of participation in the paid labour force rose by much less than is often believed. As before the war, precise statistics are elusive. Some of the apparent increase in women's employment arose from the transfer of women from previously under-recorded occupations into statistically visible ones, such as munitions work. The numbers in domestic service fell sharply, throwing many women into unemployment, which was high among women in the first year of the war. Women entered the armed services for the first time, in ancillary roles as clerks and drivers; the first women's police force was established. Skilled male manual workers, supported by Labour Party women, were hostile to the entry of women into 'diluted' versions of their jobs – skilled tasks subdivided and lower paid – due to understandable fear that this would provide an opportunity for employers permanently to downgrade the status and pay of their occupations while continuing to confine women to low-status jobs; they also opposed dilution by unskilled men. By 1917 the *Labour Gazette* estimated that one in three working women was directly replacing a male industrial worker. Most wartime women workers were either meeting expanded demand in occupations which had traditionally employed them: in textiles or making footwear; or were in jobs specific to war needs, such as the manufacture of munitions, which were often highly paid, though dangerous and unpleasant, but ceased with the war. Many female manual workers benefited, like male workers, from full employment, regular pay and overtime during the war, but few held on to their gains after the war, when their jobs disappeared or they were expected to relinquish them for returning soldiers. Middle- or lower-middle-class women were more likely to retain the white-collar, mainly clerical jobs which had increased during the war.

4

'In Want of Union': Industrial Relations in the Early Twentieth-century Pottery Industry

Richard Whipp

Introduction

The six towns in the 30 square miles of north Staffordshire, known as the Potteries, was one of the principal products of industrialization in Britain. In 1900, the Potteries region arguably constituted the greatest concentration of ceramic industries in the world. The area accounted for almost a third of the world's ceramic export market. The output of the Potteries was exceptional, in terms of quality and of variety. The 'Six Towns' were regarded within Britain as 'a great industrial district'. Eighty per cent of the country's pottery workers lived within a 5-mile radius of Stoke Town Hall. In 1911, 46,000 workers were employed directly by the industry, 80,000 indirectly.[1]

Many powerful images of the Potteries have emerged. It has been convenient to represent the industry as technologically backward, unsophist-icated in management, and parochial. The best-known feature of the area was the apparent harmony of the potbank and its industrial relations. The reputation has much to do originally with the views of Arnold Bennett, a locally born writer, made popular by the success of his novels based on the area.[2] The strength of the image of social tranquillity is matched only by its inaccuracy. Great damage has been done, therefore, to the historical record of not only the Potteries but also to our wider understanding of industrial relations within the United Kingdom.

The primary objective of this chapter is to present an alternative account of industrial relations in the pottery industry. Far from being straightforwardly peaceful, the industrial relations of pottery manufacture reflected both the differences within capital and labour as well as the divisions between them. Contrary to general belief, conflict was endemic and widespread in the pottery industry. A detailed reconstruction of the period 1900–25 reveals the richness of the structures and social relations across the industry. The received view that national collective bargaining became established in British industry at this time will be tested by the potters' experience. In so doing, the conventional view of the so-called 'origins of British industrial relations' is called into question.

The secondary purpose of the chapter is rather different. The aim is to show how a preoccupation with the structural form of industrial relations is of limited use. Clegg and others have defined industrial relations as the study of the rules governing employment. Collective bargaining then becomes the bargaining over such rules between trades unions and employers, as well as the making, interpretation and administration of employment rules. Early writers, too, saw the history of trade unionism as the history of the development of collective bargaining.[3] This approach is too narrow: it minimizes wider social pressures, ignores the varied motivations of employer and employed and reduces industrial relations to bargaining procedures alone. The intention in the following pages is to demonstrate the wealth of influences on industrial relations: from within and outside the workplace, through structural determinants as well as the experience of those involved, and to include the highly unpredictable dynamics of power, compromise and chance.

The chapter is divided accordingly into three main parts. Part 1 reconstructs how the relations between employer and employed took place on multiple levels, appropriate to the complex division of labour, the fragmented union structure and the range of managerial approaches. The second section is then able to demonstrate the limited significance of national-bargaining institutions: they appear as particularly impermanent. Part 3 not only shows conflict to have been an essential part of potbank and Potteries life, it also advances a composite explanation of the record of disputes; an understanding drawn from economic sources, together with social and political imperatives. The problem of the timing of conflict is also addressed. The chapter concludes by emphasizing the potential contribution to the analysis of industrial relations by combining the insights and conceptual tools of more than one discipline.

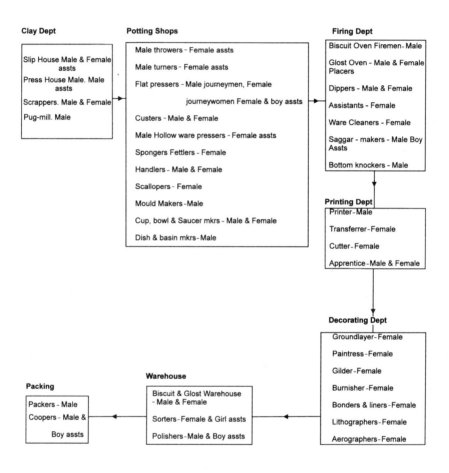

Figure 1 The Production Process and Division of Labour of Pottery Manufacture
Source: C.J. Noke and H.J. Plant, *Common Commodities and Industries. Pottery* (1924). C. Binns, *Manual of Practical Potting* (1922). *The Times Engineering Supplement*, 2 April, 1913, pp. 25–30. E. A. Sandeman, *Notes on the Manufacture of Earthware* (1921).

1 Chaos or Natural Order?

The pottery industry mirrors the infamous complexity of British industrial relations.[4] During the 1908 disputes, it was noted how 'among the whole body of manufacturers it would be difficult to find half-a-dozen who had received a precisely similar set of notices'.[5] The fragmentation of the pottery companies and workforce gave rise to an intricate pattern of industrial relations. The Donovan Commission of 1974 highlighted two aspects of industrial relations in the United Kingdom: the informal and the formal. The informal relations are those between workers or unionists and employers in the workshop or plant, as opposed to the formal level where unions and employers bargain in a regional, industrial or national setting. The informal level involves customary, often unwritten understandings; the formal relies on written agreements. This distinction supplies a useful starting point for understanding how potters organized their forms of bargaining. Yet, the outstanding feature of the pottery industry's industrial relations, and the main reason for the pattern of conflict, was the multiple levels at which bargaining operated.[6]

Five levels of bargaining were distinguishable in pottery. The levels ranged from: the individual or workshop level; to the plant; the occupational group; the subindustry; or the industry-wide level. Phelps-Brown observed in relation to the 1900s that 'four out of five employees made their own bargains' and how 'the immediate relations between employer and employed at the place of work remained remarkably unregulated'.[7] It was entirely consistent with the social relations of the potbank[8] that bargaining was predominantly between the individual or workgroup and the employer. A sample of the union's dispute files shows almost 80 per cent of the bargaining problems related to individual companies. In a second sample of disputes, 35.42 per cent of the disputes involved individual potters, and 47.92 per cent workgroups.[9]

Three reasons lay behind this pervasive small-scale bargaining. First, management preferred to handle individuals or workshops rather than confront questions affecting a whole potbank. In October 1908 Cauldons issued notice to all its employees telling them that 'every one employed on these works will be under one month's notice from this date . . . during the month each person will be seen with a view to possible rearrangement of their work and wages'.[10] Second, the technical differences between occupations in the potbank meant that common issues did not emerge. Third, the piece-rate system reinforced the individual basis of bargaining because it relied on the pricing of single items produced by one worker or small group. Owners had perfected this type of bargaining from the annual hiring system of the early nineteenth century.[11] In 1908, it was estimated that 16,000 workers had given in notices to their employers and, after the 1911 arbitration board, 3,000 notices were still being negotiated. When industry-wide bargaining became more apparent later in the period, it took months to deal with the deluge of individual issues on the potbanks as each potter interpreted the national agreement.[12]

Work-group bargaining arose naturally from the primary social groups which made up the potbank (*see* Fig.1). Such groups wrestled with the issues and problems specific to their workshop, which were not easily transferable or understood by others. In November 1913, Cauldons' enamellers in one dispute over their pattern difficulties and low prices, negotiated management recognition and the alteration of apprentice allowances.[13] Women's occupational groups also developed similar bargaining techniques, especially among the skilled lithographers, transferrers and paintresses. Group bargaining was the natural extension of the strength of work-group control.[14]

Individual or workshop bargaining was the most direct contact point with the union for many potters.[15] Moreover, it was from these localized work-group questions that many of the larger industry-wide disputes developed. The sanitary pressers' dispute of 1907 grew originally from the introduction of one article on a single potbank. When more formal systems of negotiation were in operation, the head office of the union was still directing that 'all individual notices on both sides to be dealt with at the factories concerned'. The localized forms of bargaining were so embedded within the potbank that, when the union and manufacturers tried to establish a fixed, annual settlement date for the industry, many work-groups simply ignored the procedure.[16]

While union and worker bargaining operated mainly within the potbank, it seldom covered the whole workforce. The division of labour separated the workers while relatively few issues arose which were common to all the workshops on the potbank. Differences in skill, status and work experience militated against factory-based action. Contrary to some authorities on British trades unions, the potters do not fit the standard image of powerful 'factory consciousness'.[17] Of the 72 recorded issues which arose between Grindleys and the union in 1912–13 or the 20 subjects arising at Johnsons over the same period, none relates to disputes involving all the workforce of a plant.[18] Rarely were issues seen by all workers to be a common threat on a potbank, resulting in total workforce mobilization. One clear example occurred at the New Hall works in 1920 over arbitrary wage deductions from a group of women workers.[19] The collapse of the National Council of the Pottery Industry sponsorship of works committees after 1918 resulted from their lack of any real social base.[20]

By contrast, the occupational group within an area of the Potteries provided a remarkably strong basis for bargaining. It was far easier to establish common prices and practices for a single occupation (such as flat pressers) in an area than to attempt to combine the divergent interests of widely different occupations in a potbank. Union-dispute files indicate that under 10 per cent of bargaining activity took place at this level.[21] The extent of these occupational groups' actions may have been small but in qualitative terms their impact was far greater. Their activities were less frequent than at the workshop level because they were fewer in number. Tactically, the (often skilled) occupational group of an area mobilized only when questions of sufficiently common importance arose. The saggarmakers of Burslem and Tunstall showed their occupational consciousness in their letter to the NEC in 1920. It explained their new area price list where: 'our idea has been to supply a long felt want for a definite list of sizes . . . We should think that the saggarmakers should be called together not only in Burslem but throughout the district'.[22]

The 'trade' or 'district' prices for an article or pattern became in due course markers for occupational or craft bargaining. The strongest area-bargaining units were the craft or skilled groups. Examples included the male pressers and ovenmen, or the female transferrers and paintresses. It was often the craft area-based groups that responded to the problems of an isolated work-group. This happened in 1907 when the Cauldons' sanitary dispute was generalized to cover the whole sanitary subindustry.[23] As an analysis of the union's dispute files shows (*see* Fig. 2), the craft and skilled occupations appear to have dominated the union's bargaining activity. This was perfectly consistent with the strength of the skilled work-groups on the potbank, *allied with* their area solidarity with their fellow skilled potters. Moreover, it was the craft groups at the potbank and area level which were responsible for the main recorded episodes of bargaining during the period: episodes which historians have mistakenly taken for industry-wide bargaining (*see below* Part 2). After the 1920 general settlement, it was noted how negotiations were 'an all year business, with departmental meetings called for saggar makers, glost placers, odd men, dippers, biscuit bedders, hollow ware placers, kilnmen and handlers'. The national agreements of the later part of the period were essentially amalgamations of layer upon layer of departmental or trade-group bargaining. Nor was sectional bargaining divisive. Many of the craft and trade groups' demands served as blueprints for smaller or less-skilled groups.[24]

An attempt was made to establish bargaining units based on the seven sub-industries. These proved to be far weaker than the occupational group level. Employer and union involvement varied markedly because of their relative strengths within a sub industry and according to trade conditions. In 1907, the china manufacturers, as a result of foreign and domestic competition,

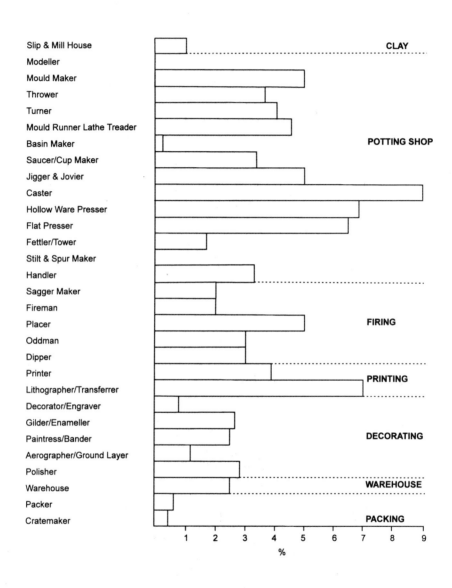

Figure 2 Level of Union Dispute Activity 1906–24
Source: CATU COLL, Union Dispute Files 1906–1924 covering 288 recorded disputes

were 'dropping down to prices never heard of before' through 'want of cohesion among the manufacturers'.[25] In contrast, the jet and rockingham and sanitary masters were well organized.[26] Yet attitudes to subindustry bargaining varied between manufacturers. While the jet and rockingham masters readily negotiated, the sanitary owners refused. The sanitary masters 'were determined to fight the men at any cost' and had 'formed an employers' federation, on the lines of the engineering employers'. Pottery workers found it equally difficult to maintain subindustry organization. Sanitary organization and bargaining was especially active in 1909–12, when casting provided a central issue, but collapsed during the war when the market fell.[27] China developed a more stable bargaining unit covering Longton largely as a result of strong union pressure in the area from 1909 onwards.[28] Stoneware never bargained at this level and, even in 1926, still lacked a standard wage scale.[29] The diversity of products and firms within earthenware (the largest subindustry) always limited the applicability of any agreements that might be reached. The subindustry level of bargaining was therefore impermanent and, where it did exist, varied greatly in its strength and coverage.[30]

2 The Importance of National Structures

The view that industry-wide collective bargaining was established in British industry by the 1900s and has since been the norm is a popular one.[31] The pottery industry cannot confirm the picture. Bargaining on this scale was attempted only in 1916 and, even after that date, the term is of limited use in the Potteries.

The differing settling times used by sections of the industry made industry-wide bargaining impossible until World War I. The dispute phases of 1900, 1906–8 and 1911 never involved the entire industry, although the *Labour Gazette* and the language of some press reports suggest the opposite. The 1900 episode principally involved the printers and transferrers trade. In 1911 the negotiations of that year involved 'sectional (occupational) committees'. It was observed 'by the manufacturers that the notices given by the men were by no means general'.[32] In 1916 it was noted that:

> ...this year, however, we believe a precedent was fixed by the workers, inasmuch as instead of apprising the manufacturers of their demands individually, or in individual groups or classes, as has long been the custom, a general formal notice was served upon the secretary of the Manufacturers Association by the secretary of the Pottery Workers' Union.[33]

The apparently epoch-making event did not mean that industry-wide bargaining was established. Manufacturer and union action remained highly sectional. The tensions between individual, workshop and wider collective forms of bargaining continued. The work-group and area-based occupational group remained strong and active after the erection of industrial bargaining forums. Both management and workers were anxious to retain the local forms as the potters' union recognized. In 1920 the National Society of Pottery Workers (NSPW) informed the manufacturers' federation that 'the above increases shall apply to slip and mill-house hands and kiln firemen, but the Union recognises the right of Employers to pay these workers at the rate per hour arranged between the individual employer and employee'.[34] It was the customary strength of the lower levels of bargaining which ensured they remained in operation in the late 1920s when the attempted industrial forms broke down.[35]

Historians attribute great significance to the apparent shift from the informal to the wider formal modes of bargaining in British industry during the early twentieth century. Price argues that the 'transition from an unformalised to a formalised system of industrial relations was the critical event in modern labour history whose significance can hardly be underestimated'. Earlier, Rowe considered the change as predetermined. In his words: 'the establishment of collective bargaining on a national basis must be viewed as a more or less inevitable process of evolution'.[36] In the pottery industry the dynamic of industrial relations was rather different.

There is evidence to suggest that industrial relations did become increasingly formalized during this period in the pottery industry. Arnold Wethered, in 1924, thought the National Council of the Pottery Industry, established in 1917, was 'quite the leading example of what a Whitley Council can be'.[37] Leading pottery owners wanted formal agreements. In binding the union to written procedures, the strength of customary action might be minimized and workers brought under greater managerial control. The owners' attempts to establish an arbitration and conciliation board for the industry were fuelled by desire to create appropriate rules. In 1908, a manufacturer observed how 'trades unionism is now more than ever before a great fact to be reckoned with in industrial affairs' and 'it is widely recognised that it forms a great safeguard against rash or ill-considered action by the operatives. Trades Union leaders are usually conscientious, well informed men, who may be relied on to discharge any unpractical demands by the rank and file'.[38]

Union leaders also favoured the creation of more formal industrial relations. They saw real benefits were obtainable. Yet they did not enter formal negotiations blind to manufacturers' interests. The officials' aim was to establish a degree of order in wages and conditions, to make employers accountable and limit manufacturers' freedom of manoeuvre. This was an immense achievement when set against the previous century's experience of chaotic prices with firms underpricing one another. In 1892, 1900 and in

1907 a section of the manufacturers had tried to destroy the potters' unions. Keeping masters to public, formally recognized agreements appeared a great feat. In 1911, therefore, the union forced Furnivals to alter their treatment of their pressers by using their association's agreement with the union. In a practical way, formal recognition of the union by manufacturers was used as a means of recruiting members to the NAS.[39]

The outcome of these national industrial bargaining arrangements in the pottery industry was problematic. They did not have the effect on the potters' union of 'rendering them comparatively harmless' as has been argued more generally.[40] Manufacturers continued to act unofficially when they felt their interests were threatened by formal agreements.[41] The institutional, formal procedures were not complete in their coverage. The richness of workshop custom and independent, informal bargaining were never easily brought under control by union or manufacturers. The 1907 sanitary dispute rested on the masters' attempt to break the six-week notice custom. From November 1912 through to January 1913 at Twyfords, a leading member of their manufacturers' association, a running dispute was fought over two trade customs: the right to second firing and the ability of workers to check the counts. Thomas Twyford was quite clear that, 'I will have my business conducted in my own way' and he refused to negotiate or be involved in the conciliation committee of two masters and two union representatives. The struggle for control of production in the potbank continued to be fought over wages, prices and allowances in their local settings. Even during the war, when formal, industry-wide bargaining was at its strongest, independent action by workers and separate bargaining was common.[42]

The development of a formalized system of industrial relations was not only partial but highly unstable. The disparate motivations and actions of workers and masters never allowed them to direct their constituents effectively. The arbitration and conciliation board had been nominally in existence since 1868.[43] Yet, between 1891 and 1908, no board operated because the unions were 'sick of the name of arbitration'. Owners sometimes referred to it as 'the first and most successful of the Labour Arbitration Boards in the Country' yet it sat officially only between 1908 and 1911.[44] The board's importance was limited because, during its life-time, 'sectional strikes were of fairly frequent occurrence'.[45]

The fragility of the formal bargaining procedures reflected the weakness of the manufacturers' associations.[46] Between 1890 and 1910 *ad hoc* groups of masters combined during disputes with workers yet they failed to take collective action on any larger scale. The subindustries experienced widely differing trade conditions, technology and labour relations.[47] As a leading manufacturer observed in 1906, 'the pottery trade, from the time of

Wedgwood to now, has invariably been in want of union. There are the different sections ... and each has fought its own hand'.

Government intervention, the war and the growth of the unions' strength led to a period of temporary collaboration between manufacturers. Legislation regarding workers' compensation and industrial illness resulted in temporary collective action by the more-established firms. This centred on resistance to the implications of the Lord James's inquiry of 1900–02, the Workman's Compensation Bill in 1906 and the lead-poisoning investigations of 1908–10.[48] These episodes, combined with 'labour troubles' and 'the Insurance Bill' had, by 1914, 'impressed upon manufacturers, as perhaps nothing else could have done, the urgent necessity for combination'.[49] The immediate problems of raw material and labour supply during the war produced a war committee of manufacturers' associations in 1914; this became the British Pottery Manufacturers' Association (BPMF) in 1918.[50] The actions of the new organization, however, explain their limited effectiveness. The association's membership list shows that over half of the employers did not join. The smaller masters were absent. When trading was disrupted and prices fell in the 1920s, enforcement of the association's regulations became a problem. The cohesiveness of industrial bargaining suffered accordingly.[51]

The ambitions of the National Council (formed in 1917) were to establish uniform pricing in the industry, repel foreign competition and even help create a new transport system. Such hopes were hallmarks of the 'reconstruction' era.[52] The council's standing rules, though, quickly expose its limitations. A two-thirds majority was required for motions to be carried; the statistical, research, organization and wages committees were designed as information gatherers. The council could not compel manufacturers or potters to accept its decisions. There were no powers to enforce agreements. The council was an entirely voluntary body.[53]

The attempt to embrace the industry was short lived. The 1920 and 1924 disputes did involve a committee from the Council. In 1920, however, a government investigator found that, in relation to the works committees' scheme, 'the vast majority of operatives know little or nothing of the recommendations of the joint industrial council'.[54] In the 1920s, union members questioned the council's relevance. The Union's annual delegation of 1922 was asked if the payments to the council were justified. In 1923 a delegate concluded that the council 'looked like doing little or nothing in the actual interests of the workers'.[55] Many manufacturers did not want the council to deal with industrial relations; they preferred the body to operate as a means of lobbying government. The fall in attendance by manufacturers from 1921 further undermined the council's efficiency.[56] The National Council failed to alter fundamentally the industrial relations of pottery manufacture. At best it temporarily reinforced normal industry-wide bargaining between 1917 and 1924. As one of the Council's architects, Henry Clay, confessed: 'the previously existing machinery for dealing with wage questions was left to function undisturbed'.[57]

3 A Rich Record of Conflict

In spite of the evidence presented here, the reputation of the pottery industry is one of stable industrial relations untroubled by conflict. Williams maintains that there has been a 'remarkable record of industrial peace in the pottery industry'. He cites, remarkably, the uniformity of bargaining forms as a key reason for the lack of conflict. Yeaman makes the claim that 'there has been no strike or dispute since 1899'. These conclusions are odd. The industry's nineteenth-century experience shows that the potters participated in many major industrial battles and that the contest for the control of production was a continuing theme. The centrality of conflict to industrial life in general makes the claims of Williams and Yeaman especially unusual.[58]

Industrial conflict is often equated with the strike.[59] Yet conflict may be expressed in many forms. Scullion and Edwards distinguish between what they call the behavioural, institutional and structural variants. The behavioural form is where conflict is recognized and expressed by participants; the institutional arises where conflict is manifested through customary procedures and practices; structural conflict exists when the forces making for conflict are implicit within a given situation and they may remain unexpressed.[60] Studies of contemporary industrial conflict confirm the variety of its expression and point to the strike as a relatively exceptional form. The typical strike has been found to be the spontaneous, small-scale and short stoppage. Even though this form is common in industry, it has gone largely unnoticed by official statistics, and the pottery industry is no exception.[61]

Contrary to the conventional view, the pottery industry of the early twentieth century exhibited conflict in all its forms. Ignored by successive generations of historians, pottery manufacture in fact contained potent sources of contest. The 'day-books' of union activists record the high incidence of small-scale, short-term disputes involving between one or half-a-dozen workers and lasting no more than a day. The majority of these tiny events never required union recognition nor action. It was the density of this routine form of conflict that led the union in 1911 to require that members reported the outcome of their disputes to the lodges so that the union might record their incidence.[62] The large-scale co-ordinated strike was in fact the exception.[63]

In terms of Stearn's strike model, much of the potters' strike activity was, to use his word, 'unsophisticated'.[64] Yet there was a broad spread of the types of potters' strike action. At one extreme was the spontaneous, unofficial, possibly violent strike action. In 1907, during a dispute at Doultons, sanitary workers fought a group of blacklegs, forcing them to shelter in Hanley police station.[65] At the other extreme was the calculated, planned offensive over a major issue. In 1881, 1890, 1906–8 and 1920, for example, these strikes were played out with deliberate union ritual and theatre. They involved the entire apparatus of bands, daily marches, mass meetings in the main squares of the Six Towns, backed up by the organization of temporary stewards, collectors and the trade committees.[66]

In the first three decades of the twentieth century, the pottery industry witnessed some of the most notable episodes of conflict within its 200-year history. It was said of the 1908 disputes that 'never in the history of the trade probably, has a more serious crisis arisen'.[67] The main phases of dispute activity seem to have fallen in 1910–15 and 1919–20: 1908–9, 1916–17 and 1923–4 were years of active, but less intense, conflict.[68] The early 1900s and 1920s were relatively quiet.

The dispute which involved large sections of the workers in a subindustry occurred in 1900 when a dispute involving printers, transferrers and ovenmen in earthenware arose over a wage-increase claim. The conflict of 1906–8 in the sanitary subindustry was really a series of rolling strikes concerning the introduction of casting. The 1906–7 disputes were touched off by a workers' offensive as prices rose. In 1908 masters counter-attacked with wage cuts as prices fell.[69] The disputes of 1911 were over wage levels in earthenware, sanitary and tile sections and the rules surrounding the arbitration board.[70] The strikes of 1913 involved jet and rockingham, tiles and the cane and white makers, while 1914 witnessed disputes over wage structures in earthenware and china.[71] The 1919–20 disputes were over the reduction of wages by manufacturers. During 1923–4 workers attempted to recoup the wage losses which had followed the extensive price cutting of the early 1920s.[72] How is such a record to be explained?

A number of explanations exists for the pattern of industrial conflict nationally during this period. The industrial peace of the early 1900s has been related to the depression in industry, unemployment and the willingness of employers and unions to continue operating such collective-bargaining machinery as already existed. The period 1908–13 is generally agreed to have been a time of intense friction.[73] Burgess highlights the conflict that arose over the exercise of managerial prerogatives as employers changed working arrangements in response to changing market conditions.[74] Hunt emphasizes the role of the trade cycle and labour market. In 1908, he argues, the strikes were in a period of high unemployment and restricted to well-organized workers. By 1910 the economic conditions had changed, the demand for labour was high enough for the less well organized to act. The intensity of disputes activity is explained by the experience of stagnant or falling real wages coming on top of eight years of high unemployment.[75] During the war, strikes were less frequent. Conflict did occur in South Wales and on the Clyde, for example, but these were largely due to a combination of factors not easily or consistently reproduced elsewhere.[76] After the 1919–20 boom, the collapse of world prices, combined with the government's policy of rapid deflation, led to lower prices and widespread attempts by employers to reduce wages. The effects of depression and unemployment made for defensive strike action and led to the defeat of a number of key industrial groups, including the railway workers, miners, dockers and building trades.[77]

How does the pottery industry compare with the general trend? Though the pottery dispute record broadly resembles the national sequence, the explanation of the potters' experience involves features unique to their industry. First, the general accounts of the period minimize the composite causation of conflict which is highlighted by the potters' experience.[78] The disputes of 1908 in pottery involved at least five main separate issues: the 15 per cent price increase; a revision of counts; a change of ware sizes; the abolition of good-from-oven; and the limitation of apprentices. These questions were in turn entangled in the creation of the arbitration board and the conditions which masters and workers laid down for its operation. The 1911 general earthenware dispute was also complex in character, although made up of a different set of elements.[79] Secondly, disputes are too easily taken to be isolated, one-off events, whereas they may be related to a prior sequence of acts. The 1908–11 conflicts apparently stand out as the first major strikes for a decade. The action of the workers, however, is intelligible only in the light of the wage reductions and defeats of the 1890s and the fact that the potters perceived they had not benefited from the series of technological changes. Conflict had been implicit (in the Edwards and Scullian sense) within the relations of master and worker over the organization of production for more than ten years. For Noah Parkes, the trade union organizer in 1908, 'the great improvements in the pottery industry in the last twenty years had gone vastly in favour of the masters and now the potters wished to take their share'.[80] Similarly, memory was an important feature. Workers did not forget the past actions of employers: memories informed their action. As one observed in 1908, 'eight or nine years ago a section of the employers unwisely adopted the attitude that the workmen's unions were a negligible quantity, and could be ignored. The spirit begot a feeling of bitterness and antagonism on the part of the men which has led to many of our difficulties.'[81]

The broad explanation for the potters' main dispute activity of the period rests on three main causes: wages, the cost of living and the organization of work. A review of conflict in the pottery industry at every level shows wage or piece price changes to be the dominant concern of both sides. In a market economy, wages were central to the potter in terms of purchasing power and status. Wage-rate disputes were often the focus of conflict because they embodied changes in working conditions or relations in the potbank. Casting was disputed throughout the period in wage terms in public, whereas the underlying issues involved skill and status differentials and the ability to control the introduction of new technology. Disputes over wages were not always about absolutes but relatives. The point at issue was the structure of wages. During disputes, the potters consistently cited their pay levels (1924 was the most detailed example) in relation to workers in other industries.[82]

Wages remained at the forefront of the potters' demands while the rationale behind the union arguments changed. In the late nineteenth-century, the union had argued that workers should profit from buoyant demand just as they had suffered from periods of depressed trade. By the 1900s, in common with other unions, the NAS not only thought their wages should reflect 'commercial prosperity but that a social criterion should govern wages'. In other words, with skilled and unskilled workers threatened by the trade cycle and technological change, minimum levels were demanded. Once established, these levels became a clear point of dispute. The 1924 dispute rested largely on Clowes's assertion that 'we want to put in a minimum rate below which no one shall go'. Minimum wage levels, and the cost of living became strong reasons for the disputes of 1908–14. Lovatt and Hollins built large parts of their cases in 1908 and 1911 on the calculation of a 15 per cent increase in the cost of living during the previous decade. In 1919–20 and 1923–4 minimum wage levels, especially for low-paid potters, were among the main planks in the union's arguments.[83]

The organization of work was a powerful influence on conflict. How new machinery was introduced and the changes in working practices were high priorities, especially for the skilled groups. It was the pivotal workers, the hollow-ware and sanitary pressers, the printers and ovenmen who were directly threatened. They were also the best-organized groups within the industry and union. The diffusion of improved jiggers and jollies, the introduction of casting or printing machines and the intensification of oven work occurred irregularly yet gradually throughout the period. Therefore, almost every major dispute includes references to these principal changes. The fear and anger of hollow-ware pressers towards the new technology was based not so much on the adverse effect on working conditions as on the threat of unemployment. In the first phase of casting innovation, some of the highest-paid workers in the industry faced the sack. At one potbank in

1908, it was discovered that two casters could do the work of five pressers: the firm was able to 'dispense' with 19 men. During the 1924 dispute, the bitterness of Booth and Clowes towards the manufacturers who had by now decimated their calling was apparent. Clowes could barely control his anger over the effect of casting when he met the masters that year. As he told the chairman of the manufacturers' association: 'I do not smile at it, because there are 110 hollow-ware pressers unemployed – men who have been to the war. It is nothing to smile at, Mr. Bullock.'[84]

The precise timing of industrial conflict in the Potteries was determined by the interaction of the trade cycle with employer strategy and to a lesser extent political activism. Generally, conflict in the pottery trade was related to industrial performance. The major dispute phases of 1900, 1906–7, 1911, 1913, 1919–20 and 1923–4 occurred in periods of increasing output, exports and employment.[85] The trade cycle clearly influenced the thinking of trades unionists. Sam Clowes argued that the 5 percent price rises of 1907 had put 300,000 in the masters' pockets and the workers now wanted their share. Workers and union officials especially kept a close eye on the trade returns in the *Pottery Gazette*.[86] This explains why the disputes of 1923–4 occurred in what appears to be a generally depressed decade elsewhere. The export and output figures began to rise slightly in 1923 and therefore Clowes, Hollins and Tunnicliffe built their claims for wage minima and rises around the discernible trade improvement.[87] Dispute activity between subindustries was also governed by perceived economic performance.[88] Union growth was allied to the trade cycle. Union membership levels were closely related to strike action (although strikes themselves can affect union growth). 1891–3, 1900, 1906–7, 1911, 1913–14 and 1919–20 were all peak years for output, exports and union membership. The disputes of 1923–4 witnessed the only period between 1920 and 1929 when union membership rose.[89]

The perceptions and actions of employers were related to the trade cycle, as much as those of trades unionists, but with different outcomes. Employers were prepared to endure strikes and stoppages during depressed trading because the loss of profit was relatively small. In 1907 it was argued that the sanitary manufacturers would have been more likely to entertain price and wage rises early in the year. When demand dropped from mid-year, the masters were prepared to sit out a two-and-a-half-month strike.[90] During 1920–1 employers attempted a 20 percent wage reduction on two grounds. The reassertion of foreign competition and the general drop in demand made a public case possible for their action. Coincidentally, the union was financially weak with funds savagely reduced by the unemployment pay expended as a result of the coal strike.[91]

Some authors have argued generally that the periods of conflict 1908–14 and 1918–21 owed much to the political debates of those years.[92] Without doubt, industrial conflict in the pottery industry during this period was primarily the result of issues generated from within the potbank allied with worker and employer strategies. The social and political arguments had an indirect influence only: they formed a backdrop to some of the main disputes. The unemployment campaign ideas of the SDF were echoed in the platform rhetoric of Booth in the 1900s.[93] Union officials were prominent in the growth of the local Labour party, and the years 1918–20 were noted for 'the present solidarity of labour in the district' with the highest number ever of council seats won by the Labour party. The war period was less traumatic for the potters than some of the engineering and mining districts because government contracts were few and the intervention of the Munitions Act was felt far less. Clearly the developing socialism of union officials, such as Clowes, Hollins and Lovatt, influenced their long-term goals, as their speeches indicate. But it was the short-term tactical considerations of the potters, arising from the changing organization of work, which were the immediate causes of industrial conflict during this period of the potters' history.[94]

Conclusion

This study of the pottery industry suggests two main conclusions. The first relates to pottery manufacture alone. In the light of the preceding reconstruction of such a range of industrial negotiation and conflict, the passive image of the potters and their supposedly 'cosy' relationship with their employers can no longer stand.[95] The findings of this paper are profoundly different from the conventional view. Williams et al.[96] conceive of industrial relations in an entirely institutional fashion: they see the subject involves only the formal apparatus of national bargaining. It is hardly surprising, therefore, that when they tried to impose this rigid and exclusive conception on the early twentieth-century pottery industry, they should find so little evidence of industrial conflict or that they should have discovered how varied a texture of relationships existed. Rather than being bound by this restrictive view of industrial relations from above, the analysis presented here has attempted to open up the subject of industrial relations in the pottery industry by combining an awareness of the spread of official, institutional arenas across the industry, with the rich mixture of relationships which operated below them.[97]

Industrial relations in the pottery industry can more productively be seen as composed of many different categories of social relations which arose from the production process. Besides the relatively infrequent, sober-suited meetings of employers and union officials at the North Staffordshire Hotel, a diverse array of informal negotiations was conducted every working day throughout the Six Towns. These exchanges could involve, for example, a single owner and a potter or they could be between all the potters of a given occupation and a group of employers in one subindustry. The fragmented production process (with its manifold skill divisions and the wage hierarchies associated with subcontracting) generated multiple interests and matching grievances. Each owner of a skill, each occupant of a step on the potbank status ladder, either individually or in a group, developed customary means of regulating their work. They bargained sectionally and produced their own versions of the 'mere chaos' of British industrial relations.[98] As in the motor industry this century, there were too many competing forces within, as well as between, the 45,000 potters and their 500 masters for them to be contained by the orderly relations suggested by previous commentators on the Potteries.[99]

The second main finding goes beyond the confines of pot-making. This recreation of the structure and dynamic of industrial relations in the early twentieth-century pottery industry, focusing on the patterns, sequence and experience of employment relations, also calls into question some of the existing perspectives of British industrial history. The search for the origins of British industrial relations verges on the ahistorical when dealing with the first decades of this century. There has been an overconcentration on the extent to which industries succeeded in establishing formal, national collective-bargaining machinery, thereby obtaining a 'mature', so-called 'system' of industrial relations. Price's assertion, for example, that the transition from an informal to a formalized system of industrial relations was the critical event in modern labour history contains a major assumption. The statement assumes that the transition process was a singular occurrence, never to be repeated.[100]

An alternative position, which encompasses structure and process, rejects that assumption for a number of reasons. Above all, as the pottery case shows, the official bargaining apparatus (including the heralded NCPI in 1917) was inherently unstable and unreliable given the uncertain combination of forces within the industry. Secondly, those involved certainly did not regard the new council as even the precursor of a regulated 'system' as their testimony indicates.[101] What they recognized at the time was the *potential* for a more formally organized method of regulating industrial disputes: a potential which was not realized in this period, as the manufacturer who considered the industry to be 'in want of union' saw only too clearly.

Moreover, what the pottery industry highlights is the impermanence of those schemes that sought to organize and codify industrial relations during this period. In the space of 25 years, the industry exhibits a succession of unsuccessful attempts to formalize different aspects of its industrial relations.

These included: the conciliation arrangements of 1899–1901; the arbitration board of 1908–11; and the ill-fated National Council of 1917. Essentially, neither the conditions nor the will existed to ensure the success of the formal apparatus. As Walker's examination of the jute trade in Aberdeen in the same period reveals, the recognition and acceptance which are the bases of such arrangements have to be 'a habit of mind and a continuous relationship as much as a once and for all publically conferred capitulation'.[102] That 'habit of mind' and 'continuous relationship' existed at the officially unregulated shopfloor level of bargaining; it was never fully established or even partially maintained at the higher, formal levels of subindustry boards or national councils. The general pattern of the creation and destruction of different variants of industrial-relations machinery during the nineteenth century has been documented elsewhere.[103] It might be more fruitful for historians to explore the work of sociologists, such as Ramsay or Penn, who see the long-term profile of British industrial relations, not as a linear progression towards formal 'maturity', but in terms of cycles of attempted regulation and control of employment triggered by periodic crises of productivity and profit.[104]

Lastly, an appreciation of the structural features of industrial relations, together with the close attention paid to *the dynamics of conflict,* offer a way forward for uncovering further the historical reality of everyday employment relationships. By accepting the highly complex reasons behind disputes and, therefore, the range of possible forms of their expression, there is no longer the need to concentrate purely on strike incidence to assess the militancy or otherwise of a workforce.[105] Nor is it necessary for historians to rely solely on union-organized action as the plea made by the NAS in 1911 for potters to report their individual disputes to the union shows. A more comprehensive history of industrial relations can be arrived at by researching the intersection of the needs and aims of those involved with customary and formal codes which provided the context for their activities. Studies of the 1980s[106] indicate that such patterns are still essential in understanding contemporary bargaining forms as the national industrial relations machinery of the 1970s has been dismantled. The very nature of industrial conflict has meant that it could not be so easily controlled, as past officials and managers have found to their cost; neither can it be encapsulated as straightforwardly as some historians have maintained.

5

Management, Labour and the State in France 1871–1939: Industrial Relations in the Third Republic

Roger Magraw

I do not intend my workers to discuss their conditions of work: if these do not suit them, let them go elsewhere . . . I have hundreds to replace them. Besides, I *am* the Master, I *intend to be* the Master, and I *will be* the Master in spite of everything. Longwy steel employer in 1905.[1]

Introduction

In the post-1945 period, French industrial relations were frequently described as 'immature'. Whereas most Western European employers appeared willing to negotiate with 'moderate' trades unions, in France a tough *patronat de combat* still viewed unions as illegitimate. The union movement, still a minority phenomenon, was fragmented along ideological lines. Such characteristics were seen as the legacy of more than a century of often-violent class conflict. French employers had been fragmented by atavistic religious and political divisions, often at odds over such issues as protective tariffs. Jealousy of rival firms often made them reluctant to join employer associations. Yet, with a handful of a typical exceptions, all had rejected state interference in industrial relations and recognition of unions as legitimate vehicles for the expression of workers' grievances.

Consequently, union membership remained low.[2] *Joining* a union was, in much of private industry, rarely a 'normal' step but in itself an act of commitment. Unionization was a minority phenomenon reserved for a handful of activists viewed as subversive troublemakers by management. Occasionally, during a favourable conjuncture (1918–20; 1936) masses of workers surged into unions and voiced radical demands. But, as the political tide turned, these neophytes would flood out as rapidly as they had flooded in, leaving the skeleton of union organization once more in the hands of the *minorites agissantes.*

Moreover, employers regarded strikes as breaches of contract, even as acts of 'mutiny'. In 12 per cent of the strikes that occurred between 1895 and 1899 two-thirds or more of the strikers were sacked.[3] Some 3300 rail strikers were dismissed in 1910, 20,000 after the defeated strike of May 1920.

Various consequences, it is suggested, flowed from this situation. Because they were either unable (through employer intransigence) or unwilling (because of their own 'extremist' views) to recruit the mass of workers and, thus, to force employers to negotiate, union militants had a highly *'political'* attitude to industrial relations. Many, at least until 1920, were fascinated by the syndicalist myth of the General Strike and dreamed that the activist minority could sweep the unorganized rank-and-file into a quasi-revolutionary movement, paralyse the capitalist economy and establish a decentralist 'Socialism' of worker control. The strike waves of 1906–8 and 1919–20 had strong syndicalist overtones. Others view strikers' 'political' goals as more pragmatic. Because unions were too weak to force the *patronat* to surrender, their aim was to attract public attention to persuade the State to pressure employers into concessions – hence the advent of a left-of-centre government, potentially sympathetic to labour, sparked off optimistic strike waves in 1879–80, 1899–1900 and 1936. Often, too, unions would seek to make use of the solidarity shown by left-wing municipalities towards strikers to counterbalance their own shopfloor weakness.[4] In the 1890s barely 3 per cent of *chefs-lieux* in France were controlled by the socialists but, by 1929, more than 25 per cent of these were held by the Socialist or by the Communist parties.

Management Strategies in the Early Third Republic

Any attempt at a brief categorization of employer strategies in the early Third Republic must inevitably be over-schematic. French industry remained highly diverse. Much of it had concentrated in the nineteenth-century upon up-market, semi-luxury products (silks, porcelain...) reliant still on 'artisanal' labour. Revisionist historiography, questioning earlier scorn for such 'archaic', 'Malthusian' enterprises, has claimed that such industries competed effectively in domestic and foreign markets.[5] By 1914, however, some sectors of French industry – Lorraine steel, the northern coalfields, cars, Alpine hydroelectricity – were as large and as 'modern' as any in Europe.

Despite attempts to respond to the rise of organized labour by developing a web of protectionist, social-imperialist and social-reform projects that could unite the fractions of the capitalist elites, ideological and political diversity continued to characterize the French industrialist class. Some industrialists still yearned for a quasi-authoritarian neo-royalist or Bonapartist regime; others had been won over to the conviction, as early as the 1860s, that long-term social stability could best be achieved by a democratic Republic established in alliance with the petty bourgeoisie and the peasantry. Some were Roman Catholic, others Protestant or militantly laic.

One distinctive feature of industrial relations in large industry (mining, heavy metallurgy, engineering), which may appear incongrous in a 'liberal-democratic' Republic, was the persistence of forms of quasi-authoritarian paternalism. This could be viewed as one logical response to an endemic labour shortage – the product of a precociously falling birth rate, of the tenacity with which peasants clung to the land and of widespread distaste for heavy industrial labour. Paternalism sought to stabilize a hereditary work-force, kept loyal via a blend of deference, gratitude and fear.[7] The creation of such 'new types of Bastille' (Zola) was not simply a form of neo-feudalism characteristic of old-style Catholic-Royalist families. 'Deference' was most likely in isolated company towns with a resident owner, like de Wendel in Lorraine, who knew each employee by name. Yet paternalism was also developed by large *Sociétés Anonymes* run by absentee boards of directors.[8]

The model paternalist company town did not tolerate independent unions. Management calculated that it made sound economic sense to use company resources to finance schemes that made strikes unlikely – medical treatment, child care, pensions. Schools and technical classes were established as earlier reliance on child labour gave way to the desire to produce a labour force with basic literacy and numeracy. 'What the factory needs is workers just sufficiently educated out of . . . coarseness and foremen whose qualities have been revealed by exams' (L. Reybaud). Catholic religious orders that ran these schools participated in the ubiquitous surveillance system that earned some company towns their reputations as clerical theocracies. Fathers of large families were rewarded and praised for breeding the next generation of 'tireless little workers'.[9]

Workers, explicitly treated as 'children', were kept isolated from outside contacts. At Bethune, high walls around miners' cottages excluded prying journalists. Paternalistic ideology emphasized the importance of housing in moulding a reliable work-force. A house – even if company owned – gave workers a proprietorial sense and kept them away from the lure of café politics. Many had gardens or allotments. There was, however, unconscious irony in management's praise of the moral virtues and robust health of the 'worker-gardener' because as at Carmaux, many firms had earlier sought to improve the timekeeping and labour discipline of 'peasant-miners' by breaking their links with their small farms.[10] Wives attended housekeeping classes to learn to use home-grown vegetables to make nutritious meals – a key factor in the ability of paternalist companies to keep wages low. Regular inspections led to prizes for neat homes and allotments – or to fines for untidiness or squalor. Company stores reduced the scope for independent small shopkeepers who might function as the focus for autonomous popular sociability or politics. Surveillance of workers frequently extended to close supervision by foremen of polling booths.

The heyday of authoritarian paternalism was in the 1870s and 1880s. But Grand 'Combes in the Gard coalfield remained a virtual 'theocracy' until at least 1914[11] and Le Creusot remained 'an Oceania with Schneider as Big Brother'. His statue dominated the square, surrounded by figures of loyal workers gazing up in awe. The town's eery atmosphere disconcerted visitors. There were few cafés and, with the men in the engineering plant, the women in kitchens or allotments and the children in training classes, the streets seemed deserted. Lorraine steel masters copied Schneider's methods and were largely successful in preventing the labour movement from establishing a foothold there. Segregated company housing helped to preserve a form of apartheid which kept French workers apart from immigrants who were coming to monopolize the hard and dirty jobs in steelmills and iron mines. Meanwhile, technological change within the steelmills (the Bessemer process, electric ovens, automatic temperature gauges) undermined the job-autonomy of the teams of puddlers and *mouleurs* whose skills had hitherto been essential. Independent *cafetiers*, who dared to permit their premises to be used for union meetings, found their water and gas supplies cut off by company-controlled municipal councils.[12] The strikes of 1905 proved to be a false dawn for the Lorraine labour movement.

Yet, elsewhere, sophisticated managers became aware by 1890 that old-style authoritarian/clerical paternalism was under challenge and that strategies had to be adapted. Violent strikes shook Carmaux, Montceau-les-Mines, Decazeville. Le Creusot was hit by bitter conflict in 1899–1900 which forced Schneider to sack 2300 strikers and to introduce 'yellow' company unions. Accounts of paternalism written in a tone of Foucaultesque despair, as if every blueprint for totalitarian social control was effectively implemented, lack plausibility. Not all attempts to divide loyal French company workers from transient immigrants succeeded. Labour turnover remained high despite attempts to create a stable, hereditary labour force. And the fall in the birth rate at Montceau, from 34 per cent to 14 per cent between 1880 and 1910, must indicate the failure of effort of this Le Playist management to reward workers who fathered large families and thus, it was hoped, ensured the future supply of 'tireless little workers'.[13]

In southern coalfields, where seams were difficult and profits low, intransigent management sought to 'bust' unions, and strikes were often quasi-messianic eruptions.[14] At Decazeville, however, paternalist strategies were modified in the wake of the violent strike of 1886 against company electoral surveillance. In the era of the Republic and of trades unions, older methods of labour control no longer appeared appropriate. The new manager Fayol – later France's leading management theorist – introduced policies which he had pioneered at Commentry (Allier). 'Fayolism' involved the withdrawal of management from attempts to dominate miners' sociability and electoral politics. It accepted that teams of hewers should have some autonomy and was prepared to co-operate with elected miners' safety delegates. Management authority should, instead, be guaranteed by establishment of a clear command hierarchy. A qualified managing director, free of meddling interference from 'amateurs' on the company's Administrative Council, should be in sole command. He should make long-term investment plans and be willing, in the wider interests of the firm, to abandon unprofitable pits irrespective of the protests from the communities who might suffer. Within the pits, company engineers and foremen should be highly trained and have control over hiring and firing.[15] This shift towards hard-headed, professional management administration can be observed in other coalfields.[16]

The most far-reaching change in industrial relations occurred in the huge northern coalfields. Here seams were easier to work, profit levels higher and management thus more willing to make concessions. One breakthrough took place in 1890 when, under pressure from miners, the government intervened to attempt to cut accident rates by insisting that miners had the right to elect pit-safety delegates.[17] By 1893, in the 'Arras Convention', the miners' union won collective-bargaining rights. In return for guarantees on safety, pensions, hours and a sliding wage prices scale, union leader Basly promised the northern coal-owners that he would seek to control strike militancy. His union became an electoral machine which sought to send deputies to Parliament to speak for miners' interests. The revolt of a militant syndicalist *jeune syndicat* failed to undermine Basly's dominance, and strike rates in the Pas-de-Calais coalfield fell in the years before 1914.

Northern coal-owners were the backbone of the national coal employers' federation (*C. C. H. F.*). This was less cohesive than its German counterpart and had difficulty reconciling the interests of northern *Sociétés Anonymes* with the smaller, less affluent, southern mining companies. The *C. C. H. F.* acted as an effective Parliamentary lobby, however, which kept a low profile to avoid public criticism. Its members agreed that their common goals were to minimize State interference and to prevent the growth of a national miners' federation and national pay bargaining. The mutual antagonism between Basly and quasisyndicalist southern militants played into their hands. From 1906 the *C. C. H. F.* organized a national antistrike fund.[18]

In the pre-war decades, management initially faced the problem of falling prices and profits during the 'Great Depression' (1875–95), and then problems of adjustment as rapid industrial growth after 1896 accelerated the transition towards the industries of the 'Second Industrial Revolution'. It was in response to such problems that new management strategies were introduced.

In the 1830s, technocrats from the Grandes Écoles, such as C. L. Bergery, had pioneered professional management and had argued the need for silent, obedient workers, trained foremen and piece-work bonus schemes. But it was during the 1880s that factory regulations became more complex and draconian. Contemporary photographs show a full panoply of clocks, factory gates, bells, rules posted on walls ... Workers' rhetoric now dubbed the factory a '*bagne*' (prison).

Inevitably, attempts to tighten discipline and raise productivity could generate resistance as well as obedience and submission. Workers valued 'traditional' freedom to chat, drink, come and go as they pleased, play cards ... Quasi-autonomous teams of skilled workers (glass-blowers; porcelain workers ...) had learned how to keep down the pace of work to help older workers and to prevent 'overproduction'. Glass workers broke 'excess' bottles at the end of a shift ... Skilled shoemakers and metal workers in the small Parisian *boîtes* changed jobs at the first sign of employer intransigence.[19]

After 1880 technological changes and new employer strategies threatened such practices. Turret-lathes and universal millers deskilled some engineering jobs and new gas ovens enabled glass employers to replace skilled glass-blowers and to break their subsequent strikes.[20] The apprentice system had long been in crisis in many trades but now, even the informal practices, whereby know how was passed on from older workers to the young, were being undermined.[21]

Concern for efficiency led to a vogue for discussion of 'Taylorism'. École des Mines professor, H. Le Chatelier, became the leading European proponent of Taylorist ideas. The debate over 'scientific management' involved more than the *patronat* concern with costcutting or continuous-flow production. It reflected the growing obsession with French decadence, nurtured by concern with falling birth rate, VD, crime, juvenile delinquency, alcoholism and anarchist bombs. For 'Taylorism' offered a mirage of effective control over skilled workers whose independence was viewed as the key to syndicalist dreams of worker control. Reassertion of managerial authority on the shopfloor held the key to national productivity and competitiveness. Significantly Renault, an early supporter of Taylorism, shared with Le Chatelier an admiration for the reactionary 'crowd theory' of Le Bon.

In practice, barely 1 per cent of workers were employed in 'Taylorized' plants by 1914. Even Renault merely attempted a quick and cheap 'fix' by piecemeal introduction of a few Taylorist practices – bonus payment schemes, time-and-motion study, factory laboratories, standardized machine tools, rational planning of factory space. Modernizing patrons (for example Michelin) remained suspicious that Taylorism was too 'theoretical', too costly and would give excessive power to engineers.[22]

Most employers simply opted for a rough-and-ready home-grown proto-Taylorism. In practice, this meant piece-work payment schemes, backed up by the use of tough foremen (ex-NCOs), to enforce tighter factory regulations.[23] Unsurprisingly, it was these 'bosses' cops' who bore the brunt of the worker backlash which assumed the scale of a genuine revolt against discipline. In 1885–9 12 per cent of strikes involved job-control issues, by 1910–14 25 per cent. In Paris, strikes by skilled and by semiskilled engineers' workers often began with violence involving foremen. In the Lyonnais payment systems, speed-ups and time-and-motion study – as at Berliet in 1912 – generated dozens of strikes.[24]

Some managers sought strategies to reduce worker resentments. Some new factories had better cloakroom facilities and a more pleasant working environment. Some industrialists flirted with 'ergonomics', a new science that studied the human body and sought ways to use the 'human machine' which could extract the maximum productivity with the minimum physical or psychological stress.[25]

The Republic made considerable efforts from its early years to 'normalize' industrial relations. A number of prefects were from the *'nouvelles couches sociales'* and felt a certain hostility to Catholic-royalist industrial plutocrats.[26] In 1884, worried by strike outbursts engendered, in part, by workers' hopes that they would get support from Republican officials, the Opportunist government legalized trades unions – in the hope that a 'moderate', 'nonpolitical' union movement on the English model would emerge. Republican municipalities began to sponsor *Bourses du Travail.* Later these became notorious for their attempts to foster an autonomous worker culture and to synchronize syndicalist strike waves. But in origin they represented an effort by the reformist bourgeoisie to provide job centres and to co-opt a 'moderate' labour leadership. They were, thus, part of the 'juridico-ideological structuring of social space according to what was suitable for the owners of the means of production'.[27] Strikes were now treated as a disease not a crime, the approach to them became 'pathological not penal'. In 1874, 18 per cent of strikers had been jailed. By 1885, this fell to 0.8 per cent.[28]

The success of such strategies remained limited. Employer hostility inhibited unionism in many sectors, not least the fast-expanding engineering industry. Unskilled workers, immigrants, recent migrants and women workers (nearly 40 per cent of the labour force) proved hard to organize.

One must not assume, however, that non-unionized workers were docile and passive. A. Cottereau has detailed the pragmatic, informal direct action used by shoeworkers to resist employers. In Paris this involved frequent job changes: in Fougères in the west it could involve 'pluri-activity' – a willingness to move back into agricultural labour during disputes with employers.[29] Moreover, strike rates rose more rapidly than unionization levels. Between 1870 and 1890 there were, on average, 150 strikes per annum, for much of the decade before 1914 annual rates were above 1000. This militancy coincided with the years of revolutionary syndicalist leadership of the main trade union confederation, the *CGT* – although the exact causal relationship between these two facts remains problematic. The *CGT*'s notoriously weak organizational structure made its contribution to industrial relations similar to that of a man standing on a table bawling instructions during a bar-room brawl! Nevertheless, there is evidence that strikes co-ordinated by (syndicalist-dominated) *Bourses du Travail* were larger, involved more workplaces and were more likely to 'succeed' than unorganized strikes.[30]

Workers continued to exhibit a largely negative attitude towards employers and managers. The rhetoric used by strikers to describe these was largely 'archaic' – vampires, bloodsuckers, parasites, tyrants, seigneurs – rather than Marxist. But its message was clear. Workers did not share the St Simonian or Schumpeterian respect for employers as dynamic, productive entrepreneurs.[31]

During the 1890s, laws regulating child and female factory labour and introducing compensation for industrial accidents were passed.[32] But the principal attempt to transform industrial relations was made by Millerand during Waldeck-Rousseau's ministry. The 1899–1900 strike wave which greeted the new government gave urgency to Millerand's assertion that real efforts were required to prevent workers becoming disillusioned with the Republic's unfulfilled promise of social justice. His attempts to enforce the 1892 Act, however, which had enabled either party in an industrial dispute to call on *JPs* to conciliate, by a tripartite *Conseil National du Travail*, on which state bureaucrats from the new Labour ministry could meet regularly with employers and unions, and by compulsory arbitration, proved stillborn. Syndicalists viewed this as a plot to tame labour organizers, while employers saw it as illegitimate *dirigiste* interference with their prerogatives. Schneider insisted that he would accept 'the intervention of *nobody* from outside the factory in contact I have with my workers'. St Etienne silk employers, praising the self-regulating capacity of the local *fabrique*, begged government to 'leave it to us to arrange things between employers and workers'.[33]

Hopes that State intervention might create the climate for calm industrial relations proved, therefore, unfounded. In only 16 per cent of industrial disputes between 1910 and 1913 were *JPs* called in – usually by workers – to conciliate. Only 6 per cent of strikes between 1898 and 1914 witnessed employer negotiations with unions and only 1 per cent of disputes in 1906–14 were *settled* by collective bargaining. Employers often made wage concessions rather than agree to recognize unions or to bargain on non-wages issues. Large and small employers alike evaded the law introducing a weekly rest day passed in 1906 in an effort to head off a General Strike for the 8-Hour Day – prompting one Radical to ask, 'What shall we say to the working class when everytime a law punishes them it is enforced and when one benefits them it is ignored!'[34]

One-hundred-and-thirty-nine factory inspectors struggled valiantly with the thankless task of enforcing factory legislation. Often, indeed, they 'transcended their limited policing powers by trying to create conditions for progressive, solidaristic forms of industrial relations via participation in social reform ... and via establishment of working-relations with trade union locals'.[35] Experiments with more consensual styles of management/union consultation attempted in State naval yards, however, were ignored by the private sector.[36] P. Stearns's claim that there was a trend towards collective bargaining on the events of 1914 seems implausible.[37]

Indeed, in the years after 1906, the Republic appeared keener to repress than to 'integrate' unionism. In the face of 'syndicalist' strikes, Clemenceau posed as 'France's Number One Cop'. Links between the State and employers became closer. The use of troops against strikers, which had fallen in the 1870–80s, rose markedly. In Lorraine in 1905, the Radical prefect called in the Army to protect Catholic neo-royalist steel bosses who financed racist, 'yellow' company unions! Union rights of public-sector employers (for example, postmen) were restricted. Strike violence often stemmed from the actions of *agents provocateurs* paid by the police to infiltrate syndicalist groups. Of the 88 really violent strikes that occurred in the Third Republic, 11 were in 1904, 20 in 1906, seven in 1911.[38]

Meanwhile, Employers' Associations more than doubled their membership (to 420,000) between 1899 and 1913. These copied German counterparts (*ZVDI*) by organizing strike insurance funds, blacklists, supplies of scab labour, lockouts and company unions.[39] The culmination of the joint State/employer offensive came when striking railmen in 1910 were called up into the Army under threat of being treated as 'mutineers'. The hitherto moderate railmen's unions – divided between 'craft' and general workers – had grown impatient with the growing reluctance of Radical governments to protect them against speed-ups and 'rationalization'. To smash the emerging syndicalist revolt on the (strategically vital) rail network, the Government backed a hardline *patronat* which insisted that 'we *cannot* consider a Trade Union, with its unrepresentative demands ... as authorised to present itself to us in the name of all our personnel ... and as constituting a useful intermediary between them and us'.[40]

By 1910–14 syndicalism was at an impasse. Strike rates remained high, but failure rates were rising. Despite *CGT* attempts to encourage industrial unionism, labour organization remained feeble in 'modern' sectors of industry (steel, engineering, chemicals). As old craft concerns over job control collapsed and the 'new' proletariat deficient in consciousness and solidarity emerged the way was open for pragmatists in the *CGT* (such as Jouhaux) to argue that it was imperative that unions move towards a more 'realistic', economistic strategy and to aim at larger, more stable membership.[41] Then the war came.

War, Union Sacrée, Labour Schism: 1914–21

Although it is tempting to label World War I as a 'watershed' in French labour history, it remains difficult to offer any unequivocal characterization of its significance for industrial relations. One could argue that working-class support for the war effort, barely dented by relatively modest and (largely) economistic strikes in 1917–18, marked a crucial step towards 'integration' of workers into the Republic synthesis. Moreover, the *dirigiste* role of the State in wartime planning drew the *CGT* into active collaboration with the war effort and raised hopes among labour reformists for a postwar new deal in which unions would be consulted by bureaucrats and employers on industrial and economic planning.

Conversely, some historians have emphasized that war weariness, deteriorating living standards and working conditions and the lure of Bolshevism gave the industrial unrest of 1917–18 quasi revolutionary overtones. Moreover, the rapid dismantling of wartime *dirigiste* machinery and return to *laissez-faire*, and the paucity of social reform, engendered working-class bitterness, a quasi syndicalist strike wave in 1919–20 and, when this was defeated, growing support for the new Communist Party (*PC*).[42]

Wartime government moved inexorably towards interventionism. It allocated scarce raw materials and food and recalled skilled workers from the trenches.[43] Albert Thomas, a reformist socialist who became Under-Secretary of State for Munitions, played a key role in war production and in labour relations. Syndicalists accused him of hawking a banal productivist rhetoric around factory canteens while turning a blind eye to profiteering by big private armaments contractors. But some have attributed to him a strategic goal of drawing a reformist *CGT* into a tripartite, corporatist industrial relations system in the interests of national efficiency and social harmony. In 1915–16 he held talks with union leaders and leading metallurgical and engineering employers in the hope of securing union collaboration with new technologies and work practices. By shifting demand towards mass-produced, standardized products, war production encouraged the spread of Taylorism, but only to an atypical minority of firms (Renault, Berliet, Michelin, the Paris-Orléans locomotives workshops, Penhoët naval dockyards, Bourges arsenal). Most firms simply raised production via longer hours, cuts in piecework rates, speed-ups, by ruthless exploitation of non-unionized workers (immigrants, women or *mobilisés* subject to military discipline). Many employers' earlier scepticism about the value of Taylorism was now compounded by worries that the projects of Thomas or of Clémentel for State support for industrial 'rationalization' (mergers; standardized/interchangeable parts) were steps down the slippery slope to collectivist *dirigisme*. André Citroën was, however, an advocate of industrial mergers and of scientific management. 'War', he insisted, 'taught us the value of organisation of work, of methods which allow . . . delicate operations without use of skilled labour.'

The wartime State provided unemployment relief, family allowances for troops' dependants and a Minimum Wage Bill (1915). Moreover, Jouhaux was given official status as a 'National Commissioner' and union officials sat alongside bureaucrats and doctors on committees that monitored factory conditions for females. A *Comité d'Action*, composed of reformist socialists and union bureaucrats, sought to consolidate and build upon this unprecedented trade union presence in domestic planning. Old syndicalist shibboleths were discarded in the hope that henceforth unions would be consulted over new technologies and economic planning and could collaborate with bureaucracy and *patronat* in a 'productivist' alliance to boost France's economic efficiency, to break her 'Malthusian' shackles, and to allow higher wages within a planned mixed economy.[44] Even Merrheim, hitherto a leading syndicalist opponent of the *Union Sacrée*, was gradually persuaded that 'revolution' would involve the education of the labour movement about how to run a modern economy. As Secretary of the Metalworkers' Federation (*FM*) Merrheim was drawn willy-nilly into negotiating with the State over conditions in war factories and appreciated Thomas's efforts to pressure employers to negotiate with unions.[45]

By 1916–17 Thomas also sought to head off rising industrial unrest by pushing the *patronat* to grant cost-of-living wage increases and to accept compulsory arbitration. In the mining sector, government not only fixed prices, directed labour and established a nine-hour day but used prefects to force even the authoritarian Gard coal companies to sign collective contracts with the Union. Miners thus remained largely aloof from the 'political' strikes of 1917–18.[46]

At Renault (Boulogne-Billancourt) grievances built up in the first half of the War as a heterogeneous, largely non-unionized work-force of some 20,000 faced longer hours, exhausting speed-ups, rising accident rates and tough discipline.[47] These pressures were not really relieved by new company *oeuvres*–canteens, crèches, sports' clubs.[48] In 1917 Thomas stepped in to end strikes for higher wages triggered by rapid inflation. He introduced conciliation machinery, a sliding wages/prices scale, and workers' election of shop stewards. Renault sought to get 'loyal', long-term company workers elected and to confine their role to that of transmitting management decisions downwards. In practice, leading shop stewards were usually syndicalists critical of the war, and of Thomas's 'productivist' rhetoric, of Renault's authoritarian management style and of war profiteering. Some of the most outspoken were sent to the trenches! Yet the relative industrial calm at Renault in 1918 suggests that Thomas's intervention achieved *some* of its objectives.

Nevertheless, there was another side to French labour's wartime experience. The *CGT* lost 80 per cent of its membership in 1914–15. The already weak Metalworkers' Federation proved much less capable of defending skilled workers'; shopfloor conditions than did its British counterpart, the ASE.[49] War-industry workers faced falling real wages and deteriorating conditions of work as earlier laws regulating factory conditions were relaxed. Meanwhile, large industrialists received government grants for machinery and had priority access to raw materials. Only in 1917 did Clémentel succeed in using Government control of imported raw materials to clamp down on their prices and profits. Hence, the strikes of May 1918 reflected worker's war weariness and political anger. In the industrial towns around St Etienne, where unionism had traditionally been weak in heavy metallurgical industry, the strikes assumed a quasi-insurrectionary character against an 'arrogant, intransigent, feudal management' (Merrheim). Lukewarm support from local textile and mining unions and hostility from the *CGT* ensured defeat for the Stephenois metal strikers.[51] But their bitterness foreshadowed the quasisyndicalist unrest of 1919–20, and many of those involved were prominent in the birth of the Communist labour movement.[52]

The support for Communism stemmed from disillusionment with the failure of the elites to 'reward' the working class for their wartime efforts. *CGT* leaders set out a 'minimum program'. This included rail and mine nationalization, the Eight-Hour Day, social insurance and involvement of unions in collective bargaining and in postwar industrial planning and reconstruction. Their slogan was 'maximum production in the minimum time for the maximum wage'. They hoped that, via the *I. L. O.*, such concessions to labour could be internationalized, thereby weakening employer accusations that French competitiveness would be undermined.[53]

Their hopes were soon dashed. Thomas had lost his post in late 1917, and Clemenceau's Government in the last months of the war adopted a hostile tone towards organized labour. With Clémentel's departure in 1919, hopes for quasicorporatist economic planning disappeared. Wartime economic regulation was dismantled with indecent haste. Although a few modernizing technocrats (such as Rateau of the electricity industry) perceived potential advantages in management collaboration with moderate unions who could 'guide workers onto the sensible path', most employers saw piecemeal quasipaternalistic schemes as an *alternative* to regularized collective bargaining.[54] Bolstered by the conservative electoral victory of 1919 the *patronat* staged a classic display of its legendary intransigence. Employers' Associations lobbied Parliament to obstruct a social insurance bill – denounced as a 'scroungers' charter', alien to the 'French mentality', overbureaucratic and unfair to the self-employed. They praised the alternative of *private* company insurance schemes. A measure designed to ease social tensions ended by exacerbating them.[55]

The one major concession was the Eight-Hour Day, rushed through Parliament to head off a threatened metalworkers' strike scheduled for May 1919. *CGT* reformists and Thomas argued that it would prove a *stimulus* to managerial innovation and an incentive to rationalization and, thus, prove compatible with higher productivity and with efforts to combat the 'spirit of routine' on both sides of industry. Labour Ministry bureaucrats, whose job was to liaise with industries in the application of the 48-Hour Week, were enthusiastic about the measure. There were to be no resultant pay cuts, but employers reliant on scarce skilled labour or involved in seasonal rush jobs were promised 'flexibility'. Meanwhile, during 1919, 577 collective contracts were signed. The previous peak (1910) had witnessed only 252.

Illusions that France was moving towards industrial compromise and orderly collective bargaining were rapidly shattered. Quasisyndicalist strikes in the metal industries repudiated productivity deals offered by the *CGT* leadership as a quid pro que for rapid employer implementation of the Eight-Hour Day.[56] Workers in other sectors followed their example.

The *patronat* had always been more hostile to concessions on hours and on union recognition than to mere wage demands. American rejection of the Eight-Hour Day confirmed their opposition to *unilateral* French measures. The engineering employers' federation (*U. I. M. M.*) reneged on its deal with the *F. M.* By 1921 10 hours remained the norm in provincial industry. Prefects allowed wholesale exemptions to a range of employers, so that only 27 per cent of workers were now covered by the Eight-Hour Act. F. Poncy of the *Comité des Forges* insisted that France's international competitiveness required *longer* hours and *less* State meddling in industrial relations.[57]

During 1919–20 employers faced the challenge of militancy from a work-force whose level of unionization had risen to unprecedented levels.[58] Nevertheless, unionism remained a minority phenomenon, clearly divided between reformists, and neo-syndicalists. Aided by a sympathetic government and by rising unemployment, the *patronat* staged a victorious confrontation with organized labour and then set about dismantling union bargaining rights. As in 1910, the showdown took place on the railways. Here the State had played a strong *dirigiste* role in 1914–18, co-ordinating the activities of the private companies. Despite enormous pressures on the work-force, there had been few strikes because railworkers had been subject to quasimilitary discipline. But, by 1920, a newly united rail union had enrolled 80 per cent of the labour force (374,000).

Faced with the enormous costs of postwar re-equipment and the potential cost of the Eight-Hour Law, the companies began vigorous 'rationalization'. They hoped to Taylorize locomotive workshops, abandon wartime cost-of-living allowances and to break the union. When Parliament rejected railway nationalization neo-syndicalist activists seized control of the union but the government helped the companies to defeat the ensuing May 1920 General Strike. Some 18,000 railmen were sacked and union membership plummeted.[59]

Meanwhile, coal employers were clawing back ground conceded during the War. The miners' union (*F. S. S.*) made demands for representation on mixed commissions and for a minimum wage. The *C. C. H. F.* stonewalled against concessions on national bargaining rights and won government support to resist strike threats. Its president rejoiced that the 'deplorable lowering of *patronat* authority' was being reversed and congratulated his members on resisting the threats from *dirigisme* and from union power. 'Alone with your workers you have calmly resisted ... problems which would have benefited not at all from being referred to others than the interested parties themselves'. The *C. C. H. F.* profited from fomenting divisions between the 'reasonable' neo-Baslyite union leadership of the north and the 'excitable and dangerous' neo-syndicalist minority unionism of the south.[60]

1921–1935

Such fratricidal rivalries – now institutionalized into the division between reformist *C. G. T.*, Communist *C. G. T. U.*, neo-syndicalist *C. G. T. - S . R.* and Catholic *C.F.T.C.* – helped to make the following 15 years a bleak age for the labour movement. Years of almost unbroken centre-right government cemented the reconsolidation of capitalist hegemony. Union membership remained below a million and was particularly weak in large private industry. The *C.G.T.*, whose main bastions were in the public service sector (post office, civil service), remained too weak to be taken seriously as a 'social partner' by government or employers.[61]

The vogue for collective contracts did not survive 1920. By 1935 there were only 29 in French industry! Strike levels oscillated around 5000 per annum, but failure rates were very high, reaching 58 per cent in 1931 and 70 per cent in 'job-control' strikes, though both these and 'violent' strikes' were now rarer because of the decline of syndicalism.[62] The Employers' Confederation (*C. G. P. F.*), dominated by the big metallurgical engineering and mining lobbies (*C des F*; *UIMM*; *CCHF*), relied on the weaknesses of organized labour to maintain its dominant position.[63] These were accentuated by massive recruitment of immigrants into heavy industry. By 1930 one industrial worker in seven was foreign. Most were recruited by private agencies, but the government negotiated general terms with foreign governments involved, notably Italy and Poland. Lacking elementary civil and political rights, subject to police surveillance and encouraged by coal and steel employers to focus their social lives round clerical ethnic associations, immigrants remained insulated from the labour movement. The *C. G. T.* secured a role, alongside Labour Ministry officials, in directing immigrants away from skilled big-city craft jobs. *C. G. T. U.* efforts to recruit immigrants proved largely unsuccessful. Undoubtedly, immigration handed the *patronat* a trump card. It 'unblocked' the labour market, kept wage levels down in the 1920s' boom and fragmented labour on ethnic and cultural lines.[64]

The vogue for 'scientific management' made the rhetoric of 'Taylorism', 'Bédaux systems' and so forth the buzz-words of the 1920s.[65] When *CGT* and *SFIO* reformists emphasized their admiration for 'American' methods, however, and urged collaboration between moderate unions and technocratic management to create 'modern', high-wage economy, their message remained anathema to the far left *and* to most *patrons*.[65] Even Citroën remained wary of high-wage strategies and refused to view shorter hours as a potential incentive to productivity increase. One study of 70 firms suggested that only nine had adopted four or more 'Taylorist' ideas. Most simply sought to boost productivity via speed-ups utilizing existing machinery and processes. Large firms remained reluctant to espouse ruthless 'rationalization' which might threaten the socio-political balance by driving smaller 'archaic' firms to the wall. Nevertheless, France *was* a European pioneer of Taylorization of car, armaments, rubber, chemical and locomotive plants. The *C. G. P. F.* campaigned in 1927 for mergers and for interchangeable parts. Productivity growth reached 2.9 per cent per annum 1924–9 – the highest rate until the 1950s. Mergers reached 44 per annum 1927–30, three times the 1919–24 level. France became Europe's largest car exporter.[67] *C.G.T.U* attempts to 'target' car plants like Renault proved unsuccessful, however Unionization rates at Citroën hovered around 1 per cent. Assembly lines, time-and-motion study and bonus-payment schemes characterized the car factories. With the steady decline in the proportion of skilled workers, syndicalist dreams of shopfloor control ebbed away. Factory discipline was maintained via tight vetting of job applications, blacklists, surveillance of canteens and cloak-rooms by paid company informers and – after 1930s – by Fascist-led company unions. Use of widely varying bonus-payment schemes further fragmented ethnically and culturally heterogeneous labour forces. Citroën did offset the pervasive sense of insecurity engendered by such strategies by using paternalist initiatives (creches, sports' clubs, holiday camps) to foster an *esprit maison*. Latent worker resentment found expression largely in ruses designed to slow the assembly lines although, by 1932–5, tiny Communist cells within the car plants were beginning to win support by concentrating on practical 'bread-and-butter' grievances.[68]

Despite friction between regional coalfields, and the inability to challenge the hold of the *Comité des Forges* on the *C.G.P.F*, the coalowners' association (*CCHF*) grew stronger. Northern coalowners' strategy involved fomenting rivalries between French and Polish miners, negotiating a coal price/wages sliding scale with the *CGT*, neo-paternalism (72 per cent of Pas-de-Calais miners lived in company houses) and 'rationalization' to preserve profits during the Depression. Between 1929 and 1935 production rose by 35 per cent while the wage bill fell by 25 per cent because of lay-offs and closures of difficult seams. Mechanized 'longwall' mining and Bédaux-individualized payment systems eroded the autonomy and solidarities of coalface hewers' teams. Miners' complaints of increased work pace, dust, noise, rising accident rates and loss of 'dignity' eventually produced an audience for *C.G.T.U* activists on the eve of the 1936 strike explosion.[69] In the narrower, irregular seams of southern pits hewer-team autonomy persisted and managerial control relied on Fayolist principles of hierarchical 'administration of labour'. The *CGT* collaborated with the *CCHF* in lobbying for reduced rail-freight rates to help struggling coalfields, leaving the *C.G.T.U* to attempt to unionize immigrants and lead the occasional strike.[70]

In Lorraine the hegemony of steel barons remained virtually unchallenged. Most Italian workers remained too cowed by police surveillance or threats of deportation to risk involvement with the *C.G.T.U*. French workers – largely skilled, supervisory or white collar – remained enmeshed in a web of 'paternalist' schemes. The *patronat* used their Parliamentary clout to obstruct social-welfare legislation that might threaten their control of family allowan-ces and welfare schemes. Via control of municipal councils, they dominated the public space of the steel towns. They financed ex-servicemens' associations and orchestrated war-commemoration rituals in adroit efforts to nurture the popular patriotism of a frontier region. Further technological changes within the steel mills eroded the remaining job autonomy of furnace workers. Omnipresent company spies reduced most 'protest' to whispered conversations in the privacy of cafés. Unions were pitifully weak, as was the vote for leftist parties. This remained equally true at Le Creusot, where the *CGT* had 74 members in a work-force of 10,000 in 1930![72]

As early as 1865, a railway manager had argued in favour of company towns where rail employees 'are not exposed to the demoralising influence of big cities..., more easily kept under surveillance... and contained'. Company houses, allotments, subsidized coal, canteens, grocery stores and apprenticeship schemes were designed to produce a loyal, hereditary work-force. Though the strikes of 1910 and 1920 rather dented the image of old-style paternalism, the latter received little support on the Nord rail network where manager Dautry had constructed 30 'garden-cities' in which the cheap houses and allotments were managed by committees of cadres and elected workers. Such projects, Dautry claimed, 'contributed to the avoidance of [industrial] conflicts', and were adopted by other rail companies. The *P. L. M.* housed 6,000 employees and one-fifth of the 400,000 worker allotments were worked by railway families. Dautry then took his blend of modern neo-paternalism and technocracy to the ailing State network. He introduced children's holiday schemes, health clinics, gymnastic exercises (soon copied by Peugeot, Michelin and others). Dautry dismissed old-style clerical/authoritarian paternalism as counter-productive. He read Sorel, Proudhon, Durkheim, not just Le Play, and insisted that railmen should be treated as skilled, proud adults, who deserved to be consulted on proposed technological rationalization. This did not prevent *all* strikes. But nor did it *seek* to prevent the acceptance of railworkers' unionization rights. A *Statut de Personnel* allowed union consultation on discipline and promotion. Some 40 per cent of railmen were unionized, yet even *CGTU* activists rarely attacked Dautry directly, and the low involvement of railmen in the 1936 strikes was probably a consequence of such relatively enlightened managerial strategies.[73]

Management and the Depression

In France, the Depression arrived late but was prolonged. It prompted management to lay off workers – particularly immigrants – to cut paternalist welfare expenditure and to intensify 'rationalization'. Schneider and Michelin undertook fresh time-and-motion studies. One-hundred-and-forty-four major firms adopted the Bédaux system.[74]

But the crisis was more than a short-term management problem. It threatened the very stability of French capitalism by wrecking the *modus vivendi* between large industry and its political clientele of small businessmen and white-collar employees. A war of all-against-all erupted. Economically precarious small *patrons* denounced the 'sheltered' cartels who dominated the *CGPF*[75] and claimed to be unable to afford the costs of their contributions under the 1930 social insurance law. Export sectors (such as silk), denounced heavy industry for securing higher protective tariffs, and car firms resented steel masters' attempts to prop up domestic steel prices. Despite universal calls for deflationary spending cuts, each sector looked to government for subsidies for itself. Rentiers wanted a stable France, while industrial exporters favoured devaluation. The dreams of 'modernizers' like Tardieu or the technocratic electricity magnate Dutoeuf, for a new French conservatism freed of old ideological squabbles, committed to a concentrated and rationalized industrial capitalism and willing to tolerate moderate trade unionism and piecemeal social reform, were wrecked.[76] The upsurge of labour militancy which accompanied the Popular Front encouraged the *patronat* to espouse neo-corporatist or quasifascist blueprints that offered a 'strong' State which would impose unity on the squabbling fractions of the bourgeoisie, dismantle union power and modernize capitalism.[17]

1936–1939 Labour Revival and the Revenge of the Patronat

In early June 1936 the *CGPF*, after discussions with Blum's new Popular Front government and with *C. G. T* leaders, made unprecedented concessions to labour in the *Matignon Agreements*. Yet, within three years, the workers had lost most of these gains.

The *CGPF* delegates signed the *Matignon Agreements* to end a massive wave of sit-in strikes which were paralysing industry. Since 1934, the balance had tilted in favour of labour as fear of Fascism prompted a truce in the internecine feuding on the left and led to the reunification of the *CGT*. The confidence engendered by the new mood of unity allowed the 'new' working class of engineering factories to express pent-up grievances that had built up since 1920. The *CGT* suddenly expanded to over 4 million, with its blue-collar unions dominated by Communists whose party had swept to power in local and national elections in working-class *banlieues* of major cities. At Renault, where a tiny handful of activists had kept the unions and the *PC* cells alive, *CGT* membership rose to 25,000, *PCF* affiliations to 6,000!

The *patronat* had not simply made panic concessions, however in the spring of 1936, engineering employers had already debated the advantages of signing collective agreements with the metal-workers' union. The *Matignon Agreements* fell into three parts.[79]

(1) 'Voluntary' employer acceptance of collective contracts with the *CGT* (the 'most representative union'). In 1929, 112 of these had been signed. In 1930–5 the annual average was 22.[80] Seven per cent of French workers, a mere 2 per cent of metal workers, were covered by such agreements. Some 4,500 collective agreements were signed in the 12 months after Matignon! Management also accepted the institution of shop stewards.

(2) The *CGPF* agreed to accept wage rises established after arbitration by Blum – who would take responsibility for the consequences. The average wage increase for a firm was set at 12 per cent.

(3) The *CGPF* awaited Parliamentary legislation on the 40-hour week and paid vacations. They believed that Blum had given assurances that these would be introduced with 'flexibility'. The *full* ferocity of the employer backlash was, thus, launched only in late-1936 when Blum surrendered to *CGT* insistence, prompted by memories of employer evasion of the 1919 Eight-Hour Law, on a strict formula of a 'week' of five eight-hour shifts with no overtime, weekend working or special exemptions.

Matignon engendered much soul searching within the *patronat*. At Peugeot (Sochaux) sit-in strikes first stupefied a hitherto 'complacent' management, then pushed them into drastic reforms. Further technological rationalization was introduced to offset wage increases. Professional organizers were recruited to found a 'Social Department', independent of shopfloor management, to reorganize Peugeot's long-established health, welfare and sporting facilities. Psychologists were employed to design tests to ensure 'scientific' recruitment and a *Direction de la Main d'Oeuvre* was established–modelled on a facet of American managerial strategy hitherto ignored by French employers, the 'Personnel Department'. Shopfloor supervisors were now expected to be 'social technicians' whose function was to elicit workers' opinions to gather 'statistics on the social temperature of the workshops'. Then, hopefully, workers would say not 'we are going to the *bagne*' but 'since work is a social duty, we're still better off at Peugeot'. All but irreducible hard-core malcontents and militants would be happy. According to one Peugeot worker '[before 1936] there were no relations [between management and workers]. There was the manager, there was the foreman – that's it. But afterwards . . . everything was transformed from top to bottom. It was like water into wine . . .'

More common, however, was recognition of the need to renew and strengthen employer organization to re-assert managerial control. Hitherto the *CGPF* was loosely organized, overdependent on *ad hoc* financing from heavy industry and largely indifferent to the participation of smaller firms. These now accused the *CGPF* negotiators of a 'cowardly sell-out'. The northern textile employers – Roman Catholic *patrons* of family firms so intransigent that they had refused to recognize even the class-collaborationist *CFTC*[82] – walked out of the *CGPF* and provoked strikes (autumn 1936) by refusing to implement Matignon concessions.

The thesis that the accession to power within the *CGPF* of Gignoux symbolized the revolt of small industry against excessively compliant heavy industrialists who hitherto ran the organization is, however, questionable. Gignoux did urge bosses to 'act like bosses . . .'. But the *CGPF* launched a counter-attack against Matignon only once the metal and engineering employers realized that expected exemptions to the 40-hour week were not forthcoming. They then pulled out of a 'second Matignon', leaving Blum to impose Compulsory Arbitration unilaterally.

A new crop of employer organizations now sprang up. Many flirted with technocratic and quasicorporatist projects designed to revitalize not only industry but the political system. Many called for a 'third way' between *laissez-faire* and collectivism which would involve some *dirigisme* to eliminate liberal-capitalist 'anarchy'. Among these was maverick employer and engineer, J. Coutrot, who argued that the sit-in strikes had made workers and managers alike suddenly 'plastic'. A new type of industrial relations, based on 'humane and rational organisation of inequality', was now possible if employers and managers would only accept Matignon 'loyally'. If further 'rationalization' was necessary to offset increased labour costs, then unions should be consulted. The future lay with a 'co-ordinated' economy in which employers would collaborate with technocratic elements in the Socialist party and accept State controls of credit. Employers should reassert their authority through their managerial competence – the days of amateur family firms were over. 'The leaders of French industry have a magnificent opportunity to show themselves worthy of the title *"chefs d'enterprise"*. For 60 years the inadequacies of the bourgeoisie have left the field clear for Marxist propaganda without opposing it with anything constructive. We are paying for that today'.[84]

But many in the *patronat* yearned for more authoritarian solutions. Impressed by recent German and Italian experiences, they saw the overthrow of Parliamentary government and the destruction of union power as prerequisites for industrial revival.[85]

One novel feature of the crisis of managerial authority was the problem of the 'cadres'. The *patronat*'s suspicion of Taylorism had been fed by fear of losing shopfloor control to engineers. But it was precisely engineers, supervisors and low-level managers who bore the brunt of worker anger during the sit-in strikes. Many felt humiliated, 'trapped between the anvil of plutocracy and the hammer of the proletariat'. A number of overlapping organizations was soon established (*U. S. I. C.*; *S. I. C.*; *C. G. C. E.*) to represent the *specific* interests of the cadres. They sought to reverse the drift of some of their number into the *CGT* because restoration of factory discipline required the taming of union power. But, they insisted, their interests were not identical with those of employers. In early 1937, *U. S. I. C.* engineers walked out during a strike in the Nord in protest *both* at *CGT* 'tyranny' *and* at the employers' failure to involve engineers in collective contract negotiations.

To confront the *CGT* they adopted some of its organizational tactics and class analyses. The cadres they insisted, were part of a 'middle class' which *was* nothing but which aspired to be *something*. It had a pivotal role in industrial society. It stood for technical expertise and for social harmony – for it alone had the capacity to function as a bulwark between employers and workers and to defuse class tensions. It took pride in its 'patrimony' of productive skills, and contrasted its austere, thrifty values with the feckless-ness of rootless proletarians and the idle luxury of the parasitic rich.[86]

As Kolbloom insists, however, cadre organizations were, in practice, often encouraged by the *patronat*. A *CGPF* circular (spring 1937) welcomed these as a symbol of reaction against *CGT* 'dictatorship'. Meanwhile, guerrilla war was developing within industry. Despite the efforts of *CGT* officials to impress upon workers that the success of the Popular Front government and of anti-Fascist rearmament relied upon productivity increases, many shop stewards led wildcat stoppages. In car plants there was virtual 'dual power' as shop stewards flouted the authority of foremen. Seidmann characterizes the mood as a 'revolt against work' – a refusal of semiskilled workers to resubmit to hated discipline from which they had momentarily emancipated themselves in the heady days of June.[87] Seidmann's insistence that workers showed little interest in job control is questionable. In the aviation sector, workers supported their Communist-led union, were enthusiastic about recent nationalization of military aircraft factories and eager *both* to produce aircraft for the battle against Fascism and to assert worker influence over hiring, training and job procedures.[88]

Seidmann underestimates the extent to which ongoing wildcat disputes were a *defensive* reaction by workers against an employer counter-offensive. In northern pits, employers sought to reintroduce the Bédaux system.[89] In car factories, shop stewards were subject to growing management harass-ment.[90] Many employers encouraged quasi-Fascist company unions. And industry as a whole raised prices to offload the costs of Matignon on to consumers. As workers sought fresh pay rises, an escalating price/wage spiral developed. To reduce inflationary pressures and stabilize industrial relations,

Blum resorted to Compulsory Arbitration. The trades unions – other than the *CFTC* – had always been suspicious of such a curb on strike rights. But Jouhaux, although warning of the danger of compulsory arbitration in the hands of a conservative government, reluctantly accepted it to secure industrial peace.[91]

From December 1936 all disputes were to go to an arbitration board with three adjudicators – one nominee each from government, employers and unions. Although there were still 3,600 strikes in 1937, as many as three-quarters of disputes appear to have been settled by arbitration procedures, and, before the General Strike of 30 November 1938, there were only 780 strikes in that year. The *CGT* complained of major inadequacies in the system, however.

(1) Wage awards were below inflation rates. In the absence of authoritative data on local price inflation, arbitrators usually accepted employers' statistics.
(2) Complex and protracted procedures delayed settlements, allowing inflation to erode wage increases awarded.
(3) There was no machinery to force employers to accept court decisions.
(4) There was no appeals procedure.
(5) Employers refused to agree that a strike over victimization of a shop steward was a 'collective dispute'.

A revised law in 1938 defined 'collective disputes' more precisely, set a time limit for Board decisions and established an appeal court. But employers' arbitrary hiring/firing powers remained untouched, no sanctions against employer non-compliance were introduced and wage awards continued to lag behind prices. By 1938–9, the *CGPF*, initially *more* hostile to compulsory arbitration than the *CGT*, was the better disposed towards it. Arbitration boards refused to pressure employers to renegotiate expiring collective contracts, even though their refusal to do so was provoking major strikes (e.g. in the Marseilles docks). By 1939, two-thirds of all disputes were settled by arbitration, but the boards rejected 80 per cent of all worker claims. The *P. C.* urged the abolition of the system and a return to the earlier practice of debating industrial squabbles in local labour courts (*Conseils des Prud'hommes*). Unsurprisingly, the labour movement showed no desire to revive the compulsory arbitration experiment after 1945.

By 1939 the balance of power in industry had been settled by labour's defeat in the November 1938 General Strike – deliberately provoked by Daladier's government in alliance with the *patronat*. The Radical Party's petty-bourgeoisie electorate, terrified by the 1936 strikes and by the social costs of Matignon, came to view Communism as a greater menace than

Fascism.[92] In autumn 1938, therefore, Finance Minister Reynaud declared the abolition of the 40-hour week, blamed by the *patronat* for France's stagnant productivity. Leading employers acted with calculated provocation by insisting that restored Saturday shifts would be longer than those on weekdays. Reluctantly, *CGT* leaders succumbed to rank-and-file pressures to resist the Reynaud decrees with a General Strike – though many wildcat strikes had broken out and been defeated *before* 30 November, the official strike day.

Support for the strike was patchy but reached 80 percent in some sectors (engineering, mining, aviation). The strikers had fallen into a planned ambush, however. Thousands of activists were sacked. Shop stewards' powers were drastically cut. Many of the practices which employers had been forced to withdraw in June 1936 were reintroduced. The *CGT* began to disintegrate as its membership slumped to around 1 million and as the reformist, pro-appeasement *Syndicats* faction – headed by future Vichy Minister Belin and strong among postal and civil service employees – launched a crusade against Communist hegemony in blue-collar industrial unions.[99] The *CGPF* challenged the *CGT*'s status as the 'representative' federation with which employers had to negotiate. Some employers now dealt with the *CFTC*, others with more sinister semi-Fascist unions. Industrial relations characteristic of Vichy were, thus, already prefigured in the climate of 1939. With employers' associations mouthing the rhetoric of order, family, discipline, class collaboration and productivism, the *patronat* appeared as wedded to authoritarian styles of management at the end of the Third Republic as at the beginning.

6

Entrepreneurs and Economic Growth: the Case of Italy

John A. Davis

Changing Perspectives on Italian Industrialization and Economic Growth

Since the end of the World War II Italy has experienced one of the highest rates of growth in Western Europe. If this performance can be explained in part by the relatively low living standards and rates of productivity that prevailed until the 1940s, Italy's post-war economic performance has none-theless been impressive and calls into question many conventional images of the country's longer-run economic growth. Italy has long been depicted as an industrial latecomer and as an example of unbalanced economic growth, where industrialization occurred late and was accompanied by deep internal dualisms (notably between an advanced industrial north and a backward, agrarian south) and where the most modern sectors of the economy have retained an unhealthy dependence upon various forms of direct and indirect support and subsidy.

But, in the light of the spectacular performance of Italy's post-war economy, Italian historians have argued that conventional interpretations overlook longer-term processes of growth, particularly in agriculture, that have brought Italy into the twentieth century along paths that have been different from its European neighbours, but which have resulted nonetheless in comparable levels of economic, social and institutional modernization.[1]

Changing assessments of the character of economic growth in Italy over the longer term necessarily call for reconsideration of the role of the Italian entrepreneur. From Giovanni Agnelli, the founder of the FIAT motor company at the turn of the century, to the Benetton family whose spectacular successes in the 1980s personified the dynamic character of Italy's post-war small-business sector, Italy can boast an impressive list of entrepreneurs of international stature. But, until recently, these individuals have been seen as the exceptions that prove the rule. And the rule was one of a deficiency of true entrepreneurial spirit throughout the formative periods of Italy's economic modernization. Indeed, the critical role in Italian industrialization that Gerschenkron and others attributed to the intervention of the State and new investment banks in the late nineteenth century implied the lack of more spontaneous forms of capital accumulation and a truly entrepreneurial spirit in Italy.

The absence of a spirit of enterprise is also frequently cited as cause and effect of the heavy dependence of Italy's first modern industries (steel, shipbuilding, chemicals, cotton) on high protective tariffs and government contracts. This dependent and 'top-heavy' structure was already evident before 1914, but increased enormously during World War I and was subsequently further accentuated by the actions of Mussolini's regime in the 1920s and 1930s.[2] The creation in the 1930s of IRI and other State holding companies to rescue the Italian banking system – and with it a large part of Italy's industrial and manufacturing sectors – from collapse in the wake of the depression and the inflationary cycle caused by the regime's own policies after the 1927 revaluation of the Lira, left Italy after World War II endowed with one of the largest public-sector economies of all the advanced industrial nations. Until Italy's small-business sector began to reveal its strength and dynamism in the 1980s, many observers identified the disproportionate size of the public sector as a major structural defect in the Italian economy that encouraged a type of 'subsidized entrepreneurship' and 'lazy capitalism' and more generally an unhealthy interdependence between politics and business that were liable to breed corruption and inefficiency. At best, the close links between leading industrial sectors and the State meant that the Italian entrepreneur was more likely to be a financier, political negotiator and *grand commis* than an independent manager or innovator.[3]

Lurking behind this indictment of the economic and managerial shortcomings of the Italian entrepreneur, there is also a political bill of attainder. Many see the inability of Italy's pre-1914 industrialists to face up to the realities of a modern economy, and in particular to abandon outdated paternalistic and authoritarian attitudes in the face of the rise of a mass labour movement, as a key factor in the violence of Italy's industrial relations before and after World War I, and hence also a major contribution to the collapse of Italian liberalism. Although business leaders remained ambivalent to the rise of Fascism in Italy after World War I, the readiness of the greater part of Italy's leading industrialists to accommodate to Fascism after the March on Rome and to Mussolini's dictatorship after 1925 offers further evidence of the weak commitment of Italian entrepreneurs to democracy and representative government.[4]

Italy's 'Lazy Capitalism' Reconsidered

The central question driving the study of Italian entrepreneurship in the 1960s and 1970s was, therefore, the *absence* of an industrial spirit in Italy (significantly this search was underway before Wiener introduced the absence of an 'industrial culture' as a central theme in the debate on Britain's industrial decline in the twentieth century). In searching for the roots of the apparent weakness of an entrepreneurial spirit in Italy, historians have pointed to the overwhelming presence of foreign entrepreneurs in developing key new sectors of manufacturing and services in the earliest phases of Italian industrialization. The new silk-, cotton- and wollen-textile manufacturers that came into being in many Italian states early in the early nineteenth century were established primarily by Swiss, French, and German, rather than Italian, entrepreneurs. Even after unification, French, Belgian and German investors and advisers continued to play an important part in providing the capital and know-how for new ventures ranging from civil engineering and infrastructures to the development of the electrical industry and the creation of a new banking system in the second half of the nineteenth century.

In more general terms, and following Antonio Gramsci and subsequent Italian Marxist writings, the weaknesses of Italian industrial entrepreneurship might be traced to the absence of a true 'bourgeois revolution' in Italy, to Italy's relatively backward economic organization and social structures at the time of unification and continuing the predominance of the primary sector (agriculture and land ownership) until World War I and beyond.

Even when a modern industrial base did begin to expand rapidly after 1896, much of the country (particularly the south and islands, but also many parts of central, eastern and northern Italy) retained its agrarian character with changes owing more to emigration that to technical or organizational change. While new industries transformed Milan, Genoa and Turin into major industrial cities, many of Italy's new industries (especially textiles) were located by preference in the rural hinterlands of Piedmont, Lombardy, the Veneto and Liguria.[5] The rural preference shown by Italian manufacturers until well into the twentieth century reflected the fact that cheap and abundant rural labour was one of the few comparative advantages enjoyed by Italian producers. But the tendency to exploit labour through draconian and archaic factory regulations, combined with the absence of effective welfare and educational institutions, also made for explosive industrial relations.

Another major theme in the history of Italian entrepreneurship has been the ambivalence shown by the Risorgimento ruling class towards 'industrialism'.[6] Central to this ambivalence was the idea that Italy could achieve modern economic growth without industrialization, a belief that could be traced back to Cavour's insistence that the economic future of the new Italian state would be determined by agriculture. The belief that Italy should follow an agrarian path to economic growth, combined with a widespread concern that Italy should avoid the social consequences of industrialization and urbanization that in England had produced the menacing Coketowns of Manchester and Oldham, became if anything more pronounced after unification in ways that deeply coloured the outlook of Italy's first industrial entrepreneurs.[7]

The best-known representative of this generation is Alessandro Rossi, founder of the great Rossi woollen works at Schio in the alpine foothills of the Veneto which, by the end of the century, was the single largest textile enterprise in Italy. A tireless advocate of the interests of the Italian manufacturers, Rossi was the first to attempt to found employers' associations. He was a nationalist, a keen supporter of protectionism, a firm believer in the need for the Italian government to ensure that Italy acquired strategically essential industries (steel, shipbuilding, chemicals), and a devout Roman Catholic. The organization of the Schio works reflected both Rossi's managerial modernity and his authoritarian paternalism. The rural setting located production close to supplies of raw materials and above all low-cost labour – the great part provided by the daughters of peasant families from the surrounding region. Rossi was quick to adopt new technologies and was among the first to introduce powered looms, so that, despite its rural location, production at Schio was organized along rational managerial principles to achieve maximum efficiency. Workers were subject to strict discipline that extended beyond the workplace, but were also provided with housing, welfare, educational and, not least, spiritual facilities.[8]

Rationality and Context: Italian Entrepreneurial Strategies before 1914 Reconsidered

Alessandro Rossi's Roman Catholic paternalism had many counterparts in France and Belgium in the same period and, while not all the Venetian, Lombard and Piedmontese textile manufacturers shared Rossi's religious zeal, the larger concerns followed similar patterns of organization.[9] But does it make sense to categorize these strategies as the product of a deep-seated hostility to industrialism and a desire to attain modernity without the social threats inherent in the development of vast industrial metropolises?

These concerns, it must be said, were stated very explicitly by contemporaries. There are few better witnesses to this than Giuseppe Colombo, founder of Italy's electrical industry, who could recount with pride in the 1880s that Milan remained a commercial rather than an industrial city:

> Large industries have great resources, but they also suffer great crises and when these occur they have terrible consequences for the places involved. To concentrate in the city vast numbers of workers who are employed in a relatively small number of large factories, all engaged in similar types of production, is to risk dangers to which smaller industries engaged in a wider range of production – but on a smaller scale and whose work-force is therefore more scattered and divided – are much less susceptible.[10]

It was also perhaps typical that Colombo looked to technology to provide solutions. He believed electrical energy to be the answer because, by permitting the industrialist to place a small electric motor in each household, increases in productivity could be achieved within the structure of domestic industry. In this way, modernization could actually strengthen the role of the family as the fundamental unit of production, so avoiding the political, moral and social disadvantages of mass production.

In many ways, however, Colombo's views also vividly anticipated more recent and post-industrial managerial strategies, and his concerns may not have been totally unreasonable in the light of the absence of infrastructures and facilities to accommodate large groups of workers in Italy's new industrial cities. When the expansion of the urban engineering, metal-working and car industries began to turn Milan, Genoa and Turin into major industrial cities at the turn of the century, the inadequacies of Italy's urban housing stock and the absence of welfare and educational facilities would become powerful incentives for collective organization and militant protest among a new, and in large part, immigrant labour force.

Closer study also reveals that Alessandro Rossi's political and religious ideas were not necessarily antithetical to the modernization of production, or to the adoption of rational and effective managerial strategies. The rural preferences of Italy's nineteenth-century textile entrepreneurs can now be seen as a rational and effective competitive strategy that enabled Italian producers to take advantage of an important comparative advantage. Italian manufacturers had no choice but to operate in difficult and unforgiving markets because the feebleness of domestic demand forced them to concentrate on exports, and in particular to specialize in primary-worked products (thrown and twisted silk and cotton yarns, for example) for sale to foreign finishing industries (especially the Lyon silk manufacturers). Producing for uncertain and unpredictable export markets, the Italian textile manufacturer could retain some elements of flexibility through employing a peasant labour force. Most rural industrial workers were women or children whose earnings supplemented the peasant family income so that, when demand for textiles fell, the 'peasant workers' could simply be reabsorbed back into the peasant labour force.[11]

Rural Enterprise and Economic Growth

Preservation of the links between industry and agriculture can be seen as a rational entrepreneurial strategy that allowed Italian producers to exploit a narrow but critical comparative advantage (cheap labour), at the same time offering important flexibilities when operating in uncertain external markets. But this still leaves open the question as to whether such strategies assisted or 'impeded' economic growth. Any clear answer to that question is made difficult, of course, by the uncertainties that attach to all models of 'optimal' paths of growth. On the one hand, it is clear that the advantages of the 'rural preference' shown by Italian manufacturers were at best only relative and could not reverse their weak position in the market. On the other, the cycles of industrial and agricultural labour were not necessarily complementary, and many have argued that the exploitation of rural labour was feasible only as a temporary strategy.[12] Despite the apparent abundance of rural labour, employers were also still faced by shortages of skilled and trained workers – a problem that was exacerbated by the high proportion of unmarried women in the labour force who generally abandoned factory work when they married.[13] Continuing reliance on low-cost labour and the exploitation of 'family wages' also meant that industrial work for peasant workers did little to stimulate the development of more buoyant domestic markets, thus perpetuating the feeble consumer demand which remained one of the principal structural weaknesses of the Italian economy at least until World War II.[14]

This has been challenged but, as yet, the quantitative evidence that peasant consumption became a significant factor of demand remains thin.[15] A broader case for 'growth from below' has been constructed around the 'Venetian model' of rural entrepreneurship, however. Deriving in part from the example of early textile manufacturers, like Alessandro Rossi, the 'Venetian model' refers to the multiplicity of small, but aggressively effective, agrarian, manufacturing, financial and industrial enterprises undertaken by landowners and even wealthier peasants throughout the Veneto and other parts of northern Italy. Once landowners began integrating new, large-scale farming techniques with a range of industrial and financial ventures and investments in the second half of the nineteenth century, their initiatives gave rise to the formation of new networks – collective or co-operative enterprises, new credit and insurance organizations – that, in turn, laid the basis for further growth. By the end of the century, for example, networks of popular savings banks provided the means to mobilize agrarian savings, including those of tenant and peasant farmers, and enabled leading Venetian entrepreneurs to draw on local, as well as national and even foreign, capital. Whatever the deficiencies of the Italian state in this period in terms of infrastructures, the expansion of small enterprises before 1914 had begun to equip the Venetian region with a capillary network of modern financial and commercial institutions capable of sustaining further growth.[16]

A strong and self-assertive sense of autonomy was part of this form of entrepreneurship, making the deficiencies of the Italian state in some ways unimportant. The Venetian-style enterprise was jealously self-regulated, with strong emphasis on the all-embracing paternalism pioneered by Alessandro Rossi and subsequently replicated more widely. Paolo Camerini's industrial complex at Piazzola in the Brenta, for example, constituted an early twentieth-century mix between 'an autarchic industrial feudal estate and a welfare community'.[17]

Autonomy and self-sufficiency were characteristic of an enterprise culture that grew out of the willingness of an otherwise conservative and elitist landlord class to engage in a range of commercial, financial and industrial investments. This may explain why, in the late nineteenth century, the Veneto was to produce some of Italy's leading and most dynamic entrepreneurs: men like Ernesto Breda and Giuseppe Volpi. By the end of World War I, Ernesto Breda headed the fourth largest industrial concern in Italy, which included the Breda locomotive and rolling-stock works in the new Milan industrial suburb of Sesto San Giovanni. Breda was the cousin of Vincenzo Stefano Breda, the head of Italy's first steel foundry that was built with support from the government at Terni in 1884. But Vincenzo Stefano Breda had first made his name through the Venetian Association of Public Construction Enterprises which he founded in the 1870s – a company that became one of the biggest public works contractors in Italy. This association offers an example of the network of entrepreneurial experience and financial resources that was available in the Veneto and which, together with networks of popular savings banks founded at the end of the nineteenth century, 'played a central role in the constitution of a connective tissue of economic activities, that provided the base for a range of small enterprises in the Veneto and beyond'.[18]

Like his cousin, Ernesto Breda moved from his original Venetian base to become one of the leading figures in the development of Italy's engineering industry. But, as in the case of Vincenzo Stefano, support from the government and leading banking interests was also to be a critical factor in the success of Ernesto Breda. When, in 1885, the government established preferences for Italian-built railway locomotives, Ernesto Breda took the opportunity to reorganize the Milanese Elvetica engineering company, and the new market for railway locomotives – of which 500 were produced at the Elvetica works between 1887 and 1904 – enabled Breda to transform what had previously been a generalized workshop into a much more specialized and rational operation. Drawing on experience in the engineering industries in Germany, Holland and Denmark, the rationalization of production went a step further with the opening of a new factory in Sesto San Giovanni in 1906 – along with the AFL Flack steel foundry equipped with the first Martin-Siemens furnaces and the first automated steel-rolling mills in Italy, the OSVA machinery factory and the Ercole Marelli electrical equipment firm, the new Breda workshop transformed Sesto San Giovanni into Italy's most advanced engineering town by 1914.[19]

Another figure closely linked to the world of Venetian enterprise was Giuseppe Volpi who played a major role in shaping the Italian economy. Like Breda, Volpi established close links with the *Commit*, which was a key investor in the development of the Italian electrical energy industry. Volpi played a major role in strengthening the ties between the electrical industry, banking and government, and, as Mussolini's finance minister, was to be the architect of the development of Mestre as a new industrial port on the Adriatic.[20]

Whatever may have been the importance of entrepreneurial autonomy in their formative years, the Bredas and Volpi provide examples of entrepreneurs whose industrial ventures became increasingly dependent on close support from leading banks and ties with influential political groups that alone could ensure markets and contracts. Nor was the combination of agriculture and capitalist enterprise peculiar to the Veneto alone. Alberto Banti, for example, has shown how, in the late nineteenth century, the landowners of Piacenza developed close links with national banking interests and established their own consumer co-operatives, credit associations and employers' associations. Maria Malatesta has traced similar developments among the big landowners of Lower Lombardy, who were also precocious in establishing close ties with major Milanese financial and insurance groups and pioneered the introduction of farmers' banks and insurance banks. Like their counterparts in the Veneto and Piedmont, the Lombard landowners were also quick to introduce welfare facilities for their workers, and generally to act as surrogates for public welfare. As in the Veneto, the picture that emerges is of a robust and assertive laissez-faire capitalism that was intolerant of interference either from the state or from organized labour, a capitalism that chose to ally itself closely with the values and authority of the Roman

Catholic Church, but otherwise was prepared to rely very much on its own resources.[21]

It should be noted that this insistence on the emergence of an aggressively dynamic and largely self-sufficient capitalism in Italy in the late nineteenth century also challenges the assumption that free-enterprise capitalism and liberalism were necessarily linked. Both Silvio Lanaro and Alberto Banti have stressed that the successful Italian agro-entrepreneurs showed little interest in liberalism in either theory or practice: they exploited the weakness of the Liberal state to regulate their own affairs, but showed little patience with attempts to mediate relations between capital and labour. At an early stage, they rejected liberalism in favour of corporatist and nationalist programmes.

Worker Peasants and the Origins of the Small-enterprise Economy.

Leaving aside the political significance of Italy's aggressively modernizing agro-entrepreneurs, in economic terms the debate on the 'Venetian model' suggests that, by concentrating too heavily on the most modern and advanced sectors of the Italian industrial economy, historians may have overlooked the impact of more rough-and-ready forms of capitalist development on Italy's economic growth in the late nineteenth and early twentieth centuries. These debates also suggest other, hitherto neglected, elements of continuity, in particular the links between Italy's dynamic post World War II small-business sectors and earlier forms of peasant entrepreneurship.

Geographically, Italy's small-enterprise economy has tended to be concentrated in the regions described as the 'Third Italy': that is, the greater part of northern and central Italy, leaving out the great industrial triangle of Milan, Turin and Genoa (the 'First Italy') and the south (the 'Second Italy') and including the upper Lombardy, the northern and western Veneto, Emilia, the Romagna, parts of Tuscany and the Marches. Until World War II, these were predominantly regions of small tenant farms (and especially share-cropping farms) where agricultural work had, since the mid-nineteenth century, been combined in various forms with industrial employment.[22]

The impact of industrialization and economic growth on the peasant economies of these regions varied enormously. In many cases, the shift towards more intensive capitalist farming caused the rapid disappearance of peasant farms as the peasants were replaced by armies of landless agricultural wage-labourers (*braccianti*). In other cases, the expansion of new industries (especially textiles in the pre-alpine hill country of northern Lombardy and the Veneto) into rural areas in the nineteenth century brought about typical cases of 'proto-industrialization', in which growing dependence on industrial employment over a short number of generations again turned peasant workers into landless industrial proletarians. This occurred in the Biella region of northern Piedmont, a major centre of the Italian wool industry, where attempts to mechanize weaving in the 1870s provoked bitter struggles between industrialists, like the Sella family, and the predominantly male master weavers who fought to retain control over their trade. Their defeat led to the centralization and, in large part, feminization of wool production, the proletarianization of the workforce and, in this case, massive emigration.[23]

But there was another possible outcome. In the upper Milanese districts of Brianza and Como, where the peasants reared silkworms and worked in the silk-reeling and throwing mills as well as growing corn, the rapid expansion of the silk industry (Italy's principal export commodity and major foreign exchange earner until the 1930s) was accompanied by the formation of families of peasant workers who, over time, became worker peasants. In this region, the peasant families were often able to engage in industrial work without losing their links with the land because the landowners were unwilling to forgo the opportunities for cheap production of silkworms offered by the peasant farms. It is not clear whether that process could be replicated in areas where silk was not a principal product of peasant agriculture, but the particular conditions that obtained in the Brianza and Como regions may have made possible the emergence in the 1930s and 1940s of small independent peasant farmers with relatively wide industrial and managerial experience.[24]

In certain circumstances, and within certain regions of northern and central Italy, therefore, peasant farms may have become vectors of economic growth in ways that would question any attempt to explain Italy's economic development solely or exclusively in terms of external and exogenous forces. More research will be needed, however, before it is possible to tell how general this process may have been. It would seem that the emergence of small independent family enterprises occurred in only a relatively small area of earlier peasant share-cropping, and, in most cases, relatively late. It may be that the rise of family enterprises had more to do with the conditions created by the later abolition of the former share-cropping system, and that, in the case of the Comasco and Brianza, the particular circumstances of silk production created conditions that were exceptional rather than typical.

Enterprise in the South

One area where the model of rural enterprise as a broader motor of economic growth stubbornly refuses to function is the south, and the reasons for this continue to be fiercely debated. Carlo Trigilia has recently argued that the obstacles to the development of small enterprise in the south have historically been cultural, and have been particularly evident in a reluctance to develop forms of collective organization capable of creating the infrastructural prerequisites for self-sustained growth. Pointing to the absence of trades unions and mutual aid societies in most of southern Italy in the nineteenth century, Trigilia's arguments lend further support to the notion of 'amoral familism' coined some 40 years ago by the American sociologist E. C. Banfield. Looking for an explanation of the absence of a spirit of co-operation in the south, Banfield argued that lack of trust encouraged southerners to rely exclusively on their families. By pursuing strategies that sought only to maximize gains for the individual family, they created conditions of anarchical competitiveness that precluded the development of broader, horizontal institutions (such as co-operatives or credit associations) that might have helped the growth of family-based enterprise.[25]

The family-based strategies that Banfield identified as inimical to economic growth are curiously similar, however, to those which Corner suggests transformed Brianza peasants into small capitalist entrepreneurs while, in the predominantly Roman Catholic Comasco, trades unions and other collective structures were as notable for their absence as in the south. But the attempts to explain why rural enterprise did not give rise to economic growth in the south solely in terms of cultural constraints fail to take sufficient account of contextual factors: in particular, the different conditions of agriculture in the south; the different agrarian relations that prevailed; the different nature and impact of emigration; the absence of extensive industrial by-employment and of provincial market towns capable of offering centres of consumption comparable to those in the north; the absence of valuable export commodities requiring primary transformation processes like silk; and in general, the overwhelming poverty and precariousness of rural society in the south.

It has often been argued that poverty and precariousness precluded the development of a southern entrepreneurial class, and that the narrowness and uncertainty of economic opportunities encouraged an aversion to longer-term investment, the absence of specialization and a preference for a proliferation of short-term and primarily speculative operations. But a number of recent studies has suggested that southern entrepreneurial strategies should be seen instead as rational and logical responses to prevailing markets and conditions. Because the highest value-added southern products – citrus fruits, olive oil, wines, almonds and other specialist Mediterranean products – were dependent on chronically unstable and unpredictable foreign export markets, southern entrepreneurs looked to ways of reducing their exposure by various forms of risk spreading – the principal reason for the tendency to a wide range of short-term investments.[26]

Even an economic institution like the great latifundist estates that have long epitomized the 'backwardness' of southern agriculture and landlordism may take on a new 'rationality' in these terms. In a detailed reconstruction of one of the biggest latifundist estates in Calabria in the nineteenth century, Marta Petrusewicz concludes that, far from an archaic symbol of backwardness, the combination of extensive cereal farming and traditional pasturage with the production of high value-added cash crops for export on the latifundist estates consituted a new and delicate economic system that enabled southern landowners to engage in commercial production for chronically uncertain export markets. When export markets were unrewarding, the latifundist economy could fall back on cereals and pasture, compensating at least in part the absence of export markets through the internal consumer market composed of the peasant families that worked the estates. Petrusewicz also argues that technological innovation did occur on the latifundist estates and might have enabled the system to develop further, had it not been for the agricultural crisis and the adoption of agricultural protectionism in the 1880s which irreparably damaged the latifundists' export markets.[27]

If the managerial strategies of the southern landowners were rational and designed to spread risks and maintain flexibility in the narrow and uncertain markets, they were also defensive. A recent study of the Sicilian citrus trade in the late nineteenth and early twentieth centuries by Salvatore Lupo shows that, while multiple short-term investment was a means of spreading risks, it was also an obstacle to structural reorganization of production and trade. The Sicilian landowners were reluctant to streamline production processes and, in response to competition in United States' markets from citrus growers in California and Florida, they preferred to exploit further their primary comparative advantages – most notably cheap labour. Little progress was made towards integrating production, processing, shipping and marketing, and the Sicilian landowners were particularly reluctant to expand processing and finishing operations (for example, the production of citric acid) even when northern banks showed interest in expanding investment in Sicily at the turn of the century. But, when banking consortiums like the Milanese *Commit* (the *Banca Commerciale Italiana*) began to invest heavily in electrification projects on the island, the majority (although not all) of the Sicilian landowners drew back for fear that collaboration with these powerful northern financial institutions might threaten their own commercial autonomy.[28]

The constraints that the southern economy imposed on entrepreneurial strategies are also demonstrated in an earlier study, by Luigi De Rosa, of the southern engineering industries in the second half of the nineteenth century. In the 1840s, the pre-unification Bourbon rulers of Naples had encouraged a number of British and French entrepreneurs to come to Naples to help establish a series of major engineering works to supply ships and marine engines for the kingdom's navy, service its railway network and meet its civil and military engineering requirements. Among these, Thomas Guppy, a Bristol engineer and a former partner of Isambard Kingdom Brunel, became the key figure in the development of an industry that expanded rapidly in the decades before the collapse of the Kingdom of Naples and its absorption in 1860 into the new Italian state. After unification, the situation of the southern engineering industry became increasingly precarious, largely because the free-trade regime of the Liberal state swept away the heavy protective barriers around which the southern engineering industry had taken root.

Despite these difficult circumstances, the industry continued to attract foreign entrepreneurs until the 1880s, when a new generation of able and well-trained Italian managers began to take control. But, despite their skill and the modernity of their outlook, they, too, proved unable to make the industry prosper. Not only did the southern industries lack government protection and orders, but they had no alternative markets to turn to. Unlike their competitors in northern Italy, which were able to meet the gradually strengthening demand for industrial and above all agricultural machinery, the poverty of southern agriculture offered no comparable support. In the closing decade of the century this, combined with government preference for northern industries, enabled northern companies to take over the slender markets of their southern competitors.[29]

The examples of the southern citrus trade and the engineering industries demonstrate the real constraints that hemmed around industrial development and economic growth more generally in the south. The prevailing conditions of high risk and uncertainty forced southern entrepreneurs into defensive positions, and often made it more profitable for them to exploit these conditions rather than overcome them. Diego Gambetta has recently argued that the Mafia can be understood as a business (however illegitimate) that provided protection and security in an environment and an economy where uncertainty prevailed, and it is certainly true that the poverty of the southern economy and its resources placed a special premium on the creation of monopolies in general.[30] In that sense, the particular circumstances of the southern economy gave rise to forms of entrepreneurship that were often directed at strengthening, rather than overcoming, the structural obstacles to growth, and encouraged forms of parasitic entrepreneurship and above all the formation of monopolies that helped block the development of those networks of commercial and financial activity that were features of Italian regions where more spontaneous processes of growth did take root in the nineteenth and early twentieth centuries.

Entrepreneurs and Italy's Leading Sectors Before 1914

The southern entrepreneurs operated in conditions that were not qualitatively different from their counterparts in the north. It is not surprising, therefore, that many of Italy's most innovative industrial managers before

1914 were concerned to find ways of lessening the uncertainties that hedged around market-oriented enterprise. The entrepreneurs and managers who took charge of Italy's first major industrial ventures in the 1880s and 1890s – men like Ernesto and Stefano Vincenzo Breda, and Max Bondi, director of the Terni steel works – were strongly nationalist in their outlook and looked primarily to government protection and contracts to realize the new initiatives. Such outlooks persisted in other sectors, and the largest player in the cotton sector, Benigno Crespi, personified the combinations of paternalism, conservatism, close links with the state and a ruthless capacity for organizational modernization.

In the climate of more buoyant economic growth in the years after the turn of the century that coincided with the first administrations of Giovanni Giolitti, a more independent entrepreneurial and managerial outlook took root, and significantly this occurred first in the engineering and the new car industries. Unlike steel and cotton, engineering received no tariff protection but had to carry the burden of the cost which protectionism added to raw materials and wages.

That new entrepreneurial spirit is best represented by Giovanni Agnelli, the founder of FIAT. After service in the cavalry, Agnelli became involved in the 1890s with a number of Piedmontese noblemen who were interested in building motor cars in Turin. Numerous small car firms were starting up in these years, but Agnelli was the first to understand that the motor car had market potential that went far beyond the elite sports car. At first conditions were buoyant and the banks were keen to invest but, once the economy moved into recession after 1906, the situation changed. At this point, Agnelli began to take a closer interest in the organization of production. In 1906 he made his first journey to the United States to study American automobile production methods, and, to develop these more fully, FIAT acquired a small factory at Poughkeepsie, in New York state. The central message of Agnelli's American experience was that the organization and scale of production, not the cost of labour, were the keys to success: in 1908, with financial backing from the *Commit*, Agnelli began to reorganize production, technology and plant to move FIAT into production for mass markets.[31]

Yet it is difficult to generalize from the FIAT experience. There were no comparable organizational changes, for example, at the Alfa-Romeo car company.[32] But even the car companies that did not introduce major organizational changes were experimenting with new forms of labour management that provoked fierce opposition. The growth of industrial employment in Piedmont was particularly rapid in the decade after 1900, rising from 49 industrial workers per 1000 inhabitants to 100 by 1910 (the comparable figures for Lombardy went from 83 to 134 per 1000 against the national average that in 1910 was still 64 per 1000). In Turin, the engineering industry alone employed 28,000 workers in 1910 – seven times more than a decade earlier, and one-third of the city's total labour force.[33]

It is not surprising, therefore, that the car industry should have become the flashpoint for labour relations in the city, because it was here that the competition for skilled labour was strongest and here that wages were highest. In some ways, Italian industrialists were confronted even more directly than their French or German counterparts by the question of labour productivity because, in a context of relatively inelastic production costs, the exploitation of labour constituted one of the few comparative advantages available to Italian manufacturers. This had been a factor in the preference for rural industrial locations but, in an urban setting and in a new high-technology industry like engineering that required a mix of unskilled and skilled labour, as well as new and old skills, the questions of labour productivity and wage bargaining therefore took on a particular intensity and centrality.

This was powerfully endorsed by Luigi Bonnefon Crappone, an entrepreneur of French origin who, in 1906, had been a cofounder of the Turin Industrial League. Writing shortly after the start of World War I, Bonnefon Crappone enthusiastically praised the intelligence and tenacity of Italian workers:

> I have always felt the greatest admiration for these men who after a day of heavy labour proved themselves able not only to defend the interests of their fellow-workers with tireless tenacity and vivacity, but also to discuss and debate the most closely prepared arguments that their employers put to them.[34]

Written in a spirit of wartime conciliation, the statement contains more than an element of ingenuity because Bonnefon Crappone had been one of the most intransigent leaders of the pre-war Turin engineering employers. He was also, however, a keen publicist of one of Italian industry's greatest comparative advantages:

> Industrial ventures here have revealed a wonderful asset: the Italian worker. At the outset, this is a somewhat rough and primitive instrument, but one that is extremely straightforward and very economical. . . . The Italian worker is not only intelligent and clever, he is also sober. Absinthe is quite unknown in Italy . . .[35]

The need to retain this advantage, coupled with an acknowledgement that old-style factory regimentation was no longer workable, was central to the strategies of the Turin engineering employers. At least in theory, this meant a greater openness to wage negotiation, and even a readiness to see strikes as a sign of vitality. But this was linked to a determination to improve labour productivity, flexibility, and discipline through the adoption of piece-rate pay schemes. Following established models in the United States and Britain, the piece-rate system offered the opportunity of increasing productivity by facilitating the introduction of new machinery and technologies that reduced dependence on skill. The resistance, of course, was strongest among those workers whose skill gave them the greatest bargaining power in the labour market and on the shop floor.

It was the collective resistance to the introduction of new piece-rate schemes that encouraged the employers to organize and bargain collectively. Modeled on the German Industrial Association founded in Altona in the previous year, the Turin Industrial League was established in 1906 to enable the Turin engineering employers and others to negotiate collectively with labour. Luigi Bonnefon Crappone and Gino Olivetti were the principal spokesmen of this new and aggressive entrepreneurial stance.[36] But collective action proved difficult to realize, and the Turin engineering and car employers broke ranks quickly on collective agreements. Many committed 'modernizers', like Giovanni Agnelli, remained leery, both of the League's attempts to regiment the employers and of their confrontational tactics – Agnelli, in fact, broke ranks to form a separate consortium of automobile employers. These rifts would become particularly apparent during the great 1913 strikes. Bonnefon Crappone's confrontational advocacy of mass lock-outs by the employers caused Giolitti's government to issue scarcely concealed threats to repatriate the President of the Industrial League to his native France, while Agnelli and others adopted more conciliatory positions with regard to the unions and the government.

Even in those sectors where economic pressures for collective organization were strong, employers' associations proved difficult to maintain. In the cotton industry – the principal beneficiary of tariff protection but an industry plagued by overproduction – agreements to reduce production and increase mechanization rarely lasted for any period of time. In the steel industry, too, the trend towards the creation of producer cartels ran largely counter to the instincts of the principal entrepreneurs – although in this Oscar Sinigaglia was an exception, as an employer who adopted state-of-the-art production techniques into his Ligurian foundry and as an admirer of the German coal and steel cartels. But, although Sinigaglia was to be a key figure in the formation of the ILVA steel consortium in Italy in 1911 (this was actually modeled on Agnelli's consortium of automobile employers in Turin), production practices and methods in the Italian steel-making industry remained very varied until World War I. Nor are generalizations within other industries easier, as witness the enormous differences in organization of production and management techniques in the Fiat and Alfa-Romeo factories.[37]

Set in comparative context, it is not clear that Italy's 'leading-sector' entrepreneurs on the eve of World War I differed significantly – for better or for worse – from their German, French, British or North American counterparts. Especially in the industries most engaged in new technologies, managerial strategies and objectives in Italy differed little from elsewhere while, within even these 'leading sectors', new and old remained intermixed. If older forms of entrepreneurial paternalism remained strong, this was certainly also true, not only in France, Britain and Germany, but also in North America as well. Indeed, there are so many differences and distinctions between and within each of these other economies that meaningful comparisons remain difficult and potentially deceptive.

In Italy, World War I would bring major changes, particularly as a result of the programme of industrial mobilization that was extended to the greater part of Italian industry in 1916. This greatly strengthened the ties between entrepreneurs and the state at a political level and in terms of contracts, markets and production. For Italy's most advanced companies, like Agnelli's FIAT or Ercole Marelli's Magneti Marelli, World War I constituted a critical moment of growth, consolidation and technical reorganization, free from the uncertainties of a free market and the disruptions of free industrial relations (workers in government-designated strategic industries were placed under military discipline). While these conditions prefigured those that would later be replicated by the Fascist regime through the destruction of the trades unions and the regime's military ventures of the 1930s, it is also true that British and French, as well as German, industries experienced similar forms of regimentation and control during the war. It would be wrong, therefore, to exaggerate the 'peculiarity' of the Italian experience of the war, even though the demands of the war did bring exceptional pressures to bear on Italy's economic structures and financial resources.

Nor was it the case that wartime mobilization necessarily predisposed Italian entrepreneurs immediately to Fascism. Some did become actively involved in the early Fascist movement, but the majority did not look on Mussolini as their first political preference in 1922. After the seizure of power, tactical alliances with the regime would be the order of the day. The principal concern of the majority of Italian entrepreneurs continued to be retaining as much independent control over their own affairs and companies as possible, which did not, of course, preclude profiting from the opportunities that good relations with the regime and its representatives could offer.[38] But, if Fascism carried the intervention of the state another massive step forward – through massive support to shore up, without taking over, major industrial and banking concerns – this was less the result of ideology than of Italy's vulnerable position in the international economy and the deflationary pressures that were further weakening Italy's fragile domestic economy.[39]

Conclusion

By placing new emphasis on the rationality of Italian managerial strategies, recent studies have brought into sharper focus the enormous difficulties that faced a country that was relatively poor in natural resources in this critical phase of European industrialization. While there may have been alternative paths of growth available and while, from the late twentieth century, a pattern of economic growth, that might have evolved spontaneously out of peasant homesteads and avoided all the horrors of iron, steel and chemicals, may seem attractive, contemporaries had little doubt that the changes taking place in powerful neighbouring economies gave the establishment of competitive domestic steel, chemical and engineering industries clear strategic priority. The history of those industries, and of the strategies that their managers adopted, reveals just how difficult it was to realize those objectives, just as the continuing haemorrhage of emigration before and after World War I – and, of course, again after the World War II – offers a continuing human indicator of the underlying weaknesses of domestic growth.

Against this broader backdrop, the debate on the nature and role of Italian entrepreneurship in the early phases of Italy's modern economic growth has necessarily changed. By stressing the rationality of the strategies followed by Italian entrepreneurs in the nineteenth and early twentieth centuries in the light of the markets and conditions in which Italian producers operated, recent studies have dispelled the notion of 'lazy capitalism' – indeed, the vulnerability of the Italian economy in a rapidly industrializing world often gave Italian entrepreneurship a markedly frenetic and aggressive character. But, while the conventional images of Italy as an industrial latecomer may understate the nature and complexity of the economic changes that were occurring in the half century after unification, the re-evaluation of Italian entrepreneurship reveals above all the difficult and precarious paths along which the Italian economy moved into the twentieth century. These difficulties explain why the captains of Italian industry were of necessity engaged more often in defensive than offensive campaigns.

7

Industrial Workers, Employers and the State in Nazi Germany 1933–1945

Stephen Salter

Introduction

Despite the growth since the 1960s in empirical studies of individual social groups in Germany between 1933 and 1945, we still lack a comprehensive social history of the Third Reich which assesses the specifically Nazi contribution to the modernization of German society.[1] Historians continue to disagree not only about the nature and extent of the Nazi regime's impact on German society, but also about the nature of the regime's objectives in the social sphere. Some historians stress the modernizing thrust of Nazi economic and social policies; others place emphasis on the unintended modernizing consequences of 12 years of Nazi dictatorship in Germany; while yet others regard as unambiguously anti-modern both the economic and social policies pursued by the regime after 1933 and the impact of these policies on German society.[2] In examining the experience of industrial workers during the 'Third Reich', I shall stress the overriding priority accorded by the Nazi leadership to rearmament, territorial expansion and war in determining the development of industrial relations. I shall also suggest, however, that the dictatorship promoted the extension of a number of 'modernizing' trends in relations between industrial workers and employers that predated 1933; and that its existence was, in the short term at least, quite compatible with the accelerated development of a rational, modern system of industrial relations. Finally, I shall attempt to assess the contribution of the Nazi dictatorship to the modernization of industrial relations in Germany.

Workers and Employers on the Eve of the Nazi Seizure of Power

The June 1933 census allocated slightly over 13 million Germans of working age to the employment category of 'industry and handicrafts'. Of these, more than 9.9 million were classified as 'workers' (*Arbeiter*), the remainder consisting of the self-employed (1.49 million), family members working largely in handicrafts (273,000), white-collar workers (1.33 million) and a small number of state officials (23,000). Of the 9.9 million workers identified by the census, a quarter were women. In the textiles industries, women made up well over half of all workers; in the electrical goods industries, slightly over one-third; and, in the optical and precision-engineering industries and chemicals industry over one-quarter.[3]

While Germany was, by the late 1920s, the world's second largest industrial economy, it would be a mistake to think of all – or even of the majority – of workers as employees of large industrial concerns. In 1933, over one-third (37.5 per cent) of workers in industry and handicrafts worked in concerns employing no more than five workers; and three-quarters worked in concerns employing no more than 200 hundred workers – 'small firms' by modern standards. Less than 10 per cent of the work-force was employed by a concern with more than 1,000 workers.[4] The aggregation of employment in industry and handicrafts probably conceals the employment of a greater proportion of workers in industry in medium-sized and large concerns than these figures suggest: yet, even with this qualification, perhaps only in heavy industry was the large concern – the *Bochumer Verein* steel concern with its 5,900 employees, for instance – the norm.

Almost a half (48.6 per cent) of the male industrial work-force was skilled; one-fifth (21.3 per cent) was semi-skilled; and three-tenths (30.1 per cent) unskilled.[5] The available statistics contain no breakdown of the female work-force in industry and handicrafts by skill, but figures available for individual branches suggest that only a very small proportion of the female manual work-force was skilled.[6] Characteristically, modern production methods – flow production, conveyor belts, and so on – were confined to a small minority of firms: a survey carried out in 1931 concluded that flow-production methods of all kinds were employed in scarcely 1 per cent of all medium-sized and large concerns – only in the locomotive-construction, iron and steel, optical and metal-working industries were such methods of much significance.[7] The distribution of the work-force by firm size, the skill structure of the manual work-force and the limited employment of modern production and assembly methods thus suggest a picture which, with some notable exceptions, had more in common with the skilled artisan production of the early twentieth century than with contemporary industrial concerns.

With the revolution of 1918–19 and the establishment of the Weimar Republic, the balance of power in industrial relations had shifted decisively. The right to join a trade union was guaranteed by the Weimar constitution; and workers' right to strike was recognized by private employers and by the state. Factory councils were established in all concerns employing more than 20 workers, and employers were obliged to consult such councils about proposed redundancies, working conditions and welfare policies. Collective wage agreements – rare in Germany before 1914 – became the norm; and an arbitration system was established in an attempt to reduce the use of strikes and lock-outs in industrial disputes.[8] Trade-union membership rose to 9.2 million in 1922.[9]

But the major determinant of industrial relations remained the state of the labour market. The stabilization crisis of 1925–6 brought to an end the low levels of unemployment characteristic of the postwar years, suggesting that the widespread image of economic recovery during the 'golden years' of the Weimar Republic is in need of some qualification. Yet it was the onset of the Depression in 1930 that was to lead to a decisive change in the state of the labour market and of industrial relations. In some branches of the investment and production goods sectors of industry, output shrank by up to two-thirds between 1929 and 1932.[10] Massive dismissals followed and, at the nadir of the Depression in 1932, over 5.6 million workers and white-collar workers – 29.0 per cent of the 'dependent' work-force in the German economy – were registered as unemployed:[11] if the 'invisible' unemployed are taken into account – those workers who disappeared from the official statistics – total unemployment may have stood as high as 7.7 million.[12] A further 20 per cent of the work-force was working short time.[13] The long-term trend of falling union membership during the mid-to late 1920s was reinforced by the impact of the Depression. By 1931, the last year for which reliable figures are available, union membership had fallen to 5.1 million;[14] and, by 1932, 43.7 per cent of union members were unemployed.[15]

Strike activity collapsed in the face of mass unemployment: the strikes that took place in 1932 involved only 129,000 workers, compared with the 327,000 workers who had struck in 1928; and the number of working days lost through strikes fell from 8.52 million in 1928 to 1.13 million in 1932. Similarly, the number of lock-outs, and number of workers affected by these, fell dramatically during the Depression.[16] The successful implementation of wage cuts, the halving of sickness rates and rising productivity in some industries all told the same story.[17] Under the impact of the Depression and the mass unemployment which accompanied it, workers largely lost the capacity to defend – let alone improve – their material position through collective action or job changing: on the eve of the Nazi seizure of power, the German labour movement had already been broken by the Depression.

The 'Re-ordering of Class Relations'

Initially the new government displayed a cautious attitude towards the trades unions, and it was only when it became apparent that the attacks on the unions carried out by Nazi activists in the course of the 'national uprising' was meeting no organized resistance that, late in April 1933, plans were drawn up to take over the unions. Officials of the social-democratic Free Trade Unions were unprepared for the occupation of their offices, confiscation of their funds and widespread arrests that took place on 2 May 1933. Robert Ley, the head of the Political Organization of the NSDAP, announced on 6 May the formation of a new umbrella organization – the German Labour Front (*Deutsche Arbeitsfront*, DAF) – to replace the Free Trade Unions. The liberal *'Hirsch-Duncker'* unions soon subordinated themselves to the DAF; and the Catholic 'Christian' unions were dissolved following the regime's July 1933 Concordat with the Vatican.[18] Yet the mere establishment of the DAF did not amount to an adequate framework for the future conduct of industrial relations, and it was only in the succeeding months that the shape of the Nazi 'reordering of class relations' was to be clarified.

In the early stages of this process, the DAF was by no means the most prominent institution. The embryonic Nazi trade union, the National Socialist Factory Cell Organization (*Nationalsozialistische Betriebszellen-Organisation*, NSBO), had played an important role in the displacement of the independent trades unions and sought to use its newly acquired power to seek the dismissal of Social Democrats and their replacement with unemployed Nazis, to press employers for wage concessions and improvements in working conditions, and to assume the role of representing workers formerly carried out by the factory councils.[19] Such activities quickly provoked a hostile response from employers, and the regime was obliged to act against the populist radicalism of the NSBO: on 19 May 1933, ultimate authority for the regulation of wages was transferred to state officials, the Reich Labour Trustees, subordinate to the Ministry of Labour.[20] Employers remained anxious, nevertheless, that the NSBO and DAF might seek to bring pressure to bear on them. The following six months, however, were to see a conservative consolidation of the Nazi 'reordering of class relations' unambiguously to the advantage of employers and of the ministerial bureaucracies responsible for overseeing industrial relations. The role of the DAF in the new order was defined in late November 1933 in an agreement signed by Ley, the Reich Ministries of Labour and Economics and Hitler's representative for economic affairs, Keppler. This agreement went a long way to eliminating any possibility of the DAF emerging as a substitute for the independent trades unions. In December 1933, the 'co-ordinated' trades unions were abolished and replaced by 'Reich Plant Communities' for the various sections of industry, trade and commerce, containing employers and workers.[21]

The regulation of industrial relations under the new dispensation was governed by the 'Law for the Ordering of National Labour' of 20 January 1934, which was to become the basic labour law of the Third Reich. The law was drafted by the Reich Ministry of Labour in consultation with the Reich Ministry of Economics – significantly, neither the DAF nor the NSDAP had any say in its formulation – and strengthened the position of employers at the expense of workers and of the Reich Ministry of Labour at that of the DAF. Equality of workers and employers before the law on the basis of contracts of employment and collective agreements on wages and working conditions was effectively abolished. The relationship between employers and workers was clearly established in Section 1, subsections (1) and (2) of the law:

> (1) The employer works in the factory as leader of the plant, together with the employees and workers who constitute his retinue, to further the aims of the plant and for the common benefit of nation and State.
>
> (2.1) The plant leader makes the decisions for the retinue in all matters concerning the plant in so far as they are regulated by this law.
>
> (2.2) He is responsible for the well-being of the retinue. The retinue owe him loyalty according to the principles of the plant community . . .

The factory councils of the Weimar period were abolished and replaced by 'councils of trust' to be elected by the 'retinue' of the 'plant community'. The right of workers to appeal through their trades unions to the labour courts in the event of industrial conflict was replaced by the right to appeal through the Reich labour Trustee to new institutions, the 'Courts of Honour'. The Reich Labour Trustee was to be ultimately responsible for the regulation of working conditions and the determination of wage rates; and the role of the DAF in industrial relations was confined to the collaboration of the DAF shop steward in drawing up the list for the election of members of the 'council of trust'.[22]

The 'reordering of class relations' which took place in 1933–4 thus amounted to a major shift in the balance of power between employers and workers. In practice, only representatives acceptable to the party were allowed to take their places on the increasingly impotent 'councils of trust': following council elections in 1934 and 1935, the results of which were unsatisfactory from the regime's point of view, further elections to the councils were postponed, eventually (in 1938) indefinitely.[23] Moreover, the 'Courts of Honour' were to prove quite inadequate replacements for the labour courts: between 1934 and 1936, only 516 cases (largely against small businesses) were brought before the new courts, and in fewer than 300 of these was any penalty imposed on the employer.[24] In place of the right to negotiate freely on an equal legal footing with employers about wages and working conditions, workers henceforth had to reckon with the imposition of these by an employer or by an official of the Reich Ministry of Labour who was usually sympathetic to employers. In place of an independent trade union, workers had now only the largely toothless DAF. Although membership of the DAF remained in theory voluntary, it had in practice become compulsory by the end of 1937. By the later 1930s, the DAF had expanded into a vast bureaucracy with 44,500 paid functionaries and an income from membership dues three times that of the Nazi party.[25] Yet this organizational hypertrophy was accompanied by little real power. Finally, though never formally outlawed, strikes were increasingly treated as a breach of the January 1934 law;[26] and, were any subversive intention suspected, they rapidly attracted the attention of the *Gestapo*.

The Development of the Labour Market

Within the framework established through the 'reordering of class relations' which took place in 1933–4, the chief determinant of relations between employers and workers was the state of the labour market. This, in its turn, was largely determined by the overriding priority accorded by the Nazi leadership to rearmament and territorial expansion. Three main stages in the development of the labour market between 1933 and 1945 may be identified: first, the period from 1933 to the summer of 1936; second, the period stretching from the summer of 1936 through to the abandonment by the regime of the *Blitzkrieg* as a military-economic strategy in 1941–2; and, third, the period from the spring of 1942 to the end of the war.

Stage 1

Between spring 1933 and summer 1936, continuing high unemployment was the major factor shaping relations between employers and workers.[27] With the full support of the Reich Labour Trustees, employers were able to maintain the depressed wage rates of 1930–2. According to the official statistics, nominal hourly earnings in industry in 1935 were barely above the level to which they had sunk in 1932 and remained a full 25 per cent

lower than they had been in 1928. Nominal gross weekly earnings rose by
16.6 per cent between 1933 and 1935 – largely as a consequence of the
reduction in short-time working – yet they too remained 25 to 30 per cent
below 1928 levels. Any attempt to calculate *real* hourly and net weekly
earnings is fraught with difficulties. Not only was the official cost-of-living
index subject to systematic distortion and badly out of line with rising prices:
deductions – taxes and social security contributions, but also DAF membership dues and 'voluntary' contributions to the *Winterhilfswerk* – rose from 12.9
per cent of gross weekly earnings in 1932 to 15.6 per cent in 1935. Yet it is
significant that, even on the basis of the official cost-of-living index, net
weekly earnings had risen by only 11.7 per cent between 1932 and 1935.
Werner Mansfeld, a senior official in the Reich Ministry of Labour and
principal author of the 'Law for the Ordering of National Labour', was
only one of a host of regime-internal critics of the official cost-of-living
index: Mansfeld calculated that the cost of living had risen by 7.3 per cent
between 1932 and 1935 (rather than the officially recorded 2.0 per cent)
and that, within the economy as a whole, real gross weekly earnings had
risen by only 4.8 per cent, and real net weekly earnings by a mere 1.5 per
cent.[28] This period saw no improvement, and may have witnessed a
deterioration, in working conditions: in July 1934, for example, employers
were empowered to make a large number of exceptions to the eight-hour
working day.[29]

Stage 2

In March 1936, registered unemployment fell below 2 million. It was never
again to rise above this level. During 1936, the effects of the rearmaments
boom initiated by the regime began to make themselves felt, as shortages of
skilled labour appeared in sectors of the economy central to rearmament. By
late 1938, the labour shortage had become general and acute, with a million
unfilled vacancies in the economy as a whole.[30] By 1938–9, all workers in
regular employment were changing their jobs on average every 12 months[31]
and were able to exploit their relative scarcity to seek improved earnings and
working conditions. Between December 1935 and June 1939, nominal hourly
earnings rose by 10.9 per cent; nominal gross weekly earnings by 17.4 per
cent. Weekly net real earnings, however, were only 4.7 per cent above their
1932 level by 1939.[32] Other indices of the enhanced market position of
industrial workers after 1936 were rising sickness and absenteeism rates,[33]
improvements in working conditions and recreational facilities as employers
sought to recruit and retain scarce workers,[34] and the re-emergence on a
small scale of collective action by workers.[35]

Until mid-1938, the labour market remained largely unregulated. Workers' freedom to change jobs had been seen by employers and by the regime as an acceptable means of ensuring an adequate supply of labour to those sectors of the economy expanding as a consequence of rearmament. Yet the regime increasingly came to see untrammelled labour mobility as a threat to the rearmament programme: rapid labour turnover disrupted production and led to the emergence of inflationary pressures.[36] To combat these problems, the Reich Labour Trustees were empowered in June 1938 to set maximum wage rates and the labour offices were given powers to direct workers to priority projects through a programme of 'civil conscription' (*Dienstverpflichthung*) which embraced 800,000 workers by September 1939.[37] After the outbreak of war, the scaling down of the unpopular civil conscription programme was accompanied by a series of *ad hoc* measures to direct labour from the consumer goods sector to the capital goods and rearmaments sectors of industry. Yet these measures met with only limited success. Not only was the regime reluctant to depress consumer goods production further than was absolutely necessary, it also faced widespread collusion between employers anxious to retain scarce labour and workers concerned to avoid the reduction in earnings often associated with transfer to a new firm. The chaotic contract distribution system operated by the armed forces enabled many firms to claim that they were engaged in armaments-related work and thus avoid transfer of their workers; and employers were often willing to connive at job changing to attract skilled workers to their firms.[38] Nor was the regime successful in its attempts to contain increasing earnings. The abolition of overtime bonuses and bonuses for night and Sunday working, undertaken by the regime on the outbreak of war, was abandoned as early as November 1939.[39] Between 1939 and 1941, hourly earnings rose from 8.6 per cent to 16.4 per cent, nominal gross weekly earnings from 12.6 per cent to 23.6 per cent, above their 1936 levels – the greater increase in the latter being attributable largely to a further extension of overtime. While the official cost-of-living index became even less reliable after September 1939 than it had been before, it seems likely that the small rise in real earnings in industry which may be detected in the immediate pre-war years continued into the early stages of World War II.[40]

The limited success of the regime in controlling labour mobility led to its increasing reliance on exemplary coercion of industrial workers. The period 1938–41 saw the creation of an extensive coercive apparatus, ranging from fines administered by the firms and Labour Trustees to arrest and imprisonment of workers for repeated absenteeism or breach of contract, and the creation of a network of 'labour education camps'.[41] Employers, especially in the armaments industries, were keen advocates of the use of state coercion as a supplement to their efforts to retain a disciplined workforce.[42]

Stage 3

The third phase in the development of the labour market began in 1942 with more determined attempts by the Speer Ministry to concentrate productive resources on the war effort and to direct labour more effectively. The introduction of a fixed-price contract system gave employers in the armaments and armaments-related sectors a clear incentive to contain wage costs. The second half of the war witnessed a stagnation of both nominal hourly and gross weekly earnings, and a sharp fall in net real earnings almost certainly occurred: moreover, by 1944–5, cash wages could be translated only with difficulty into the essentials of life.[43] The strengthened position of employers was evident in other areas. Thus, they were charged with requesting the allocation of workers to the category of 'reserved worker', and removal of this status normally led to conscription – an increasingly unattractive prospect from 1942 onwards.[44] Other disciplinary devices at the disposal of employers included their responsibility for the distribution of bonus ration cards and the extension within factories of medical supervisory systems designed to depress high sickness rates.[45] Behind employers stood the state and, while the main burden of coercion was to fall on foreign workers after 1942, German workers were also subject to an increasingly brutal terror apparatus: on average, over 2,100 German workers were arrested for 'labour discipline offences' each month during the first half of 1944.[46] With their freedom to exploit their scarcity value drastically reduced, confronting savage disciplinary measures, German workers during the second half of the war were powerless to resist extensions of the working week and an acceleration in the work tempo.

Branch-, Skill- and Gender-specific Developments

The three-stage model of the development of the labour market sketched above helps us to follow the changing pattern of relations between workers and employers in the Third Reich; yet it masks important differences between branches of industry and between different sections of the work-forces within these branches. Thus, after January 1933, different sectors of industry recovered from the Depression at different rates. For example, by 1936 the iron and steel industries of the Ruhr had recovered to production levels comparable with those of the pre-Depression years; yet, in the Ruhr coal-mining industry, recovery was much slower, and high unemployment and short-time working remained significant until late 1936.[47] Similarly, after the introduction of the Four Year Plan in 1936, those industries central to the rearmament programme were able to recruit workers by offering higher

wages and improved working conditions and recreational facilities, while
both the consumer goods sector of industry and the primary products sector
faced the loss of their workers to the armaments-related industries and were
unable to improve wages significantly and so to halt this development.[48]
Again, the Ruhr coal-mining industry will serve as an example. Subject to the
supervision of the Reich Coal Council and the Reich Commissar for Prices,
the industry was unable to pass on higher wages in the form of higher prices
and so was largely unable to compete with the adjacent armaments-related
industries for scarce manpower. Nor, given the nature of mining, were
improvements in working conditions easy to achieve.[49]

These sectoral and branch-specific developments are clearly reflected in
the development of earnings. Earnings' differentials between sectors widened
between 1933 and summer 1936. Within the production goods sector of
industry, nominal weekly earnings rose by between 10.6 per cent and 23.8
per cent between September 1933 and September 1936: in the consumer
goods sector, on the other hand, they rose by no more than 5.4 per cent and
actually fell in some cases.[50] Between December 1935 and June 1939, as the
labour shortage came increasingly to affect all branches of industry, this
sectoral gap appears to have narrowed somewhat; with nominal weekly
earnings rising by 20.7 per cent in the consumer goods industries and by 16.8
per cent in the production goods sector.[51] Sectoral and branch-specific
differentials continued into the war years. During the period 1939–41, for
example, nominal weekly earnings continued to rise rapidly in the iron and
steel industries, while those in the construction industry stagnated.[52]

Further distinctions may be made between skilled, semi-skilled and unskilled workers; and between male and female workers. Thus, in the
metal-working industries, the gross hourly earnings of unskilled workers sank
from 72.3 per cent of those of skilled workers in 1927–8 to 68.0 per cent in
1936 and 65.7 per cent in March 1944. In the textiles industry, by contrast,
the gross hourly earnings of unskilled workers rose from 75.3 per cent of
those of skilled and semi-skilled workers in 1927–8 to 76.9 per cent in 1936
and 77.2 per cent in March 1944.[53] Gender-specific differentials widened in
the metal-working industries while narrowing in the textiles industry, bearing
out the general picture of a widening of gender-specific differentials (even
during wartime) in those industries in which women made up less than 40
per cent of the workforce.[54]

During the war years, male skilled German workers, especially in the
armaments and armaments-related industries, became an elite within
the work-force, increasingly charged with supervisory functions. Under the
impact of conscription, mass importation of foreign workers and prisoners
of war and (from 1943) the attempted mobilization of economically inactive
women for war work, the male German work-force shrank from almost

four-fifths of the total industrial work-force in July 1939 to slightly over half in May 1944.[55] Parallel to this, the skill profile of German industry changed dramatically: in the machine-tool industry, for example, the share of the work-force made up by skilled workers fell from 51.5 per cent in 1940 to 27.5 per cent in 1944; while that made up by unskilled workers rose from 12.7 per cent to 32.0 per cent over the same period.[56] The privileged position of male German workers, especially skilled workers, *vis-à-vis* the rest of the industrial workforce helps to explain the relatively good work discipline that characterized this group throughout the war.

Rationalization, Modernization and the Atomization of the Work-force

If relations between employers and workers in German industry and handicrafts between 1933 and 1945 are to be explained principally with reference to the destruction of independent representation of workers' interests, the development of the labour market, and the position of individual industries and branches within the economy and of individual groups of workers within these industries, longer-term trends in industrial organization and employer-worker relations should nevertheless not be ignored. As was noted above, in 1933 German industry employed modern production methods on only a very limited scale. Rationalization and mechanization of production techniques were confined largely to coal mining, the iron and steel industries, locomotive-construction plants, the electrical goods and precision-engineering industries and the chemical industry: the first great wave of rationalization and mechanization in German industry had come to an end with the onset of the Depression.[57] Yet, with the economic recovery that began in 1934–5, rationalization and mechanization were to be extended. A guaranteed market for the output of those industries participating in the rearmament boom, the record profits made by firms working on state contracts, the elimination of independent trades unions, the maintenance of wage rates at Depression levels and the corporate tax system, all made greater mechanization of production methods feasible and attractive: the growing shortage of skilled workers made such modernization necessary.

Throughout the later 1930s, conveyor-belt and flow production methods found greater application in German industry than ever before. This modernization of production techniques was reflected in the dramatic increase in productivity that occurred in many branches of industry. Thus, in the metal-working industries, productivity per worker-hour rose by 32.2 per cent between 1929 and 1939; in the textiles industries, by 31.5 per cent over the same period.[58] Despite German industry's continuing reliance on universal machine tools and the shortage of the less versatile, but more productive, special machine tools, the modernization of production techniques was to be continued during the war years, as the demands of the war economy and the acute shortage of skilled workers made themselves felt.[59] Parallel to these developments, the period after 1935–6 witnessed attempts by the state authorities and by employers to introduce more rational, productivity-related, wage systems. One indicator of such initiatives was the renewed interest shown by employers in Taylorist time-and-motion studies. A national time-and-motion studies organization had existed in Germany since 1924. With the post-Depression recovery and the onset of the rearmament boom, the number of participants in time-and-motion training courses run by the 'Reich Association for Labour Studies' (*Reichsausschuss für Arbeitsstudien, Refa*) increased dramatically. In 1929, 1,650 time-and-motion engineers were trained in such courses. In 1936, this figure rose to 4,000; in 1939, to 6,000; and was to reach a peak in 1943, when no fewer than 12,000 engineers participated in the courses run by the organization throughout the year. The application of time-and-motion studies to production techniques was particularly prominent in the metal-working industry and in large manufacturing concerns; but, by 1939, it extended across German industry and was beginning to appear in medium-sized and smaller firms.[60] The more highly differentiated payment systems which were made possible by the application of more scientific techniques for organizing production were accompanied by the extension of company welfare schemes, pensions and bonuses,[61] as well as by the further development of a factory-based medical supervisory scheme which succeeded in depressing sickness rates and containing these throughout the Third Reich – even during the later war years – to levels well below those of the last pre-Depression years.[62]

Central to all these developments was a conscious attempt on the part of employers, actively supported by the DAF, the Reich Labour Trustees and, later, the officials of the Speer Ministry, to create a 'modern' industrial work-force, employed in rationalized and mechanized production, bound to the firm by a range of company welfare benefits, but denied independent representation and with little scope for determining working conditions or the work tempo, and rewarded strictly according to output.[63]

Conclusion

That the existence of the Nazi dictatorship profoundly influenced the development of relations between employers and workers after 1933 is fairly self-evident. The destruction of independent representation of workers' interests; the over riding priority accorded by the regime to rearmament, territorial expansion and war; its readiness to bolster employers' authority, and its diligence in maintaining the 're-ordered' state of class relations – all could not but have major implications for industrial relations. Yet the extent to which the Nazi dictatorship contributed to the modernization of industrial relations is less clear.

While the 're-ordering of class relations' carried out by the Nazi regime in 1933–4 was plainly a reaction against some typically 'modern' features of the development of industrial relations after 1918 – against the attempt to promote greater institutional regulation of industrial conflict through the state-sponsored labour arbitration machinery and the works councils[64] – the dictatorship also witnessed the extension of other distinctly modern trends in production and labour-management techniques which pre dated 1933. The backward-looking and anti-modern rhetoric of Nazism notwithstanding, through its rearmament policies and the economic boom to which these led, the regime provided employers with an incentive to extend modern produc-tion and management techniques; facilitated such an extension through the elimination of workers' independent representation; and thus was, in the short term, at least compatible with the modernization and rationalization of a range of aspects of industrial relations. Moreover, political disenfranchise-ment, the destruction of the dense associational life of the urban industrial working-class milieu, and the constant threat of exemplary terror, combined with the consequences of the rearmament boom – full employment, greater geographical mobility and opportunities for limited upward social mobility – to reinforce the decline in class affiliation already apparent in the later Weimar years and to encourage a retreat by workers into private and family concerns and the emergence of the individualistic and achievement-oriented behaviour characteristic of the 'modern', 'affluent' worker of the *Wirtschaft-swunder* years.[65]

Yet the longer-term *incompatibility* of the Nazi dictatorship with any stable and rational social order perhaps contributed as significantly to the modern-ization of industrial relations. Set alongside the dramatic developments which accompanied the collapse of the 'Third Reich', the Allied occupation and the reconstruction of the (West) German economy during the period 1944–8, the 'objective' social changes and the 'subjective' changes of value and attitude brought about by the Nazi regime up to 1943–4 pale into insignificance; a perspective which emerges clearly from the prominence of these 'crisis years' in the memories of those interviewed by oral historians.[66] Evacuation of urban areas during the later stages of the war; the flight of millions westward from the advancing Red Army and, later, from the Soviet occupation zone; the expulsion of Germans from large areas of central Europe after 1945 – all served to break down regional and local ties.[67]

The emergence of a subsistence economy in large parts of Germany after May 1945 and the common experiences of the immediate post war years had a levelling effect, creating the basis for the 'classless' affluent society of West Germany during the 1960s and contributing directly to shaping the 'model' industrial relations regarded with envy by British observers. The binding of workers to their factories, which took place during the later war years, continued after 1945 as workers and employers came to share a common interest in the reconstruction of their firms. The moderation displayed by the factory councils established after 1945 – moderation which extended even to the implementation of de-nazification policies – reflected not only the exhaustion of the work-force but also workers' awareness of their dependence on the technical and managerial expertise of employers in the reconstruction of the economy.[68] For their part, employers and managers seem to have become more willing to make concessions to a work-force on the skill and commitment of which they, in turn, were dependent.[69] This recognition of mutual dependence in the crisis conditions brought about by its collapse, and the changed patterns of behaviour to which such recognition led, were perhaps the most important contributions made by the Nazi dictatorship to the modernization of industrial relations in Germany.

8

Employers and Workers in Japan Between the Wars

Takao Matsumura

Contemporary Japanese industrial relations have four characteristic features: employment for life; seniority wages; mutual loyalty; and 'enterprise unionism'. These four features are closely related, but in fact different, phenomena. Lifetime employment (*Shûshin Koyô*) means that graduates from school or university are recruited and given employment with tenure until the age of retirement (at the age of 55 or, more recently, 60 in some companies). Earlier discharge, lay-off or premature resignation are rare in the case of large-scale enterprises and the public-sector companies, although these characteristics are gradually changing. But most workers have a lifetime commitment to the company. The seniority wage system (*Nenkô*) implies that wages are related to individual and personal factors such as education (whether at university, college or high school), length of service and age rather than skill. Under this system, wages rise every April in line with criteria based on age and family commitments. As well as monthly wages, workers also receive bonuses twice a year. Such bonuses are often equivalent to half the annual wage and, when workers retire, they receive a large lump sum. Mutual loyalty is the third critical feature: the loyalty and deference shown by the workers to their company are strong, and are consolidated through participation in group decision-making and consultation at all levels. As a result, trade-union membership is restricted to the permanent workers of an individual company, so that white-and blue-collar workers belong to the same union. The system does not prevent strikes but they are usually short, and Japanese working-class values are such that the struggles never go beyond company-specific issues: sympathy is never shown with workers in other companies and industries.

While these have become the dominant trends in Japanese industrial relations since World War II, their roots – albeit in more sporadic form – lie in the interwar period. What needs explaining, therefore, is how and why this system has taken shape.

In Japan a feudal system known as the *Shôgunate* existed for seven centuries until it was abolished following the Meiji Restoration in 1868. The nature of the Meiji Restoration was hotly debated by historians in the 1920s and 1930s. One group (the *Kôzaha* school) argued that the Restoration was an incomplete bourgeois revolution, with the result that Japan remained dominated by an absolute monarchy with many feudal residues even after the Restoration. A different view was held by the *Rônôha* school of historians, who argued that the Restoration constituted a bourgeois revolution that provided the basis for the formation of a modern capitalist society in which the bourgeoisie became the ruling class of post-Meiji Japan. These debates still continue but the most widely held view is that pre-war (and probably postwar) Japanese industrial relations were dominated by feudal ethics, so that employers and employees, for example, held the same concepts of *Giri* (social justice) and *Ninjô* (humane sentiment) which constituted the common base on which social relations developed.

It has often been argued that the origins of the Japanese employment system can be traced to the original practice of a small number of large commercial enterprises like Mitsui. Here, it is claimed, the traditional ethos of the Japanese family (called *Ie*) was adapted to the organization of a modern industrial enterprise, where relations between employers and employees were seen in terms of a 'family enterprise' and directly comparable to those between the head and the children in the family. Chie Nakane describes this as 'a vertical society'[1] and, in his pioneering study of the Japanese factory system, J. C. Abegglen argues that the system was based on the traditional willingness of workers and managers to see the enterprise as a family-like community in which their own welfare was dependent on its prosperity. Such beliefs were reinforced by the traditional vertical structure of social dependence.[2] It is also possible that Confucianism played a major role in generating the system, and the particular work ethos of Japanese people – including the acceptance of authority, loyalty and deference to superiors – clearly was, and is, of great importance.

But the origins of the specific characteristics of industrial relations in Japan need to be considered more specifically in their historical context. If we look at the origin of the system in terms of economic circumstances, managerial strategies, state power, and the nature of the labour movement, then it will become clear that the system was the creature of the rational, profit-maximizing behaviour of managers who were seeking to adapt their strategies to the specific characteristics of the Japanese labour market.[3]

As Mikio Sumiya and R. P. Dore argued in the 1970s, the Japanese employment system is of relatively recent origin.[4] The system by which wages were related to length of service was first introduced in a handful of government engineering works as early as the late nineteenth-century, but it was only during World War I that the system was introduced more widely in Japanese industry. Japan was on the side of the Allies, the eventual winners, and, during the five years of the war, enjoyed an industrial boom. Real net domestic product rose by 61.5 per cent in the period 1910–20, and particularly during the war years. Exports increased and, while some of the benefits were passed on to the workers, high prices in general and low real wages meant that profitability was not diminished.

The war changed dramatically the structure of the working classes in Japan. The number of workers in heavy industry, light industry and construction increased rapidly from 211,000 in 1914 to 255,000 in 1920. The number of female textile workers also grew rapidly, but not as fast as that of male workers, and the numbers in factories employing over five persons increased by 60 per cent in the same period to reach 46.8 per cent of the total work-force in 1920.

After the summer of 1915, the growing demand from Russia for munitions stimulated the Japanese economy and caused labour shortages. Most of the additional workers were recruited from the agriculture section, and labour mobility between factories increased – particularly in shipyards, machine factories and steel mills – and industrial managers became preoccupied by the problem of securing a stable supply of skilled and semi-skilled labour for their factories. They attempted to counter high mobility by wage increases and agreements between themselves to prevent poaching. This was not very effective, however. As Andrew Gordon puts it:

> By the end of World War I, Japanese managers offered an impressive array of enticements to seniority. Promotions, wage hikes, bonuses, and welfare programmes such as retirement pay all favoured senior workers and theoretically encouraged long-term employment. These benefits had emerged largely as a piecemeal response to the persistence of high turnover, although in a few cases, organized workers had demanded and gained them.[5]

During World War I, capital also became more concentrated, and the *Zaibatsu* groups established their position as leaders of Japanese industry, commerce and finance. The Industrial Club, through which the Japanese employment system was later developed and propagated, together with Chambers of Commerce and Industry and other bodies, was founded in 1916. The war also changed the labour movements in Japan. The Japanese trade union, *Shokkô Giyûkai*, had been founded in 1897, but the Peace Police Law of 1900 was designed to suppress all allegedly subversive political activities and had made it difficult for trade unionists to expand their influence among the workers. After the labour leader Shûsui Kôtoku and some of his followers were executed in 1911, the Japanese labour movements experienced a 'winter period'. Before World War I, there had been only small-scale and localized unions among carpenters, stonemasons and other skilled trades while, except for a few groups like printing compositors, other factory workers had not been organized.

The economic boom caused by the war made the trades unions more confident and aggressive, however, and after 1917 labour disputes increased rapidly. The number of disputes for wage increases reached a peak in 1919. Factory workers began to organize rapidly and the number of unions grew: in 1918 there were 107 unions, in 1919 187 unions, and in 1920 273 unions. Steelworkers, shipbuilders and machinists were particularly militant and even the *Yuaikai* (Friendly Society), which had originally been founded in 1912 by Suzuki Bunji, a Christian social reformer, as a tame and harmless institution, began to take a different form and attitude.[6]

These changes meant the abandonment of the old principles of harmony between capital and labour and the adoption of something more akin to class struggle. The *Yuaikai* changed its name to the Great Japan Trade Union Federation in 1919, and took the decision to become the national co-ordinating centre for craft and industrial unions in Japan.

The Russian Revolution had a dramatic impact on Japan because it gave hope to those who had been insisting on the need for revolutionary changes in society. In 1918 large-scale 'rice riots' took place and shook the government. Starting in a remote village as protests by housewives against the sharp increase of the price of rice, the riots quickly spread throughout the nation and involved several million people. Troops were mobilized to repress the rioters, and the repression of the riots was seen by many as the desperate act of a dying *ancien régime*. During the war, many young intellectuals had entered the labour movement, and the *Shinjinkai* (New Man Society), formed at Tokyo Imperial University and *Sakuzô Yoshino*, encouraged its members to join the *Yuaikai* and help awaken the political consciousness of the workers. The intellectuals looked mainly to guild socialism, while the Paris Peace Conference in 1919 also stimulated a new democratic movement named *Taishô* Democracy.[7]

But, by the end of 1920, all these militant movements had disappeared. The prosperity brought by World War I continued for a short while after the Armistice but, in April 1920, the boom ended. Many banks failed and the market in silk, Japan's major export commodity, shrank. The golden era of wartime had ended and, before recovery could begin, the 1922 Washington Conference on disarmament further damaged Japan's heavy industries which relied heavily on military procurement. Lay-offs were widespread in the shipyards and machine factories throughout Japan. Then, on 1 September 1923, the great Kantô earthquake brought economic activity in the Tokyo-Yokohama region to a complete halt. Out of 15,000 factories in the region, 9,000 were destroyed by fire. About 100,000 people were killed, and many companies suffered damage and laid off large numbers of workers. The number of unemployed workers after the earthquake was estimated at between 80,000 and 100,000 in Tokyo and 25,000 in Yokohama.

Throughout the 1920s the Japanese economy staggered from depression to depression until 1929 when it suffered even greater damage from the world depression. The number of unemployed was estimated by the government to be between 300,000 and 400,000, and put at 1,300,000 by *The Economist*. It was during the long-term depression of the 1920s that the characteristic Japanese pattern of industrial relations took shape. The increase in the number of factory workers during the decade was not very large (from 1,550,000 in 1920 to 1,800,000 in 1928) and the rate of increase per annum was only 1.5 per cent (compared with 18 per cent between 1914 and 1919). But, in contrast to the war-boom period, it now became a risky and difficult matter even for the skilled worker to move from factory to factory. Hence, the desire to stay with a particular company grew, and more men hoped to remain with their first employer from initial appointment to retirement. During the war, labour mobility in heavy industry had been as high as 70 to 90 per cent per year but, in the late 1920s, the rate of labour mobility fell to about 10 per cent. When turnover dropped sharply in the 1920s, managers looked on costly seniority benefits with less enthusiasm and often retreated from earlier commitments to seniority bonuses, regular pay rises or retirement funds, and tried instead to introduce efficiency-based wage systems. The introduction of these new pay-incentive formulae had been foreshadowed by translation of Taylor's *The Principles of Scientific Management* in 1913, only two years after its American publication. On the other hand, some managers preferred to try to establish a stable and trained skilled work-force within their companies to meet the rapidly increasing demands of new technologies. In the Mitsui Shipbuilding Company, the Kôbe Iron and Steel Company and the Shibaura Machinery Company, for example, technological training programmes were set up. The managers looked to employ inexperienced young boys with good educational qualifications after graduation each year in March or April; these became favoured and were expected to be the future leaders. The companies taught high levels of technology, rather than manual skills, to the newcomers, and, in the 1920s, in-company technology-training schemes, rather than reliance on courses provided by public technical schools, became standard procedure in many large companies. It was natural that workers who received such training from their companies should have developed a strong sense of loyalty, and this was how the tradition of lifetime employment developed.

Seniority-based wages were supplemented by other inducements, such as retirement funds and non-wage welfare benefits, for workers who stayed with the company. These were introduced roughly in parallel with the seniority-based wage system. Managers were generally opposed to state welfare schemes, as well as to the proposed legislation in 1920 on health insurance, because this would have meant that non-wage welfare in the company would have lost its effectiveness.

It is important to stress, however, that the lifetime employment and seniority wage systems were established only in the larger-scale companies and applied only to permanent workers. All these companies also employed a substantial number of temporary workers and women who could be laid off whenever trade was poor, and employers drew the majority of their temporary labour from a pool of mobile adult wage-earners. Those employed on this basis were given a one-week trial period; then they began as temporary workers with contracts for three months, for six months or for a year. Only after such initial contracts would a company give some of the new workers regular status.

This constituted the new employment policy of the 1920s. Another important factor was the prevalence of the subcontracting system after World War I. The coexistence of large companies, having high levels of capital and relatively high wages, with small and medium-sized companies, that were labour intensive but offered low wages, became a major social issue after the war. This 'dual structure' of the Japanese economy was of vital importance, because the large-scale companies were able to exploit the smaller ones by laying off workers and subcontractors. As a result, the smaller firms and their employees were forced to function as the shock absorbers for the depression, and thus remained outside the new Japanese employment system.

Recently, historians have questioned whether the training systems in the larger companies in the 1920s were as successful as the managers expected. In a comparative study of the employment conditions of white-collar staff (*Shokuin*) and workers (*Kōin*) in the Hitachi Company, Shinji Sugayama has shown that attempts to encourage long-term service by hiring graduates and offering seniority wages began systematically for white-collar staff in the late 1920s. It was also applied to other workers in part, bringing about a new stratification of the labour market in both large and small factories. Management efforts to elicit long-term service from workers, however, were limited in effect and inconsistent. Between 1920 and 1939, workers hired after graduation comprised only 10 per cent of all the recruits. Wages did not necessarily rise with seniority, and income differentials between junior staff and workers amounted to a factor of four in the late 1940s. When business was slow, older workers with seniority were the ones most often dismissed. The non-graduate workers recruited in the late 1920s comprised about 40 per cent, of the total while junior staff represented about 70 per cent and senior staff about 90 per cent. The percentage of non-graduate workers recruited in the late 1930s is presumed to be much lower, but this did not occur in the case of staff employees,[8] and the position of blue-collar workers was insecure. To regard relations in the Japanese employment system as 'a paradise' is therefore misleading, and Andrew Gordon is right when he says that 'If the enterprise was a family, then workers were servants using a separate entrance; if a community, workers were misfits liable to steal or cause trouble'.[9]

How then was the concept of lifetime employment established if, in reality, this did not happen very often? Two factors have to be considered. First, in Japan there was a form of apprenticeship but one that differed from its English counterpart. In England, and in many other European countries, the apprenticeship system might last for up to seven years and constituted the process through which artisans mastered the skills of their trades and became journeymen. In England in the mid-nineteenth-century such men had organized national craft unions which were able to regulate the entry of apprentices and ensure high wage rates. In Japan, there were urban craft guilds in the Tokugawa period and in Tokyo, for example, the masons and sawyers maintained their craft guilds until at least 1889, but machinists and others in modern industries did not reproduce these earlier journeymens' organizations. As a result, they were never able to regulate entry into the trade or to set wages through negotiations with their masters, and, when new technologies began to be imported from the industrialized countries in the West, it was too late to establish an apprenticeship system.

This meant that in Japanese industry there was no stratum of artisans in the English sense, and this was why, subsequently, craft and industrial unions proved difficult to establish, even though (as we have already mentioned) *Yuaikai* did attempt to create such an organization. But it was the workshop, rather than particular occupations, crafts, or even individual industries, that continued to be the basic unit of organization. A few industrial unions, such as the gun workers and the Tokyo electric machinery iron union, were established in 1920 but attempts to set up industry-wide craft and industrial unions failed and collective action never went beyond company-specific issues. Even the successor to the *Hyôgikai*, which had been the most active proponent of industrial organization, decided in 1929 to devote its energy to workplace struggles.

As a result, managers in large-scale heavy industries succeeded in expelling independent trades unions from their enterprises, and they set up instead so-called 'factory councils'. Since 1918 the government had officially encouraged the introduction of factory councils and, according to Yutaka Nishinarita, 48 shipyards, arsenals, steelmakers, machine and metalworking factories introduced factory councils in the period between 1919 and 1928. In 1919 the Yokosuka Naval Yard, with 17,500 employees, was the first to institute a factory council. The Kure Naval Yard, with nearly 29,500 employees, and Yahata Ironworks, with about 16,000 employees, followed in 1920; then the Mitsubishi Nagasaki Shipyard did the same in 1921. The introduction of factory councils in these big industries reached a peak in 1921 and thereafter decreased rapidly. But Nishinarita has also shown that there were 35 heavy industrial firms with over 500 employees nationwide that did not set up councils between 1919 and 1928, and he argues that factory councils were established mainly in the large-scale industries that were controlled either by state capital or by the Zaibatsu groups.[10]

The real issue, however, is the aim and results of the introduction of the councils. In contrast to the factory councils (or shop-steward committees) in the West which provided a means for conducting negotiations between managers and trades unionists, factory councils in Japan were designed to prevent independent trades unions from coming into the firm or to get rid of existing unions. From the beginning, the councils were designed to function as substitutes for trades unions. Managers usually allowed workers to elect council members, but the candidates were generally limited to senior white-collar workers. Managers offered workers a chance to express views on wages or work conditions, but they always limited the council to an advisory role. In the early 1920s, there were some attempts to use the councils as springboards for establishing unions, but such attempts proved ineffective and, by the end of the 1920s, managers had succeeded in banishing almost all strong unions from the major shipyards, machine factories and steel mills.

This marked a major change, because, from the late nineteenth-century to the early 1920s, the Japanese labour movement had developed primarily in the larger enterprises. In 1920 and 1921 strikes broke out in a number of major concerns – for example, at the Kawasaki Dockyards in Kobe, where 35,000 men were involved – but thereafter this changed. Independent trades unions were eliminated from the big businesses and only in medium and small-scale firms were workers able to remain organized. The result, shown in Table 1, was that industrial disputes and collective action shifted from the larger enterprises to smaller factories. Although trades unions continued to exist in the arsenals and in some of the bigger businesses, their role was limited to electing labour representatives for the ILO, and they were no longer independent trades unions. The failure of the labour movement in the larger enterprises in the 1920s and the establishment of the factory councils were, therefore, two sides of the same coin, and constituted the essential conditions for the emergence of the modern Japanese pattern of industrial relations.

Table 1 Distribution of labour disputes by number of participants (1921–31)

Year	Number of participants					Number of disputes
	1–14 %	15–99 %	100–299 %	300–399 %	>1000 %	
1921	11.0	57.8	19.1	8.9	3.2	246
1926	27.0	51.9	15.9	3.6	1.6	495
1930	30.9	53.4	11.0	3.6	1.1	907

Source: Labour Ministry, 'Labour Disputes in our Country shown by Statistics', cited in Kazuo Nimura, 'The Steady Development and the Defeat of Labour Movements in Pre-war Period', in *Rôdôundôshi Kenkyû (Labour History Review)*, No. 50 (1969), p.63.

The world depression in 1929–30 proved a disaster for Japanese heavy industry. The year 1931 was the severest, when Japan's exports fell by 70 per cent compared with 1929, and unemployment reached at least 2 million. Even the university elites were affected and the title of a popular film, *I went to University, but . . .* became a cliché of the era. In 1931 Japan came off the Gold Standard, and Finance Minister Takahashi's deficit spending policy had some effect so that Japan's recovery came earlier than it did in the West.

In 1931 Japan began the invasion of China and, after military intervention in the northern part of China (Manchuria) in September 1931 ('The Manchurian Incident'), Japanese military expenditure also began to rise steeply. Heavy industrial enterprises were among the chief beneficiaries but, despite the recovery, the labour market shifted only gradually from a situation of oversupply to one of shortage. Individual companies did not repeat the experience of World War I but behaved cautiously, continuing to employ most new recruits as temporary workers. This gave permanent workers added incentives for staying with their companies. Then, following the Manchurian Incident, a highly nationalistic climate developed. In 1933 Japan withdrew from the League of Nations and in 1938 from the ILO. Japan's war industries were now enjoying spectacular gains, unemployment virtually disappeared and wages were rising.

As a result, the trades unions also gained strength through increased membership, and, in 1936, union membership reached its peak for the pre-war period, with a total of 420,000 members, even though this was still less than 8 per cent of the total industrial work-force. But the outlook of the trades unionists remained unchanged. In March 1933, for example, one of the leaders of the Japanese Seamen's Union wrote to his friend Edo Fimmen, General Secretary of the International Transport Workers Federation, to describe his impressions of Japanese trades unions after returning from several years' service in London:

> From my experience with the trade union movement in Europe, I think that the functioning of Japanese trade unionism has in many respects not yet reached maturity. A reform is required not only in the organisation of trade unionism but to recreate a trade union spirit among the organised workers. For one month I did my best to attend various trade union meetings to tell them about trade union organisation and trade union spirit which the trade unionists in Europe have experienced in fighting for the establishment of trade unionism during the last hundred years.[11]

The number of disputes and the numbers participating in disputes decreased from the time of the Manchurian Incident until 1935 but, in 1936 and 1937, a sharp rise in disputes in small factories brought the *Sanpô* movement to life.

War with China broke out in 1937, and what was called the 'China Incident' quickly became a full-scale war as the Japanese invasion spread across China. The eventual outcome was war with the United States in 1941, and this four-year war was to be the longest that Japan had ever fought. At the time of the invasion of China there were almost no trades unionists left to oppose the invasion. On the contrary, at its annual convention in October 1937, the All Japan Labour Federation passed a resolution that declared: 'We give our most sincere thanks to the officers and men of the Imperial Army who ... with the Imperial Navy did so much to add to the nation's glory throughout China since the Incident began ... '[12] In March 1938 the National Mobilization Law was passed, providing the government with emergency powers to control human and material sources in time of war. The first regulations which were put into effect in 1939, were ordinances limiting labour mobility and controlling wages. Signs began to appear in the shops; 'waste not, want not, until we win'.[13]

From then until the end of the war in 1945, the government issued regulations in rapid succession. The National Registration System was introduced in 1939; this required individuals with special skills to register with the government, and it was then gradually expanded to require the registration of *all* workers regardless of special skills. At the same time, *all* males aged 16 to 20 were required to register whether they were workers or not. In 1941 this system was further expanded to require registration of all males aged 16 to 40 and all unmarried women between 16 and 25. In 1944 it was extended to males aged from 12 to 59 and unmarried women from 12

to 39, and, in the final period of the war, high-school pupils were mobilized
into heavy industries. The National Workbook Law of 1941 required all
workers to carry workbooks, registered with the local employment agency,
in which were recorded their employment histories, current status and wages.
The law encompassed 6 million workers, roughly three-quarters of the
nation's industrial work-force. In 1942 a comprehensive anti-turnover ordin-
ance was introduced to reduce the rising rate of labour turnover and making
it almost impossible for workers in heavy industries legally to move from one
factory to another. As labour shortages became more severe, with the
development of the war, increasing numbers of Koreans were forced or
persuaded (often by deception) to come to Japan to work in mining and
munition factories. The exact number is still not known but it is estimated
that about 3,000,000 Koreans were working in Japan when the war ended.
Their working conditions were extremely poor and, if they attempted to
escape, they were killed. In the Nagano prefecture, for example, many
Korean workers were killed once construction of the munition factories was
completed because they knew the secret layout and structure of the factories.

After the China War started in 1937, industrial relations were drawn into
the orbit of *Sanpô* Industrial Service to the Nation.[14] The *Sanpô* movement
had been founded in 1936, and was initiated by the far right of the labour
movement, the *Kyôchôkai*, and by the Home Ministry's Police Bureau. The
reason for introducing *Sanpô* into all factories was to harmonize labour-management relations, to prevent disputes, to ensure industrial peace and thereby
facilitate war production. The factory councils of the 1920s were taken as
models, and the policy was implemented through the *Sanpô* Federation, which
was officially supported by the Home and Welfare Ministries in July 1938,
before being superseded by the government-run *Sanpô* Association. 'Enterprise as one family' was a typical slogan. All other unions were eventually
dissolved, but the *Sanpô* was seen by many contemporary workers to be a
more sophisticated version of earlier enterprise unions, and most previous
trade union leaders co-operated with the *Sanpô*. All employees, from the
company president to the temporary workers, were members of the organization, and the *Sanpô* leaders declared that the traditional distinctions between
white and blue collar should be ended. A new spirit of 'industrial service to
the nation' should replace the selfish spirit of personal interest and workplace confrontation.

The impact of the *Sanpô* movement on industrial relations was considerable
and helped to diffuse in-factory training schemes in large and in small
factories where such programmes had previously been either weak or
non-existent. Instead of seniority-based wages, *Sanpô* established the formula
of the 'family-supporting' wage, that is, a minimum rate for each age bracket,
and an extra allowance for each dependant. Uniform annual pay increases to

all workers, regardless of their length of service, became the general trend after the onset of the Pacific War but, once this stage of the war began, the emphasis on harmony gave way to more practical concerns regarding attendance, efficiency and productivity. The slogan, 'Imperial Work Ethic' replaced the 'Enterprise as one family'. It was not long before life for working people became increasingly wretched and finally disastrous.

In conclusion, then, it would clearly be quite wrong to see the typical features of contemporary Japanese industrial relations as comprising an ideal that has made high rates of economic growth possible. Employment for life, seniority wages, mutual loyalty and enterprise unionism were established in a fairly haphazard fashion during the 1920s in a period of long-term depression. The changes occurred only in the larger enterprises and were possible only because they were combined with the simultaneous employment of temporary workers and of women and the development of a system of subcontracting to smaller outside companies. Immigrant Korean workers also began to play an increasingly important part in the labour-force. In return for the sacrifices they made, a certain section of the Japanese labour-force was rewarded with a relatively secure system of industrial employment. But such a system, it must be remembered, was also premised on the exclusion of an independent trade union movement.

9

The Struggle for Control of the American Workplace 1920–1985

P. K. Edwards

Introduction

The history of American industrial relations used to be written as a natural progress towards stability, wherein employers and trades unions come to accept each other's legitimacy, and conflict is peacefully institutionalized: book titles, such as *As Unions Mature*,[1] capture the tone. From the 1960s, radical analyses began to argue, instead, that conflict at the point of production had not been eliminated and that this conflict reflected a continuing struggle for control of the work process: the workplace was a *Contested Terrain*.[2] Events since the mid-1970s have underlined the point. Some employers have been vigorously resisting unionization; others, that traditionally accepted unions, have been opening new facilities on a non-union basis, while yet others, which still work with unions, have made radical changes in working practices. Renewed struggle has led to *The Transformation of American Industrial Relations*:[3] the 'New Deal' system of industrial relations, which dominated the period since the 1930s and which was based on a detailed collective-bargaining contract that inscribed rigid job rules, has collapsed. It has been replaced by a system in which flexibility and active commitment, instead of mere contract compliance, are stressed.

Such books have not only drawn together historical detail but have also provided interpretive syntheses. They have stimulated a wide-ranging theoretical and empirical debate. This chapter cannot cover all of this ground but, by focusing on one key topic, it tries to indicate how the various debates are connected. This topic is the control of the workplace: the methods of regulating how work is done, together with the influence of employers and workers over these methods. Workplace control is the explicit concern of several debates, the work of Kochan et al. for example, being driven by the argument that the New Deal system of regulation no longer met employers' needs and was therefore dismantled. The issue is implicit in other debates. That on the role of the law, for instance, is not just about legal technicalities but also about the ways in which the law helped to define and support a particular form of workplace order.

The difficulty with *Contested Terrain*,[5] its title notwithstanding, is that management is seen as the source of change and that outcomes are viewed as providing stable resolutions to struggle. This ignores workers' active role, and also neglects the influence of the State in shaping workplace regimes. The work of Kochan and his colleagues[6] is more convincing but it, too, has a limited view of shopfloor relations. It defines 'job control unionism' as that form of shopfloor activity concerned with the administration of a legalistic contract system. Job control, in fact, also embraces efforts to assert control at the point of production;[7] such unionism has been particularly significant in Britain. Because they concentrate on only the one feature of job-control unionism. Kochan et al.[8] skate over periods when the second form was an historical possibility, and they also have difficulty with times when direct action at the point of production – notably the wildcat strikes of the 1950s – arose. The underlying rationale of such actions is lost.

This is not to suggest that American industrial relations could necessarily have developed on a different path from that taken. It is to argue that the reasons why this path was taken need to be reconstructed and that, in this process of reconstruction, the ways in which what might be termed point-of-production unionism was subordinated to the contract-administration type play a central role.

Struggle over job control, in both senses, has been continuous, which suggests that different phases of history should not be separated too sharply. The 1920s, for example, were not all passivity and the 1930s were not all rebellion;[9] indeed, several key developments of the 1930s had their origins much earlier. The period from 1920 to 1985 none the less falls into four phases that may be considered in turn.

The 1920s: Prosperity and Powerlessness

In the early 1920s employers were in the ascendant. During the late nineteenth century those in industries such as steel, where craft unions had established themselves, systematically destroyed these unions. Newer industries, such as cars, came into being during the twentieth century without any union presence. World War I marked a temporary interlude: as industrial unrest threatened the war effort, the government intervened to limit employers' freedom of action and, in some cases, collective bargaining was tentatively established. These efforts were rapidly dismantled after the war. In massive strikes in the period 1919–22 employers won significant victories, notably in the steel industry and in railroad engineering shops. The 1920s were the era of the 'Open Shop' (that is non-union operation) and the assertion of unrestrained managerial prerogative.

This did not, however, mean that problems of shopfloor control had been resolved. Employers needed to find ways to persuade workers to work. A good example is one of the country's most autocratic firms, Ford. In 1914 the revolutionary Five-dollar Day was introduced.[10] Raff and Summers[11] point out that this can hardly have been a response to a shortage of labour, for unemployment was high. It was part of a policy of raising productivity by raising wages. Absenteeism and labour turnover were very high, and morale was low. Together with reforms, such as removing the untrammelled right of foremen to dismiss, the Five-dollar Day persuaded workers to tolerate the intensification of labour and increased their long-term commitment to the firm. Even Ford did not rely on total coercion and, during the 1920s, it continued to use a number of welfare programmes.

Yet Ford, like other firms, moved away from reformism. At first sight, this looks curious. Prosperity and industrial productivity were rising, so was there not still pressure towards the liberalization of workplace control? Prosperity was, in fact, much more limited that the image of the 1920s as a period of progress would suggest. Mechanization was proceeding at an increasing rate, and employment in manufacturing was stagnant. Unemployment remained high, and rising productivity was not translated into higher wages, for wages rose more slowly than in other boom periods.[12] Slack labour markets led to a reduction of problems of turnover which had bedevilled employers before and during the war. Employers who had introduced personnel departments in an effort to make hiring more systematic tended to abandon them. There was a return to the 'drive system' of autocratic foremen and arbitrary discipline. Some firms in the newer, profitable industries, such as electrical goods, adopted more progressive policies such as seniority rules for promotion and lay-off, and welfare plans but labour-market conditions did not encourage these to spread beyond the progressive minority.[13]

Interpretations differ as to the significance of the welfare capitalism practised by progressive firms. Bernstein exemplified those who saw it as a minority concern and as basically bound to all because it was designed to avoid any real challenge to management's absolute right to manage, for it offered workers welfare but no real voice. Derber,[14] citing growth in the coverage of employee representations plans from 0.4 million workers in 1919 to 1.5 million in 1928, suggested, by contrast, that it was an advance in such areas as due process (replacing arbitrary power with a rule of law), and that it brought a measure of representation to workers in mass-production industries. Most controversially, Brody[15] argued that its 'failure was not inherent in its functioning in the 1920s, but rather from an extraordinary turn in the business cycle'.

Detailed studies of progressive firms suggest that welfare capitalism was not a nascent form of industrial government. At International Harvester, the workers' councils atrophied and dealt only with trivia.[16] At General Electric, high wages and secure employment made the work desirable but workers also developed methods of output restriction and other forms of job control which suggested that they had not fully endorsed the integrative appeal of welfarism.[17] Welfarism might have helped to solve some employers' problems of labour control in the particular environment of the 1920s, and to that extent was not collapsing through internal contradictions. But it was a partial and fragile development that any external shock might well have disrupted.

An alternative to autocracy was emerging in the clothing industry. From 1910, employers had begun to recognize unions. This was due partly to an awareness of the classic role of unions in a competitive industry of taking wages out of competition; the industry was chronically prone to cost cutting, and union wages offered a means of stabilization. Political attention had also focused on sweatshop conditions. And employers, some of whom had risen from the ranks and who appear to have had some paternalist concern for their workers, may have been more prone to accept unions than were the large-scale capitalist firms in the mass-production industries.[18] Collective bargaining became well established. Its proponents saw it as a model of industrial significance in the 1930s, when the industry's experience was used as a model for others and when its leading figures played a direct role in shaping labour legislation.[19]

A final model concerned the role of the State. The war had provided a precedent for direct intervention in labour relations.[20] Another model lay in the railroad industry, where the Railway Labor Act of 1926 was the culmination of 40 years of legislation.[21] It continues to regulate not only railroads but also airlines, and was significant in suggesting mechanisms by which the State might impose rules on the conduct of industrial relations.

Such models had little opportunity of being generalized. The Great Depression changed all that. Some scholars argue that the depression was caused by a crisis of labour control.[22] There is little evidence of this.[23] Jacoby's [24] careful studies have shown that turnover and absence were much less of an issue for employers than they had been in the 1910s. Strike rates were falling rapidly. And output restriction can hardly have had more than a small effect on productivity. But workplace regulation was important in a broader sense. The success of capitalists in restricting wage increases and introducing new techniques of production meant that the productive capacity of the economy was running ahead of workers' buying power. A crisis of over-accumulation developed. The structure of labour control that emerged during the 1920s contained the seeds of its own destruction, for it generated an increasing contradiction between the creation of surplus in production and realization of surplus in exchanges.

1932–1945: Protest and Institutionalization

During the 1920s worker discontent was suppressed. Dunn's[25] account of the car industry is useful in that it does not read the situation in the light of subsequent developments. It underlines resentment against arbitrary managerial authority to hire and fire and the absence of any shopfloor rights. Such resentment came into the open in the 1930s. The speed-up of work and poor working conditions were certainly important, but at least as significant was the question of shopfloor authority. Workers aimed to limit employers' discretion on discipline, promotion and lay-offs. Their ability to do so reflected three things: their own willingness to protest, which was sharpened by experience of the Depression; employers' loss of confidence; and the State's encouragement of collective bargaining. These may be considered in reverse order.

In 1932 a Congress still controlled by Republicans passed the Norris-La Guardia Act which 'for the first time spelled out a federal labour policy favouring full freedom of association of workers and freedom from interference by employers with this right.[26] A year later the National Industrial Recovery Act contained, in the famous Section 7(a), a statement in favour of collective bargaining. It lacked effective means of enforcement, however, and it drew increasing criticism from unions. In 1935 the National Labor Relations (or Wagner) Act took over the language of the NIRA but added a more effective National Labor Relations Board to enforce the will of the legislators. In its early years the Board eagerly took up its powers.

What explains these developments? They were certainly not the result of the wishes of the Roosevelt Administration. Roosevelt had little interest in, or knowledge of, labour matters, and at best adopted a neutral stance.[27] It was the result of the work of liberals in Congress, notably Wagner himself.[28] Seeking some model on which to base a federal policy, they naturally turned to existing experiments. Influenced by drew on experience in industries such as clothing, where collective bargaining had been established: the experts interpreted this experience as showing how bargaining could become a form of industrial government.[29] The desire to intervene reflected a general dislike of what were termed 'economic royalists'. But also important was a belief that establishing a balance of power in industry was the only way to promote economic recovery. Over-powerful employers were felt to be able to hold down wages, whereas a floor on wages would revive purchasing power.

Employers fiercely resisted the legislation. Any idea that it met their wishes by incorporating and defusing protest is unsatisfactory. Their ability to prevent it was limited by their loss of influence that resulted from the Depression. In so far as it aimed at restoring profitability, moreover, it did not directly run counter to all their interests, and, during the NIRA period, they were able to gain significant benefits without giving much away to workers. Once the NIRA was in place, it provoked four reactions: out-and-out opposition to union recognition, characteristic of small firms but also some of the steel companies and Ford; sophisticated anti-unionism as practised at International Harvester, which involved a range of anti-union tactics including propaganda; pragmatic acceptance once union recognition had been achieved, involving efforts to contain and channel union influence (an approach used by most leading firms such as General Motors); and progressivism, as at General Electric, where unions were accepted without a fight.[30] In some cases, the logic of choice seems clear. GE, for example, dominated its industry, had long been on the liberal wing of firms, and its managers believed that their long experience of workers' councils would enable them to contain the challenge of unions.[31] No doubt, too tactical considerations of gaining industrial peace by making concessions willingly played a part. But there is a less clear logic in other cases, with firms in the same industry responding differently. As Harris argues, the philosophy of individual capitalists was important.

The position regarding workers is perhaps the most contentious. The militancy of the period 1933–7 contained the strands of point-of-production and contract-administration unionism identified above. Its basis was the desire for an end to employer domination within the workplace. Neither aspect was simply economic in the sense of seeking better wages and conditions. Both were political in seeking to restrain the use of power. They had different solutions and in several unions, notably the United Auto Workers, there were intense debates as differing models of unionism were defined. The point-of-production approach was most evident among Trotskyite groups such as the truck drivers led by Farrell Dobbs.[32] Drawing on the tradition of the Industrial Workers of the World, or the 'Wobblies',[33] these groups eschewed bargaining contracts and saw the permanent threat of slow-downs and similar disruption as the only way of exerting influence on employers. Contract administration was most evident in the steel industry, where rank-and-file militancy in 1933 and 1934 had run out of steam and where the Steel Workers' Organizing Committee, a body largely staffed and funded by the united Mine Workers, engaged in a 'top-down' campaign, with a contract being signed with little shopfloor involvement.

Conventional history sees the role of workers as little more than permissive: there may have been some widespread protest, but this was rapidly and naturally channelled by unions into the pursuit of a bargaining contract.[34] New Left analyses[35] underline the point of production and see mass protest as having a radical potential, which was contained by a combination of the conservatism of union leaders and the skill of capitalists and the State in incorporating it. A new synthesis[36] has been emerging which reacts against both. It argues, first, that the image of the vast majority of workers taking part in strikes is misleading. Many workers took no part in them, and, even in the massive disputes such as the sit-down strikes of 1936–7, only a minority of workers in the plants affected actively participated in the action. Studies of the formation of union locals suggest that leadership often lay with a handful of activists.[37] Second, there is no evidence of mass radicalism: workers pursued traditional goals of a bargaining contract. As Harris in particular argues, this is not surprising: workers were taking a step into the unknown and they had little experience of activism, so that to expect anything other than a cautious and uncertain approach is wishful thinking. In the context of massive employer hostility, moreover, gaining a contract was no mean feat. To stress the incorporation of protest is to assume that the alternative was radicalism. In fact, it may have been an employer counter-attack: even limited success was far from guaranteed.

Skocpol[38] has used such evidence, together with the fact that there was no correlation between periods of militancy and the passage of legislation, to argue that mass militancy was unimportant in the creating of New Deal labour laws. This is, however, to adopt too strict a test of importance. The militancy plainly functioned as an influence on legislators' thinking, and, without it, they may not have had to focus on industrial relations, as opposed to urban poverty or agricultural depression. It was also making employers aware of the costs of autocracy. Firms such as U.S. Steel, which moved rapidly to recognize unions, feared that strikes might upset their precarious return to prosperity, and sought a union contract to pre-empt what they saw as worse, namely politically motivated left-wing unionism on the shopfloor.[39]

Workplace militancy thus played a central role. But, arising as it did on a terrain dominated by the employer, it lacked the traditions to emerge into a developed point-of-production unionism. Its roots were too shallow to permit such unionism to grow. In Britain, by contrast, craft traditions remained alive. The importance of tradition requires emphasis. The Wobbly approach was never successful because it relied on spontaneity. A craft tradition, by contrast, contains elements of unity, discipline and purpose, so that issues of the speed of work and the allocation of tasks are determined by a web of customary rules. Such point-of-production unionism accepts collective bargaining, but wishes to limit formal agreement to wages and basic conditions, with the terms of the effort bargain being hammered out on the shopfloor. With the exceptions discussed below, such a living tradition never grew up in America. The lack of a working model of such a tradition, combined with the behaviour of employers and the State, meant that there was a drift towards contract administration. This was neither a sell-out nor a case of simple incorporation but the outcome of complex processes in which the politics of the shopfloor played a key part.

A point-of-production tradition has existed in some industries. In coal mining, the highly variable nature of the work task has defied tight regulation by a contract. Combined with the solidarity of miners, this has promoted more day-to-day effort bargaining than has occurred elsewhere.[40] Particularly instructive, however, is the case of Chrysler, for here was a major auto firm behaving differently from most mass-production companies. Point-of-production unionism emerged with the growth of militancy in the early 1930s, but it did not face away.[41] Precise reasons why it was established are hard to identify, though Jefferys suggests that the size of the firm's main plant and its cramped conditions may have promoted a sense of unity. Chrysler management's behaviour may also have been important: the firm had introduced an ambitious company union, and found this being turned against it as workers exploited the leverage it offered. Jefferys shows that, when the first contracts were signed in 1937, there was already a difference from the other car firms for, in Chrysler, 'district committeemen', with full rights to negotiate during working hours, were recognized by management whereas GM had already restricted recognition to a small shop committee which could be distanced from the work process. Chrysler continued to be distinctive until the late 1950s, showing that contract unionism, although the most likely outcome, was not the automatic result of the American environment: where space was permitted, different traditions could emerge.

Reconsiderations of the evidence, suggesting that the 1930s was not a period of mass class-conscious action, should not be read as denying that significant changes in workplace control occurred. As Montgomery[42] argues, and as case studies demonstrate,[43] the experience of workers was profoundly altered: for the first time, they had a sense of dignity, and also the power to enforce demands for fair treatment.

Crucial to this was one of the distinctive features of American shopfloor practice, the emphasis on seniority as the prime alternative to employer unilateralism. Promotion and lay-off ceased to be determined by the employer's decision and depended instead on a worker's seniority; as time went by, exactly how seniority should be defined came to be increasingly codified.

What explains this emphasis? Schatz[44] offers four reasons: as workers became increasingly de-skilled, they lost identification with an occupation and saw themselves as increasingly dependent on one firm; the work-force was ageing; employers had undermined alternative craft-union controls on the labour market; and, most importantly, it had been widely used in the non-union period to reduce such things as high labour turnover, and was therefore compatible with existing employer approaches. By 1945, says Schatz, even a union as militant as that at General Electric (the UE, the United Electrical, Radio and Machine Workers of America) came to see seniority as the very cornerstone of trade unionism. But in no other area were the 'achievements and legacy of the union movement more contradictory and complicated';[45] seniority increased workers' security but reduced their solidarity, and they increasingly abandoned collective struggles in favour of reliance on the individual rights inscribed in the seniority system.

This tendency was strengthened by the other major innovation of the period, the establishment of grievance systems. These spread rapidly during the late 1930s and early 1940s. Their rationale was summed up in the phrase, 'obey now, grieve later'. That is, when a production standard, for example, was in dispute, it was the duty of the aggrieved worker to accept management's instruction and to process the grievance through the machinery. The final stage was an independent arbitrator. As time went on, arbitrators' decisions defined areas of acceptable and unacceptable activity. A legalized and bureaucratic rule of law grew up which, in many ways, suited managements because managerial needs were the basic rationale, with direct shopfloor action increasingly being ruled out as a legitimate tactic.

Exactly how the emerging system of industrial relations impinged on the shopfloor depended on the way in which unionization was achieved. Where it owed little to shopfloor activism – most notably in the steel industry – there was no tradition of autonomous action, and a formalized rule of law developed relatively easily. Where unionism was imposed on a tradition of sophisticated personnel practice, as at GE, there was similarly no basis for work-group power. But, where it was built on rank-and-file militancy, as in the car and rubber industries, there was more possibility of independent worker activity. Kuhn,[46] studying tyre and electrical plants in the 1950s, found much more shopfloor bargaining about effort levels in the former than in the latter. He attributed the difference to difference in technology, which were no doubt important, but surely at least as important was the presence of a tradition of action: technical conditions at best permit bargaining to occur but, to take advantage of favourable conditions, workers need a collective awareness that they can exert leverage at the point-of-production, and a tradition of autonomous action is central to such awareness.

By the end of the 1930s, pressures to contain the insurgency of the decade were already evident. But crucial to the bureaucratization of industrial relations was World War II. The State played an active role directly, by containing shopfloor protest through measures including wage and price controls and, where necessary, military intervention in strikes,[47] and indirectly, by encouraging the formalization of personnel policy in such areas as recruitment, discipline and seniority rules.[48] The National War Labor Board aimed to remove disputes from the shopfloor through the grievance procedure, although also strengthening unions through maintenance-of-membership arrangements which provided that once a worker was in a union it was impossible to leave during the life of the collective contract. Unions found their institutional presence given important underpinning while their activities were increasingly circumscribed. The State was no longer saying that its sole aim was to promote collective bargaining, with its actual conduct being left to the parties. Instead, the aim was shopfloor order, and bargaining was no more than a means to this end.[49]

The ability of unions to challenge management and government was limited in two main ways. First, a no-strike agreement pledged them to industrial peace. Significantly, the only union to refuse the pledge was the Mechanics' Educational Society of America, a small union of skilled workers in which the point-of-production ethos remained strong. And the most substantial instances of conflict occurred in the coal industry, again a place where contract unionism was less firmly established than elsewhere.[50] Second, efforts to have a say in wider issues of war planning at national level and production planning within companies were rebuffed. On the former, labour was a junior and increasingly marginalised partner within price control and production planning bodies.[51] On the latter, plans for co-ordinated production were put forward by Philip Murray, President of the Congress of Industrial Organizations, and by Walter Reuther of the Auto Workers, but these were simply ignored.

None the less, the war was a period of substantial shopfloor protest. Pressures for production intensified, wages were controlled, and the unions' no-strike pledge closed off legitimate channels of action. In 1943, a 5 per cent 'victory tax' was the first direct taxation of the working class, and a union economist calculated that a 20 per cent increase in working time raised earnings by only 5 per cent.[52] Living conditions around the massive war plants were often poor and were exacerbated by long and difficult journeys to and from work, as contemporary accounts vividly testify.[53] Wildcat strikes over production standards became increasingly common, and union leaders found it hard to retain the no-strike pledge.[54] Such protest outside the bounds of legitimate action reflected tensions at the point of production: the tightening of production standards led to an intensification of effort, and there were no means of protest other than wildcats and absenteeism. The protest was increasingly divorced from accepted channels of influence. In Britain, shopfloor unionism attained an institutional presence, and it came to influence not only the effort bargain but also, through its role in joint production committees, managerial prerogative more widely.[55] In America, protest was increasingly insulated from the legitimate modes of union influence.

Two issues dominate interpretation of the period up to 1945. First, was there a progressive de-radicalization of the Wagner Act, as Klare[56] argues, or was it the case that there was no real radical intent, and hence no radical impetus to destroy?[57] There certainly seems to have been no radical purpose in the Act, if this means a clear policy of some kind of industrial democracy: the aims of the Act were vague, and its meaning had to be thrashed out later. Moreover, as Harris stresses, the containment of the New Deal that undoubtedly took place was not a purely legal matter: it reflected the whole political climate, which made a 'radical' interpretation of the Act increasingly difficult. Yet it remains true that government agencies and the courts played a key role in defining the nature of legitimate shopfloor action, as Tomlins[58] has shown.

This leads to the second question, of the implications of the containment of autonomous activity. As noted above, many scholars now question how strong the impetus of shopfloor action really was. The weaker it was, the less necessary is it to find some cause, such as conservative union leaders, for its supposed destruction. In addition, the extent of the shift of shopfloor power, from unrestrained employer autocracy to a detailed bargaining contract containing important rights for workers, was considerable. It was not, then, a matter of the taming of militancy in the interests of employers but of the construction of a new shopfloor order in which direct action at the point of production was certainly rendered illegitimate but in which significant job rights were also achieved. The legacy was not all negative from a workers' point of view.

1945–1975: Stability and Hidden Decay

During the late 1940s and the 1950s, the rule of law based on formal bargaining contracts became more firmly established. The story of its rise has been well rehearsed, but some qualifications of the picture of a 'system' of industrial relations, in which there was an effective truce between capital and labour for much of the postwar period, need to be entered. First, signs of decay can, with the benefit of hindsight, be identified from the mid-1950s. Union membership, as a proportion of the labour-force, peaked in 1954,[59] and employers began to resist unionization, as indicated by an increase in the number of 'unfair labor practice' charges brought against them.[60]

Second, even in the mass-production unionized sector, the system was far from firmly established by the 1950s. Detailed analyses of shopfloor control are rarer than they are for more 'heroic' periods. But available evidence suggests that labour peace was far from firmly established. Kuhn's[61] contemporary study has already been mentioned. Even within formalized collective contracts, there was 'bargaining in grievance settlement', meaning that the process of resolving shopfloor grievances was not a purely legalistic one and that bargains still took place on the shopfloor so that, for example, an issue which could be put through the grievance procedure, such as discipline, was used to exert leverage on a topic which was supposedly within the area of management rights. At Chrysler, this tendency remained particularly strong; in 1949, for example, there was a walk-out when three workers were given disciplinary lay-offs for questioning a production standard, a clear indication of the use of direct action at the point of production in preference to 'obey now, grieve later'.[62] At International Harvester a massive number of cases entered the grievance procedure during the early 1950s, reflecting the company's opposition to binding arbitration and the extensive use of piece-work; delays in the procedure encouraged workers to use strikes to break the deadlock.[63] And, despite their lack of union tradition, General Electric workers, were able to control the firm's incentive pay system, and there were many shopfloor disputes over the day-to-day operation of the system.[64]

This sort of evidence has led some observers to question the image of American workplace relations as legalized and formalized.[65] It is true that experience was more varied and that shopfloor bargaining was more prominent than the idea of a developed system would suggest. It should also be added that the concept of the 'New Deal system' applied to only the unionized minority of the work-force and to only some of them; the construction industry, for example, lay outside the scope of the Wagner Act, and its industrial relations continued to display characteristics of non-legalized system, notably a high rate of unconstitutional strikes and inter-union disputes.[66]

Tolliday and Zeitlin do not, however, stop there. They also argue, first, that bargaining at the point of production had not been eliminated and, second, that the American system of regulation, far from reflecting the progressive subordination of labour, in fact gave workers more rights and imposed more restraints on managerial authority than the British system with which some observers compared it unfavourably. On the first point, however, it seems clear that the Chrysler pattern was very unusual. Particular features of this firm did encourage shopfloor bargaining, and in others, such as International Harvester and GE, incentive pay systems gave an impetus to bargaining. But many other firms, notably GM and Ford, had never used incentive pay or allowed stewards the hold they had attained in Chrysler. All three 'deviant' firms, moreover, made strenuous efforts during the 1950s to contain the shopfloor challenge: Chrysler tried to restrain its shop stewards; by 1961 IH had eliminated its backlog of grievances and had persuaded its managers to act on them instead of just denying them; and GE moved to end its pay system. Legal developments were also restraining autonomous action: three cases, all involving the Steelworkers' union and settled in 1960, affirmed the legal underpinning for arbitration.[67] American employers and the State were moving to tighten the containment of shopfloor insurgency at the State were moving to tighten the containment of shopfloor insurgency at the very time when, in Britain, such insurgency was coming to public attention. Such action can never be totally regulated but, in America, it was being rendered increasingly illegitimate.[68]

On the second point, the real gains to workers of protection from arbitrary managerial action, together with such advances as cost-of-living clauses in collective agreements and, from the mid-1950s, unemployment insurance, should not be ignored. It was not a matter of shopfloor militancy being defeated: the 'New Deal System' had to recognize significant workers' interests. But it is also true that this system was increasingly moving away from the settlement of differences at the point of production. It is also true that Britain hardly provided an ideal against which America should be measured: strong shopfloor union organization was limited to a small number of factories, and in some aspects of shopfloor politics, notably the ability to sack union militants with impunity, British employers were more powerful than their American counterparts.[69] But the key point made by those who contrasted Britain and America[70] was not really that workers' interests were being denied in one case and expressed in the other. It was that the nature of the job-control struggle was diverging, with America moving in a legalistic direction whereas in Britain the drift was towards the settlement of issues at the point of production.[71] As Lichtenstein[72] concludes, in America 'the union effort to control the shopfloor work environment was clearly on the defensive in the post-war era: and work rules were less the product of union power than a consequence of its defeat'.

That the American situation was one of struggle and movement and not a static system was indicated by events at the end of the 1950s. In what became known as the 'employers' hard line', many firms began to demand changes in work rules and to introduce new technology, which led to some massive confrontations that were not just pay disputes but which stemmed directly from renewed struggles to control the work process.[73] The hard line is often seen as a strange interlude, with there being little effort to explain why it occurred. It probably reflected a squeeze on profits;[74] that it did not develop into a full-scale challenge to the pattern of regulation was due to economic recovery in the early 1960s which took the pressure off profits.

In retrospect, the 1960s seem more of an exceptional interlude, but, at the time, events on the shopfloor were seen as a major reversal of institutionalized bargaining. Renewed rank-and-file militancy was identified by wildcat strikes that involved not wage demands but issues of working conditions, growing absenteeism, refusals to accept the authority of union leaders, and a general questioning of the right of management to determine work standards.[75] A strike at GM's plant at Lordstown, Ohio, in 1972 was taken to represent renewed shopfloor refusals to accept tight discipline, speed-up, and an inability to deal with urgent matters of effort standards as and when they arose.[76]

The size of this 'labor revolt' was in fact exaggerated: it was limited to a small range of industries and, even in the car industry where it was most evident, wildcat strikes did not increase very dramatically.[77] Its long-term significance has also been questioned. In Europe, renewed worker militancy often received some institutional expression, as in the growth of 'qualitative demands' by German unions and the emergence of factory councils in Italy.[78] In America, workers' protest burnt itself out and produced no lasting results.[79] It remained separate from the mainstream system of industrial relations and, although capable of disturbing the calm of the system, had no means of affecting its operation.

The example of the car industry is useful, for it is one of the few in which national agreements were subject to local amendment, thereby opening up the possibility that some form of custom and practice would develop. By 1970, firms such as GM had developed what Serrin[80] termed a 'civilized' relationship with the union: each side was certainly willing to use its economic power during a strike at the end of a contract, but open conflict was limited to this period, and the union accepted a tacit trade-off wherein it did not aggressively pursue shopfloor demands on work speed, working conditions, or discipline, and the company was willing to grant wage rises and improvements in fringe benefits. In fact, the UAW kept tight control of local agreements, a practice which also suited management.[81] Autonomous shop bargaining failed to emerge.

Thus, shopfloor action was detached from any lasting institutional expression. As had been the case during World War II, there was substantial protest but workers generally lacked the means to consolidate its results. The existence of the protest also shows, however, that contract unionism could not manage all issues of shopfloor conflict: militancy was not an aberration but was a reflection of a style of activity that related to day-to-day issues of work speed and the effort bargain.

None the less, the formalized system gave workers important rights, with the grievance procedure offering arbitration to contain arbitrary managerial power and with seniority rules providing some employment security. The rigid and highly involved job classifications that went with it were seen by managements, however, as constraining their freedom of action. Although they had been among the chief architects of the system, it was they who moved to destroy it. Some efforts were made during the 1970s to modify the system. The Experimental Negotiating Agreement in the steel industry, for example, banned strikes even at the end of contracts, and was seen as a further erosion of workers' powers to challenge managerial demands.[82] Such efforts aimed at modifying the workings of the system but did not transcend it. As competition intensified towards the end of the decade, far more radical initiatives were introduced.

1975–1985: A New Order?

Until recently, conventional and radical writers, whatever their other differences, agreed that the formalized system of bargaining was the end point of development which required explanation; hence, many studies stop with the triumph of the system. As has been seen, hindsight tells us that the system had begun to decay almost as soon as it was established. But it was events during the 1980s that really forced a reassessment of the postwar period. At the start of the decade, 'concession bargaining' was the main talking-point: as firms found themselves in severe financial straits, unions were prepared to take wage cuts to allow them to stay in business.[83] Competitive pressure came from two sources. In industries such as cars, imports, particularly from Japan, were the main threat. Where there was little international competition, as in meat packing, the big unionized firms found themselves being undercut by non-union competitors. One result was the breakdown of established patterns of bargaining, in which the major firms in an industry offered similar wages and conditions, with the smaller ones following their lead. Firms now had to find their own solutions, and the standardized pattern of bargaining began to fragment.

Concession bargaining was a response to an immediate crisis. It has been followed, it is widely argued, by attempts to create a new model of industrial relations. This was characterized by Walton[84] 'as involving a shift from control to commitment: under the old system, managements sought detailed bargaining contracts, used rigid job classifications, and required workers to perform specified tasks. This was being replaced by a system stressing commitment: job boundaries were being widened and the number of separate grades was being cut; experiments, such as quality circles, were being introduced; and firms were being more open in the information that they provided to employers. Even a company such as Ford, long the most stubborn defender of managerial rights, introduced its Employee Involvement plan. For Kochan et al.[85] this represents the makings of a new system of industrial relations, embracing the strategic level of corporate decision-making as well as the system of rules at shopfloor level: some firms have given union leaders seats on the company board, and others have tried to involve unions in planning initiatives, such as Employee Involvement, instead of restricting dealings with them to the collective-bargaining contract. The rigidity of the New Deal system was being replaced with flexibility. The non-union sector, which, in the past, had tended to follow the unionized sector by establishing such things as grievance procedures, was now taking the lead with innovative pay systems that linked reward to performance, and with methods of employee involvement. The unionized sector has been responding, and a new model is emerging.

This is not, these authors recognize, the only recent development. They distinguish between asset management and value-added management. In the former, a company responds to a loss of competitiveness by closing loss-making units or shifting production away from unionized areas. The decline of employment in the industrialized north-east, and the growth of the south and west is well established.[86] But this has not worked for all firms. GM's widely publicized Southern strategy' of opening new facilities on a non-union basis in the south never overcame union opposition and its own internal difficulties. In an equally heavily publicized move, GM's new Saturn Corporation is to be established in Tennessee but with the United Auto Workers recognized before a worker is hired. Far more flexible work rules have been exchanged for union involvement in corporate planning; 'trading dollars for power has been the name of the game'.[87]

Apart from the collapse of the New Deal system, two analytical points in this account stand out: it is argued that industrial relations' scholars have tended to ignore the key role of management in the generation of change; and managements make 'strategic choices', so that outcomes depend not just on external conditions but also on managerial action. The distinctiveness of these points is, however, questionable. Accounts of the consolidation of bargaining from the 1940s stress the role of management, aided by the State, in shaping a new rule of law. And, as noted above, choice was evident in the different ways in which firms responded to the challenge of unionization. The leading role of management in the 1980s is not in question, though. Major changes in work rules have been introduced in virtually every industry, and quality circles and associated initiatives are plainly driven by management.

The role of the State in providing an environment conducive to such changes must also be taken into account. The two best-known actions of the

Reagan Administration in relation to labour were the deregulation of the transport industries, which unleashed pressure for work rule changes in the airlines in particular, and the very tough line taken against a strike of air traffic controllers in 1981. Yet also significant were changes in the NLRB, whose new chairman led a string of anti-union decisions.[88] Throughout the postwar period, unions had been finding it harder to win representation elections, but the new NLRB policy marked a further twist.

What effect has this set of changes had on workplace control? Unlike earlier developments such as the 'hard line', which involved efforts to change work rules within the conflictual system of industrial relations, current developments are claimed to transcend direct struggles for control. Instead of work speeds and job allocation being fought out, there is said to be a more co-operative spirit in which joint solutions are sought and the parties escape from a zero-sum concern with the details of job classifications into a more constructive relationship.

There certainly have been some areas of gain for workers. Among the most significant is job security. Firms such as GM and Ford have reached agreements that protect workers from job losses due to company re-organization by, for example, giving displaced workers the first claim on replacement jobs. At Ford, there have been moves towards lifetime employment. The contrast with Britain is again instructive, for in Britain the exchange of work rules for job guarantees has been rare, with firms pushing through change without any accompanying guarantees. Critics of the American arrangements argue, however, that the job guarantees are limited: they specifically exclude job losses due to competition and they relate only to current employees, the upshot being that unions have sacrificed forever the rights of new workers for some precarious protections for existing workers.[84]

On the work rules themselves, Zipp and Lane[90] studied the relocation of a GM plant. The old factory had detailed contractual provisions on seniority and job classifications but these were lost in the move to a new plant. Here, a participative style of management was much in evidence but it was in effect a cloak for tighter managerial authority: work standards were strictly enforced, and discipline was imposed more forcefully than in the old plant. Workers had, moreover, lost any way of questioning managerial decisions. The old contract had given them some basic rights and the means of enforcing them, whereas the new language of co-operation had undercut the basis of opposition and left workers individualized and open to managerial pressure. It is hard to know how representative this case is, although Wood's[91] review of developments in the car industry as a whole suggests similar conclusions, with work being intensified and with any independent mode of challenge to managerial authority being eroded.

Thomas,[92] comparing quality-of-work-life programmes in America and Japan, argues that American managements have been willing to adopt improvements in work operations that workers suggest but have resisted other changes, such as job enlargement, that might bring into question the basis of managerial authority: managements appear to be open but, in fact, wish to gain control of workers' 'secret knowledge' of the production process while minimizing any co-ordinated challenge by workers to their own power. By 'secret knowledge', Thomas means the many ways in which workers gain practical experience of how the production process really works. As Halle[93] shows in his study of chemical workers, this knowledge can be used to aid production, as when workers bend the rules to get the work out, but they can also be deployed to gain some control of the timing and amount of workers' efforts. Halle stresses that secret knowledge gave workers a realm of autonomy: it made management dependent on them and it gave them a sphere in which they could make their own decisions. This was a form of job involvement but one which, Thomas would argue, management wants to break down, replacing it with a constrained and, above all, individualized insertion into programmes in which the logic lies within managerial control. Thomas argues that the real lesson of Japan is not that co-operation can replace conflict but that arrangements such as quality circles rest on tight overall managerial control of production, with workers being placed in a dependent position and with independent unions having no place. Shaiken et al.[94] similarly argue, on the basis of a study of ten plants, that, although flexibility can broaden jobs as workers conduct minor maintenance and carry out their own inspections, it has also tied them more to machinery, increased the intensity of work, and reduced the space that they were formerly able to create for themselves; a standard practice under old arrangements was, for example, to work up a line to build a bank of work and thus earn some leisure, but now schedules are tightly programmed and such autonomy is being eroded.

A related line of criticism notes the similarity between current developments and labour-management co-operation in the 1920s, when a weakened union movement seized on co-operation as a way of selling itself to companies.[95] Co-operative experiments then were short lived and, it is argued, a compliant union movement is giving up the ability to offer independent challenges to management in the hope that managers will continue to tolerate it.

It is too early to judge which of these interpretations is correct. It is plain, however, that major changes have taken place such that what passed for a model of legalized industrial relations no longer applies. These changes should not really be seen as surprising. As observers of many persuasions have noted, American managements have never accepted the legitimacy of unions, but have been willing to work with them when there seemed to be little alternative. The New Deal period was one of pragmatic accommodation and, presented with the opportunity to escape from this, employers have taken full advantage. Some of the more celebratory accounts seem to miss the control issues. It is not a matter of moving from control to commitment but of seeking control in different ways; a policy of commitment is a strategy of control, in particular in the ways in which workers can become more dependent on their employers, and their collective secret knowledge is replaced by an individualized relationship with the employer.

Conclusions

The period since 1985 has been one of considerable change, and commentators have been cautious about reaching firm conclusions about the long-term significance of some bewildering developments. Katz,[96] for example, notes that in the car industry the system of work teams being used in some plants, in which a team takes responsibility for a set of operations without distinction between jobs, has benefits of flexibility but may be accepted only with job guarantees; and he shows that it has been resisted by craft workers. Even if it is accepted, it can create problems for management: if taken seriously it would 'inevitably lead to extensive worker and union involvement in business decision making regarding work design and the implementation of new technologies'.[97] More generally, pressure towards what Katz calls a co-operative path is counteracted by union wishes for standard wage increases and for workplace initiatives to be kept separate from collective bargaining. It is uncertain whether a new model of co-operation can be established and, even if it is, whether it will survive in the longer term.

Although the precise shape of industrial relations in the car industry is open to debate, current developments do not suggest a wholesale shift towards a non-union strategy by management. On the contrary, the major firms have been seeking ways of working with unions. As the car and other unionized industries have declined, however, unions have represented a declining proportion of the work-force. There is some suggestion that, as the remaining unionized firms are those not seeking a change of status, the rate of decline will slow down. But few commentators argue for a reversal of the trend, the result being that soon only one American worker in six will be a union member. Thus, at least three patterns of workplace control can be suggested.

First, there is the union sector on which this chapter, like most contributions, has concentrated. Continuing pressure on work rules seems likely here although, as noted above, interpretations of the nature of the accompanying workplace regimes vary. Even those who offer an optimistic view of transformation are cautious about the extent and depth of change. For example, Katz,[98] one of the proponents of a new 'human resource' model, concedes that evidence of change is patchy and states that 'few would quarrel with the claim that for unionized workers the pace and difficulty of work has intensified in the 1980s'. Other commentators are more sceptical. Wells,[99] for example, concludes that new forms of team work are not consistent with strong, independent unions: workplace change means a reassertion of managerial authority.

Second, in the large, sophisticated non-union firms, employers are likely to continue to experiment with team working and pay-for-knowledge systems. These are intended to incorporate workers as individuals within the aims of the enterprise, leaving little space for independence.

Finally, the growing sector of small non-union firms, which often use the labour of illegal immigrants who have no means of resisting intense exploitation, may well continue its familiar practices based on hire-and-fire, strict discipline, and little by way of established workers' rights. When labour conditions and the control of work are debated, this last group is often forgotten but, in many ways, it is more representative of contemporary work experience than the advanced corporations. Edwards[100] estimates that what he calls this secondary labour market embraces between a quarter and a third of the work-force. Harrison and Bluestone[101] note the expansion of low-wage, low-productivity jobs in this sector since the end of the 1970s, and speak of the 'hollowing out' of the productive core of the economy. Workers here lack any effective protection against dismissal. It is only in the unionized sector that arbitral protection operates. In this sector, workers' rights may be more firmly enforced than in some comparable countries such as Britain.[102] But for the non-union workers, protection is much weaker. It is true that during the 1980s the American doctrine of 'employment at will' came under some challenge in the courts,[103] but protection depends on the interpretations of individual jurisdictions; in any event, it is a very rare individual who has the determination to press a case against a powerful employer.

A major question concerns the extent to which union practices are read across into other firms. One view is that unions are increasingly irrelevant. The opposite is that unions are essential, for without them there would be no restraint on employers. As noted above, economy-wide wage increases were low during the 1920s, for which the weakness of unions is reasonably offered as an explanation. Writers such as Ozanne[104] have suggested that unions are necessary for wage increases to be sustained. And it is surely doubtful whether the car firms would have been so cautious in their approach and so keen to find ways of keeping workers' co-operation had it not been for 50 years' experience of the problems that uncontained shopfloor conflict could bring them. Even if they represent only a declining minority of workers, unions may continue to play a key role in influencing not just wages but also the application of the employer's authority within the workplace.

Debate on the future organization of the workplace continues apace. Reformers identify 'productivity coalitions' as means of aligning worker and management interests. Drawing on the German model in particular,[105] they argue that a system in which workers are involved in decision-making will not only improve workplace democracy, but will also contribute to productivity growth and to the development of a high value-added economy. 'Associational' unionism[106] is seen as the route forward. Alternative models propose a more oppositional role for unions, as in Shostak's[107] analysis of 'robust unionism' which is based on workplace action combined with community organizing and health-and-safety campaigns. The success of either is likely to depend on the role of the State. In 1993, the Clinton Administration appointed a commission to consider the reform of labour law. At the time of writing, it had not reported. But, seen in the context of the history of the American workplace, it is clear that decisive State interventions are rare and depend on very specific conditions. Unless economic and political conditions similar to those of the New Deal develop, it is unlikely that major legal support for workplace productivity coalitions will emerge.

Seen in long-term perspective, it may turn out that the roughly 40 years of the New Deal 'system' are no more 'typical' than are the 35 or so years of largely non-union operation that preceded it. Thus, regulation through formal contracts can be seen to be less of a key characteristic of the American system than is often thought. More fundamental has been the struggle by employers to assert control at the point of production, together with the efforts by workers to subvert, contain and contest this control. The work process itself has been a more central focus than it has in many other countries. The struggle to control it has changed its shape but, as continuing pressure on work rules illustrates, it has not yet been supplanted by a different way of regulating the relationships of capital and labour.

Bibliography and Notes

1 Entrepreneurs, Managers, and Business Men in Eighteenth-century Britain

H. G. Aitken, *Explorations in Enterprise*, (Cambridge, Mass., 1965).

T. S. Ashton, *The Industrial Revolution 1760–1830*, (London, 1948).

R. Bendix, *Work and Authority: ideologies of management in the course of industrialization*, (New York–London, 1956).

S. D. Chapman, *The Early Factory Masters*, (Newton Abbot, 1967).

J. W. Gough, *The Rise of the Entrepreneur*, (London, 1969).

I. Grubb, *Quakerism and Industry before 1800*, (London, 1930).

H. J. Habbakuk, 'The economic functions of the English landowners', in H. G. Aitken op. cit. (1965).

A. L. Beir, D. Cannadine and J. A. Rosenheim (eds), *The First Modern Society*, (Cambridge, 1989).

B. Collins and K. Robbins (eds), *British Culture and Economic Decline*, (New York, 1990).

N. F. R. Crafts, *British Economic Growth During the Industrial Revolution*, (Oxford, 1987).

M. Dintenfass, *The Decline of Industrial Britain (1870–1980)*, (London, 1992).

B. Elbaum and W. Lazonick (eds), *The Decline of the British Economy*, (Oxford, 1986).

R. C. Floud and D. McCloskey (eds), *The Economic History of Britain since 1700*, Vol. 1, (Cambridge, 1981).

E. Hagen, *The Economics of Development*, (Homewood, III., 1975).

J. R. Harris, *The Copper King*, (Liverpool, 1964).

M. Lazonick, *Managers, entrepreneurs and the choice of technique in the rings and mules in Lancashire*, (Cambridge, Mass., 1979).

D. McClelland, *The Achieving Society*, (Princeton, NJ, 1961).

N. McKendrick, 'An eighteenth century entrepreneur in salesmanship and marketing techniques', *Economic History Review*, 12, no. 3, (1960).

N. McKendrick, 'Josiah Wedgwood and factory discipline', *Historical Journal*, 4, no. 1, (1961).

N. McKendrick and R. O. Outhwaite (eds), *Business Life and Public Policy*, (Cambridge, 1986).

G. Mantoux, *The Industrial Revolution in the Eighteenth Century*, (London, 1964).

P. Mathias, *The First Industrial Nation: An Economic History of Britain 1700–1914*, (London, 1972).

P. Mathias, *The Transformation of England: Essays in the Economic and Social History of England in the Eighteenth Century*, (London, 1979).

P. O'Brien and R. Quinault, *The Industrial Revolution and British Society*, (Cambridge, 1993).

S. Pollard, *The Genesis of Modern Management: a study of the Industrial Revolution in Great Britain*, (London, 1965).

M. Savage, *Capital, entrepreneurs and profits*, (London, 1990).

J. Schumpeter, *The Theory of Economic Development*, (Cambridge, Mass., 1934).

N. J. Smelser, *Social Change in the Industrial Revolution. An Application of Theory to the Lancashire cotton industry 1770–1840*, (Chicago, 1959).

F. M. L. Thompson (ed.), *Landowners, capitalists and entrepreneurs: essays in honour of Sir John Habbakuk*, (Oxford, 1994).

2 Labour and the Process of Industrialization in the First Phases of British Industrialization

R. Bendix, *Work and Authority: ideologies of management in the course of industrialization*, (New York–London, 1956).

M. Berg, *The Age of Manufactures: Industry, Innovation and Work in Britain 1700–1820*, (London, 1985).

J. Bowden, *Industrial Society in England Towards the End of the Eighteenth Century*, 2nd ed., (London, 1965).

A. L. Bowley, *Wages in the United Kingdom in the Nineteenth Century*, (Cambridge, 1900).

J. D. Chambers and G. E. Mingay, *The Agricultural Revolution 1750–1970*, (London, 1966).

P. Deane, *The First Industrial Revolution*, (Cambridge, 1979).

M. W. Flinn, *British Population Growth (1700–1850)*, (London, 1970).

R. C. Floud and D. McCloskey (eds), *The Economic History of Britain since 1700*, Vol. 1, (Cambridge, 1981).

J. L. Hammond, 'The Industrial Revolution and Discontent', *Economic History Review*, 2, (1930).

E. J. Hobsbawm, 'The British Standard of Living 1790–1850', *Economic History Review*, 10, no. 1, (1957).

E. J. Hobsbawm, *Labouring Men: studies in the history of labour*, (London, 1964).

B. Holderness, *Pre-Industrial England—Economy and Society from 1500–1750*, (London, 1976).

E. L. Jones and G. E. Mingay (eds), *Land, Labour and Population in the Industrial Revolution*, (London, 1967).

P. Mathias, *The Transformation of England: Essays in the Economic and Social History of England in the Eighteenth Century*, (London, 1979).

P. O'Brien and R. Quinault, *The Industrial Revolution and British Society*, (Cambridge, 1993).

H. Perkins, *The Origins of Modern English Society 1780–1870*, (London, 1979).

J. Rule, *The Experience of Labour in Eighteenth Century Industry*, (London, 1981).

A. J. Taylor (ed.), *The Standard of Living in Britain and the Industrial Revolution*, (London, 1975).

E. A. Wrigley, *The Population History of England 1541–1871*, (Cambridge, Mass., 1981).

3 Women and Work in Britain, *c.*1870–World War I

1 Michael Anderson, 'The Social Position of Spinsters in Mid-Victorian Britain', *Journal of Family History*, (Winter 1984) p. 392.

2 E. Higgs, 'Domestic Servants and Households in Victorian England', *Social History*, 8, 2 (May 1983) pp. 201–10; E. Higgs, 'Domestic Service and Household Production' in Angela V. John (ed.), *Unequal Opportunities. Women's Employment in England, 1800–1918* (Oxford, Blackwell, 1986) pp. 125–50.

3 Belinda Westover, 'To Fill the Kids' Tummies. The Life and Work of Colchester tailoresses. 1880–1918', in L. Davidoff and B. Westover (eds), *Our Work, Our Lives, Our Words. Women's History and Women's work* (London, 1986) p. 64.

4 Hannah Mitchell, *The Hard Way Up*, (London 1977), pp. 68–9.

5 Lee Holcombe, *Victorian Ladies at Work* (Newton Abbot, 1973). Meta Zimmeck, 'Jobs for the Girls: The Expansion of Clerical Work for Women, 1850–1939', in John (ed.), *Unequal Opportunities*, pp. 153–78. Dina M. Copelman. 'A New Comradeship between Men and Women: Family, Marriage and London's Women Teachers, 1870–1914', in Jane

Lewis (ed.), *Labour and Love. Women's Experience of Home and Family, 1850–1940* (Oxford, Blackwell, 1985) pp. 48–52.

6 Martha Vicinus, *Independent Women, Work and Community for Single Women, 1870–1920* (London, Virago, 1985).

7 B. R. Mitchell and P. Deane, *Abstract of British Historical Statistics* (Cambridge, 1962) pp. 12–15.

8 *Daily Telegraph*, 22 March 1888.

9 *Daily Telegraph*, 3 April 1888.

10 Clementina Black, *Married Women's Work*, 2nd edition (London, Virago, 1983) p. 10.

11 R. Whipp, 'Potbank and Union: A Study of Work and Trade Unionism in the Pottery Industry, 1900–1925', University of Warwick Ph. D. thesis, 1983. Now published as: *Patterns of Labour: Work and Social Change in the Potteries*, (London, Routledge, 1990).

12 N. G. Osteruo, 'Gender Divisions and the Organization of Work in the Leicester Hosiery Industry', in John (ed.), *Unequal Opportunities*, pp. 45–70.

13 M. A. Savage, 'The Social Basis of Working Class Politics: The Labour Movement in Preston 1890–1940' University of Lancaster Ph. D. thesis, 1984. Now published as: *The Dynamics of Working Class Politics: The Labour Movement in Preston 1180–1940*, (Cambridge 1987).

14 Leonore Davidoff 'The Separation of Home and Work? Landladies and Lodgers in Nineteenth and Twentieth Century England', in S. Burman (ed.), *Fit Work for Women* (London, Croom Helm, 1979) pp. 64–97.

15 Melanie Tebbutt, *Making Ends Meet. Pawnbroking and working Class Credit*, (Leicester, 1983). Elizabeth Roberts, *A Woman's Place. An Oral History of Working Class Women. 1890–1940* (Oxford, Blackwell, 1984). Paul Jonnson *Spending and Saving. The Working Class Economy in Britain. 1870–1939*, (Oxford, 1985).

16 Mary Freifeld, 'Technological change and the "self-acting" mule: a study of skill and the sexual division of labour', *Social History*, 11, 3, (October 1983).

17 Sonya O. Rose, ' "Gender at Work": Sex, Class and Industrial Capitalism', *History Workshop*, 21. (spring 1986).

18 Eleanor Gordon, 'Women and the Labour Movement in Scotland', Glasgow University Ph. D. thesis. 1985. Now published as: *Woman and Labour in Scotland*, (Oxford, 1991).

19 J. H. Zeitlin 'Craft Regulation and the Division of Labour: Engineers and Compositors in Britain, 1890–1914; University of Warwick Ph. D. thesis, 1981. Sian Reynolds, 'Women in the printing and paper trades in Edwardian Edinburgh' in E. Gordon and E. Breitenback (eds), *The World*

is Ill-divided. Women's Work in Scotland in the 19th and 20th centuries, (Edinburgh, 1990), pp. 49–69.

20 June Hannam, 'Women Workers in the West Riding Clothing Industry, 1850–1914', University of Sheffield Ph. D. thesis, 1986.

21 E. H. Hunt, *Regional age variations in Great Britain, 1850–1914,* (Oxford 1973) pp. 115–61. Savage, *Social Basis of Working Class Politics* (1984); Jill Liddington and Jill Norris, *One Hand Tie Behind Us. The Rise of the Women's Suffrage Movement,* (London, Virago, 1978).

22 Hunt, *Regional Wage Variations,* p. 112.

23 Hunt, p. 317.

24 Hunt, pp. 111–12.

25 Hunt, c. 345.

26 Liddington and Norris, *One Hand Tied Behind Us,* p. 112.

27 Hunt, *Regional Wage variations,* p. 216.

28 Hunt, *Regional Wage variations, passim.*

29 Eleanor Gordon, 'Women, Work and Collective Action: Dundee Jute workers, 1870–1906', *Journal of Social History,* (summer, 1987), p. 31.

30 Higgs, 'Domestic Service', pp. 138–9.

31 S. Tolliday, 'Militancy and Organization: Women Workers and Trade Unions in the Motor Trade in the 1930s', *Oral History,* 11, 2, (Autumn 1983). Liddington and Norris, *One Hand Tied Behind Us,* p. 42. L. J. Satre 'After the Match Girls Strike: Bryant and May in the 1890s', *Victorian Studies,* 26 (autumn 1982).

32 E. Gordon, 'Women, Work and Collective Action', p. 40.

33 E. Gordon, 'Women, Work and Collective Action', p. 42.

34 E. Gordon, pp. 42–5.

35 *Reports* of the Annual Conference of the TUC: 1677, pp. 17–18; 1879, pp. 29–30; 1880, pp. 28–30.

36 *Report* of the National Conference of Labour Women, 1913.

37 E. Roberts, *A Woman's Place,* pp. 46–50.

38 Meta Zimmedk, *Jobs for the Girls,* pp. 165–7.

39 R. Whipp 'Plenty of excuses, no money: the social bases of trade unionism, as illustrated by the potters', *Society for the Study of labour History, Bulletin No. 49,* (autumn 1984), pp. 29–30.

40 D. Thom, 'The Bundle of Sticks: Women Trade Unionists and Collective Organization before 1918' in John (ed.), *Unequal Opportunities,* pp. 261–89. J. Bornet, 'Lost Leaders: Women, Trade Unionism and the Case of the General Union of Textile workers. 1875–1914', in John (ed.), *Unequal Opportunities,* pp. 201–34.

4 'In Want of Union': Industrial Relations in the
Early Twentieth-century Pottery Industry

1 S. H. Beaver, 'The Potteries: A Study in the Evolution of a Cultural Landscape', *Institute of British Geographers. Transactions and Papers*, No. 34, June (1966), p. 1. J. R. Remer, *Hansard*, 30 June 1927, Col. 631. *The Times Imperial and Foreign Trade Supplement*, August 1917, 'Special Pottery Edition', p. i. *Department of Commerce, Misc. Series No. 21, The Pottery Industry. Report on the Cost of Production in the Earthenware and China Industries of the United States, England, Germany and Austria. Census of England and Wales, County of Stafford.* County Borough of Stoke on Trent, Occupations 1911, Table 23, pp. 64–6.

2 A. Bennett, *Anna of the Five Towns* (London, 1902); *The Grim Smile of the Five Towns* (London, 1907); and *The Matador of the Five Towns* (London, 1912).

3 H. Clegg, *The Changing System of Industrial Relations in Great Britain* (Oxford, 1979) pp. 1–3. J. Rowe, *Wages in Practice and Theory* (London, 1928), p. 121. R. Charles, *The Development of Industrial Relations in Britain, 1911–1939* (1973). Cf. J. Cronin, *Industrial Conflict in Modern Britain* (London, 1979) pp. 23–6. R. Hyman, *Strikes* (London, 1972) pp. 66–8. J. Rubery, 'Structured labour markets, worker organisation and low pay', *Cambridge Journal of Economics*, Vol. 2, No. 1, March 1978, pp. 17–36.

4 K. Burgess, *The Origins of British Industrial Relations* (London, 1975) pp. ii–iii. R. Price, *Masters, Unions and Men. Work Control in Building and the Rise of Labour 1880–1914* (Cambridge, 1980) pp. 5, 22. For the greater uniformity of US pottery industry bargaining see McCabe, *National Collective Bargaining in the Pottery Industry* (Baltimore, 1932), *passim*, and *The Pottery Gazette* (*P. Gazette*) 1 Jan., (1920), p. 43.

5 *P. Gazette*, 1 June (1917), p. 480; and National Council of the Pottery Industry (NCPI), Mins, 18 July (1921). *P. Gazette*, 1 March (1908), p. 347.

6 Clegg, *Industrial Relations*, p. 15. I. Boraston, H. Clegg and M. Rimmer, *Workplace and Union* (London, 1975) p. 165. E. Batstone, I. Boraston, S. Frenkel, *The Social Organisation of Strikes* (Oxford, 1978) p. 14.

7 E. Phelps-Brown, *The Growth of British Industrial Relations. A Study from the Standpoint of 1906–1914* (London, 1959) pp. xxvi & 279. Cf. G. D. H. Cole, *The Payment of Wages* (London, 1918) p. 90.

8 A. potbank is the local term for a pottery factory. The Potteries refers to the 'Six Towns' of Tunstall, Burslem, Hanley, Stoke, Fenton and Longton in north Staffordshire.

9 Out of a sample of 393 clearly recorded bargaining episodes from

1906–24, 313 (79.64 per cent) involved only a single firm; 78 (20.36 per cent) concerned manufacturers' organizations or groups of companies. Of a sample of 288 recorded disputes from 1906–24 102 (35.42 per cent) related to individual workers; 138 (47.92 per cent) to work-groups; 17 (5.9 per cent) to a whole factory; 25 (8.6 per cent) to a collection of workers across a subindustry and 6 (2.08 per cent) related to an entire sub-industry. Ceramic and Allied Trades Union Collection (CATU COLL) Hanley. Each letter in the collection is referred to by L and a reference number. The National Amalgamated Society of Male and Female Pottery Workers (NAS) was formed in 1906; in 1917 the name was changed to the National Society of Pottery Workers (NSPW).

10 *P. Gazette*, 1 Nov., 1908, p. 1315.

11 CATU COLL: L450, 13 Dec., 1919, dipper to central office. L630, case of John Forrester, presser, 9 June 1910, Furnivals. L724, sanitary presser, 26 Jan., 1912. L568a & b, individual notices handed to Mr Wakefield and Mr Utting, turners, 10 Feb., 1923. Cf. Cole, *Payment of Wages*, p. 5. W. H. Warburton, *The History of Trade Union Organisation in the North Staffordshire Potteries* (London, 1931), p. 149.

12 CATU COLL: L497, S. Clowes (Organizer from 1908 and General Secretary from 1918), conference notes 3 March 1924. 1920 wage negotiations statement, para. 5 and wage settlement, p. 2 1924 Accountant's Report p. 10. *P. Gazette*, 1 Nov. 1911, pp. 453–4.

13 CATU COLL: L572 group of Twyfords' mould makers 14 Jan. 1920. L489, work-group led by A. Chaney and J. Savage at Copelands to J. Lovatt, 14 Feb. 1924. L473, Cauldon's enamellers, 12 Nov. 1913.

14 In loc. cit. L601, hollow ware pressers 24 Aug. 1911. L310 R. Houson & Co.'s slip makers 15 Nov. 1916. L567, Wedgwood's liners 20 Sept. 1923. L52 female throwers Bourne & Son, 28 Feb., 1916. For a similar phenomenon in the early car industry see J. Zeitlin, 'The Emergence of shop steward organisation and job control in the British car industry', *History Workshop Journal*, 10 (1980), pp. 119–37.

15 L220 Minton's jiggerers and jolliers to S. Clowes 25 April 1923.

16 Sam Clowes's scrapbook, 21 March 1907. L153, J. Lovatt to J. Howard, 11 Feb. n. d. L441, J. Stevenson on behalf of Six warehouse workers, 15 Dec. 1919. See also L437 & L550. National Executive Committee (NEC) mins, 15 April 1916, 26 Oct. 1916. Emergency Com. Minute Book, 20 March 1923, p. 73. NEC mins, 17 Feb. 1923 and 24 Oct. 1925.

17 Bell, in A. Flanders and H. Clegg (eds.), *The System of Industrial Relations in Great Britain* (London, 1967) p. 246. H. Beynon, *Working for Ford* (Harmondsworth, 1973) p. 98.

18 M. Jones, *Potbank* (London, 1961), pp. 162–5. L376 Grindley's file, L384 Johnson's file. See also D25, 'Rates of Pay at Melling pottery 1913–1916'.

For examples of workers' 'pricing committees' within firms see S. Clowes's scrapbook, 21 & 30 March 1907.

19 *P. Gazette*, 1 Jan., 1920, p. 94.

20 L573, Worcester works joint wage demand, 11 May 1919. National Council of the Pottery Industry (NCPI) mins, 10 Mar. 1922; 15 Sep. 1920 and 19 March 1924. W. Machin found that managers in particular were very suspicious of works committees as a threat to their authority, *P. Gazette*, 1 Feb. 1920, p. 191.

21 See footnote 9.

22 L433, Hanley District Com. to central office, 16 Sep. 1915. L447 sanitary pressers, 1 Jan. 1920. L273 hollow ware pressers' district prices, 21 Nov. 1908. L116 J. Alcock of saggar makers committee 27 January, 1920.

23 *P. Gazette*, 1 March 1907, p. 475.

24 The seven subindustries were: earthenware, china, jet and rockingham, sanitary, electrical, chemical ware and tiles. In loc. cit., 1 Dec. 1921, p. 1828. CATU COLL, 1920 wage negotiations, p. 4, and 1920 printed wage settlement, p. 5. L82, terms of agreement of departmental demands, March 1919. *P. Gazette*, 1 Nov. 1911, p. 1263. See Price, *Masters, Unions and Men*, pp. 46 and 500 for the positive role of leading groups.

25 *P. Gazette*, 1 Jan., p. 212 and 1 March, p. 475 and 1 May 1907, p. 597. *The Times Imperial and Foreign Trade Supplement*, 2 December 1918. S. Clowes's scrapbook, 27 March, 1907.

26 *The Labour Gazette*, 1908, pottery industry report. *P. Gazette*, 1 March 1907, p. 478. CATU COLL, L240 terms of settlement of jet and rockingham dispute 25 March, 1913.

27 CATU COLL, L174 sanitary agreement 28 May 1909, L715, L721, sanitary workers com. to A. Llewellyn 28 March 1912 and L106, sanitary agreement 25 March 1918.

28 *P. Gazette*, 1 Sep. 1917, p. 896 and 1 Sep. 1911, p. 1033. CATU COLL, L178, J. Lovatt to J. Arrowsmith, sec. of china manufacturers' assoc., 29 July 1914.

29 NEC, mins. 22 Sept. 1917, and L334 Minutes of Stoneware trade conference, 26 March 1926.

30 *P. Gazette*, 1 Aug. 1910, p. 920 & 1 Sept. 1907, p. 1198. CATU COLL, British Pottery Manufacturers' Federation (BPMF), Operatives Wages, March 1919.

31 V. Allen, 'The origins of industrial conciliation and arbitration', *International Review of Social History*, Vol. IX, (1964), pp. 237–54. Burgess, *Origins of British Industrial Relations*, p. 291. Rowe, *Wages*, pp. 65, 70, 74 and 84.

32 CATU COLL, L1 H. Clay to S. Clowes, 14 Feb. 1928. For variation in settling times see L203, Wilemans to NSPW 10 Feb. 1923, and L313, Conference of china manufacturers and operatives, 21 June 1912. *Labour*

Gazette, 1900, pottery industry report. *Times I. F. T. Supplement*, 13 April 1911 and 4 Sep. 1920.

33 Op. cit., 1 April 1916, p. 425.

34 *Times I. F. T. Supplement*, May 1918. 1924 Wage Inquiry. CATU COLL, L552a, March 1920 agreement. Cf. Batstone, *Social Organisation of Strikes*, pp. 51 & 61.

35 CATU COLL, Annual Delegation report, 1928, p. 2. 1924 Wage Inquiry, p. 1, when the 1920 departmental demands remained unsettled. NSPW, *Handbook of Agreements* (Hanley, n.d.) p. 21. 1931 wage negotiations, *passim*. L490, letter of S. Dodd (chairman of BPMF) to A. Hollins, 21 March 1931.

36 Price, *Masters, Unions and Men*, pp. 55 and 95. Rowe, *Wages*, pp. 132, 143 and 176. A. Shadwell, *Industrial Efficiency* (London, 1906), p. 340. G. Allen, *British Industries and their Organisation* (London, 1937), p. 9. Clegg, *Industrial Relations*, p. 3. V. Allen, 'The origins of industrial conciliation and arbitration', p. 254. R. Bean, 'The Liverpool dock strike of 1890', *International Review of Social History*, Vol. XVI, (1971), Part 1, p. 69. S. Pollard and P. Robertson, *The British Shipbuilding Industry 1870–1914* (London, 1979), p. 157.

37 1924 Wage Inquiry, p. D.

38 *P. Gazette*, 1 Jan. p. 91 and 1 April 1908, p. 470. R. Price, 'Labour, the Labour Process and the Dynamic of Labour History', mimeo. 1982, p. 20. C. Goodrich, *The Frontier of Control* (London, 1920, 1975 edn.), pp. xxiv and 225.

39 See footnote 9. *P. Gazette*, 1 July & 1 Nov. 1890; 1 Aug. 1891 and 1 April 1895. 1 March 1907, p. 475. NCPI Mins, 1920, p. 314. CATU COLL, L617 J. Lovatt to A. Llewellyn, 16 Jan. 1911.

40 Cf. Burgess, *Origins of British Industrial Relations*, p. vii. Benwell Project, *The Making of a Ruling Class* (Newcastle-upon-tyne, 1978), pp. 39–41.

41 CATU COLL, L723, J. Lovatt to A. Llewellyn, 18 Nov. 1911.

42 S. Clowes's scrapbook, 26 March & 15 April 1907. CATU COLL, Twyford's correspondence L736–740. *P. Gazette*, 1 May 1916, p. 534 and 1 June, p. 651.

43 Op. cit., 1 Oct. 1908, p. 1186. Webb Trade Union Collection, L.S.E. Vol. XLIV, pp. 175–9. *The Staffordshire Knot*, 31 Oct. 1891. *The Workman's Times*, 12 Dec. 1890 and 14 Aug. 1891. W. Owen in *TUC Report 1893*, p. 84.

44 *P. Gazette*, 1 June 1907, p. 716, 1 Jan. 1908, p. 91 and 1 April 1911, p. 453.

45 As in the nineteenth century the fundamental difference between manufacturers and the unions centred on the exclusion 'good from oven' and apprenticeship rules from the board's jurisdiction. *P. Gazette*, 1 March

1908, p. 349. *The Staffordshire Advertiser* (*S. Advertiser*) 22 Feb. 1908. See also Phelps-Brown, *Growth of British Industrial Relations*, p. 186 for the voluntarist basis of most forms of conciliation and arbitration at this time.

46 See J. H. Clapham, *An Economic History of Modern Britain*, Vol. III (Cambridge, 1938) p. 214 for manufacturers' pricing or trading associations. Ashworth, *An Economic History of England*, pp. 99–100 for the growth of associations 1880–1900 in response to declining prices and the growth of unions, and pp. 387–8 for the unofficial pacts between employers. R. Charles, *The Development of Industrial Relations in Britain, 1911–1939* (London, 1963) pp. 39–41 for the early twentieth-century growth of employer organizations specifically to fight trades unions. H. A. Turner, *Trade Union, Growth, Structure and Policy* (London, 1962), p. 373 for the detailed 'divisions of interest' between cotton firms and the role of unions in forcing them to act jointly. Clegg, in Flanders and Clegg, *System of Industrial Relations*, p. 197 for the definition of price and bargaining associations.

47 *Staffordshire Knot*, 27 June 1891. *P. Gazette*, 1 Aug. 1890; 1 June 1892; 1 Sep. and 1 Nov. 1898. *Royal Commission on Trade Disputes* (1900) Cd. 2826 p. 281, Q. 4990–1.

48 PRO. HO/45/1018/B11239P, letters of 'Joint Com. of Allied Manufacturers' to Home Office, 10 Sep. 1900. *P. Gazette*, 1 July 1906, p. 823; 1 Oct. 1910, p. 1125 and 1 Nov. 1911, p. 1263.

49 Op. cit., 1 Sep. 1914, p. 1081.

50 Op. cit., 1 Aug. 1920, p. 1052. *Times I.F.T. Supplement*, 2 July 1917, and 1 Dec. 1918. CATU COLL, L593 notes on joint com. of manufacturers, 7 Sep. 1915.

51 *The Committee of Inquiry into the Workman's Compensation Act* (1920), Vol. I, Cd. 908, Q. 18669 shows that under half the firms were in the BPMF in 1920. 1924 Wage Inquiry, pp. P and F2 also indicate only 187 firms. NCPI, mins, 1 July 1921 show 235. *P. Gazette*, 1 May 1921, p. 794. The Rules and Regulations of the British Earthenware Manufacturers Association, 30 Oct. 1916, pp. 3–9 contain little effective sanctions against members. G. E. Stringer, *New Hall Porcelain* (London, 1949), p. 65.

52 *P. Gazette*, 1 Jan., p. 60 and 1 Feb. 1918, p. 139. The National Council of the Pottery Industry, Reprinted from *The Staffordshire Sentinel* (n.d. Jan. 1918?). *Report of a Conference of Operatives and Manufacturers on the Pottery Industry*, 5 May 1917 (Darlington n.d.) for the advisory roles of Henry Clay, Arnold Rowntree and E. H. Wethered. For the climate of reconstruction: Charles, *Development of Industrial Relations*, p. 86. A. L. Bowley, *Some Economic Consequences of the Great War* (London, 1930) p. 21ff.

53 For the standing orders and functions of the council and its committees

see Minutes, 11 April and 11 January 1918. CATU COLL, L209 & 210, Frederick Hand (secretary to the council) to A. Hollins, 19 Sep. 1919.

54 NCPI, Mins, 17 Oct. 1918, p. 71 & Organisation Com. 17 March 1920.

55 CATU COLL, A. Delegation, p. 111 and 136.

56 NCPI, Mins. 2 May 1922, executive com. and 2 Jan. 1925.

57 H. Clay, *The Problem of Industrial Relations* (London, 1929) pp. 162, 165 & 167. See also, G. D. H. Cole, *Workshop Organisation* (Oxford, 1923) p. 122 and Charles, *Development of Industrial Relations*, p. 196 ff., for a similar view.

58 B. Williams, 'The pottery industry' in D. Burn (ed.), *The Structure of British Industry* (Cambridge, 1958), pp. 298–300. W. Yeaman, 'The geographical factors influencing the major changes in the pottery industry of North Staffordshire 1945–1965', unpublished MA thesis, University of London, 1968, p. 150. On the nineteenth century see: Warburton, *Trade Union Organisation*, pp. 50–4 and 80–99.

59 J Griffin, *Strikes. A Study in Quantitative Economics* (1939), pp. 20–2, as cited in Hyman, *Strikes*, p. 17.

60 P. K. Edwards and H. Scullion, *The Social Organisation of Industrial Conflict and Resistance in the Workplace* (Oxford, 1982), p. 12ff.

61 Batstone, *Social Organisation of Strikes*, p. 51. J. Cronin, *Industrial Conflict in Modern Britain* (London, 1979), p. 12. Cole, *Organised Labour*, pp. 124–5. D. Brody, *Steelworkers in America: the non-union era* (Cambridge, Mass., 1960). *The Labour Gazette* records only official disputes for this period.

62 CATU COLL, A. Lawton daybook *passim* and example of 7s 6d payment to group of women towers on strike. NEC, Mins, 1 Feb. 1916. Annual Delegation, 1911, p. 9. Financial Ledgers Vol. I to III small grants to individuals and groups on strike.

63 *P. Gazette*, 1 Oct. 1909, p. 1169.

64 P. Stearns, 'Measuring the evolution of strike movements', *International Review of Social History*, Vol. XIX (1974), pt. 1, pp. 4–27, using the criteria of size, workers involved, frequency, planning, timing, duration and goals.

65 *P. Gazette*, 1 May 1907, p. 598 and 1 Sep. 1910, p. 1039. Cf. R. Price, 'The other face of respectability: violence in the Manchester Brickmaking Trade, 1859–1870', *Past and Present*, Feb., No. 66 (1975), pp. 110–32.

66 Modern Records Centre, MS28/CO/1/B/24/4 Handbill, 6 Dec. 1881. *Workman's Times*, 14 Nov. 1890. S. Clowes's scrapbook, 30 March, 4, 16 & 17 April 1907. *P. Gazette*, 1 Dec. 1920, p. 1828.

67 Op. cit., 1 April 1908, p. 471 and 1 April 1911, p. 399.

68 *Report of the Chief Correspondent on the Strikes and Lock-outs of 1900*, Cd. 689, pp. 68–9 & xlviii.

69 S. Clowes's scrapbook, 17 April 1907 and 17 April 1907. *S. Advertizer*, 22 Feb., p. 5.

70 *P. Gazette*, 1 April, p. 453 and 1 May 1911, p. 572. *The Times*, 13 April, p. 12; 28 April, p. 6 and 10 Aug. p. 8, 1911.

71 *P. Gazette*, 1 April 1913, p. 452 and 1 March, p. 331 and 1 May 1914, p. 602.

72 CATU COLL, Wage negotiations notes 1924.

73 Burgess, *Challenge of Labour*, pp. 82–4. A. Levine, *Industrial Retardation in Britain, 1880–1914* (London, 1967), p. 105.

74 Burgess, *Challenge of Labour*, pp. 82–4.

75 E. H. Hunt, *British Labour History 1815–1914* (London, 1981), pp. 321–2.

76 G. D. H. Cole, *Organized Labour* (London, 1924), pp. 70, 121 and 182. J. Hinton, *The First Shop Stewards Movement* (London, 1973). R. Holton, *British Syndicalism* (London, 1976).

77 G. D. H. Cole, *History of the British Working Class Movement* (London, 1937), pp. 182ff. and 192.

78 Batstone, *Social Organisation of Strikes*, p. 50. Hyman, *Strikes*, pp. 63 and 120.

79 *P. Gazette*, 1 March 1908, p. 347 and 1 Sep. 1911, p. 1016.

80 *S. Advertizer*, 22 Feb., 1908, p. 5. CATU COLL, L736–740, Twyford's disputes. See footnote no. 60.

81 *P. Gazette*, 1 Jan. 1908, p. 90.

82 The Board of Trade and Ministry of Labour reports in the *Labour Gazette*, 1900–24 show that the vast majority of the officially recorded disputes concerned piece prices/wages. A sample from the union's dispute files confirmed that out of 146 clearly documented small-scale cases, 52 concerned piece prices; 41 wages; five hours; 28 organization and conditions of work; 11 apprenticeship and 19 dismissal. *P. Gazette*, 1 Sep. 1911, p. 1016. 'less well paid for skill than any other trade' as J. Lovatt put it. 1924 Wage Inquiry, 'Schedule of Comparative Wages' using the trade board Act figures. Cf. *P. Gazette*, 1 Oct. 1908, p. 1186 and compare Lovatt's statements with Clapham, op. cit., p. 474 that before 1914 'there was no general familiarity with cost of living figures' in bargaining.

83 Cf. W. Owen to Hatherton Arbitration 1879, *The Potteries Examiner*, 22 Nov. 1879 with, *S. Advertizer*, 22 Feb. 1908, p. 5, and *P. Gazette*, 1 Oct. 1919, p. 1109. See also A. Briggs, 'Social background' in A. Flanders and R. Clegg, *The System of Industrial Relations in Great Britain* (Oxford, 1967), pp. 12–13. 1924 Wage Inquiry, p. 131.

84 *P. Gazette*, 1 June 1907, p. 716. CATU COLL, Wage Inquiry, p. 67.

85 See monthly reports of the *Labour Gazette* on pottery.

86 S. Clowes, *P. Gazette*, 1 March 1908, p. 458.

87 CATU COLL, 1924 Wage Inquiry, p. K1. See also, Cronin, *Industrial Conflict*, pp. 58, 97 and 101.

88 *P. Gazette*, 1 June 1907, p. 711. China production was concentrated in the two towns.

89 See *Labour Gazette* in loc. cit.

90 *P. Gazette*, 1 June 1907, p. 716 and 1 March 1908, p. 348. E. Hobsbawm, *Labour's Turning Point* (London, 1948), p. 155. Cronin, op. cit., p. 129.

91 *P. Gazette*, 1 Aug. 1921, p. 1392.

92 Burgess, *Challenge of Labour*, p. 168. Cronin, op. cit., p. 112.

93 J. Booth, *S. Sentinel*, 28 March 1907.

94 S. Clowes, *S. Advertizer*, 1 Feb. 1908, p. 7. *P. Gazette*, 1 April 1917, p. 407 and 1 Dec. 1919, p. 1355. For a similar conclusion on the relationship between industrial and political issues see M. Savage, *The Dynamics of Working-Class Politics: The Labour Movement in Preston, 1880–1940* (Cambridge, 1988).

95 The word is used by A. H. Morgan, 'Regional consciousness in the North Staffordshire Potteries', *Geography*, March (1942), p. 99.

96 See footnote 58 *supra*. See also M. Jones, *Potbank. A social enquiry into life in the Potteries* (1961) pp. 165–6.

97 On the consensus-oriented accounts of industries developed in the 1950s (when Williams produced his view of the pottery industry) see R. Loveridge, 'Occupational change and the development of interest groups among white collar workers in the U.K.: a long-term model', *British Journal of Industrial Relations*, Vol. x, No. 3 (1972). Cf. M. Buraway, *The Politics of Production* (London, 1985).

98 The term was first used by G. D. H. Cole, *The World of Labour*, p. 211, as quoted in J. H. Clapham, *An Economic History of Modern Britain. Vol. II* (London, 1938), p. 335.

99 See footnote 58. R. Whipp and P. Clark, *Innovation and the Auto Industry* (London, 1986), pp. 87–171. Cf. S. Tolliday and J. Zeitlin, *Shopfloor Bargaining and the State* (Cambridge, 1985).

100 Price, *Masters, Unions and Men*, pp. 55 and 95. See also C. J. Wrigley (ed.), *A History of British Industrial Relations, vol. II: 1914–39* (Brighton, 1986).

101 G. Eyre Stringer, *New Hall Porcelain* (London, 1949), pp. 63–6.

102 W. Walker, *Juteopolis. Dundee and its Textile Workers, 1885–1923* (Edinburgh, 1979), pp. 292 and 313.

103 Allen, 'Industrial conciliation and arbitration', in loc. cit.

104 H. Ramsay, 'Cycles of control: worker participation in sociological and historical perspective', *Sociology*, Vol. 11, No. 3 (1977), September. R. Penn, *Skilled Workers in the Class Structure* (Cambridge, 1985). For a further discussion of the temporal dimension see R. Whipp, 'A time to every purpose': an essay on time and work, in P. Joyce (ed.), *The Historical Meanings of Work* (Cambridge, 1987).

105 See also H. Gutman, *Work, Culture and Society in Industrializing America* (New York 1976), p. 297.

106 E. Batstone, *The Reform of Workplace Industrial Relations: Theory, Myth and*

Evidence (Oxford, 1988). K. Sisson (ed.), *Personnel Management in Britain* (Oxford, 1989).

5 Management, Labour and the State in France 1871–1939: Industrial Relations in the Third Republic

1 P. Stearns, 'Against the Strike Threat: Employer Policy towards Labour Agitation 1908–14', in *Journal of Modern History (1968)*.
2 In 1913 there were fewer than 1 million unionized workers in France and, at the peak of the postwar industrial militancy in 1919–20, under 2 million. Comparable British figures were 4 million and 6.5 million. See e.g. J. L. Robert, *La scission syndicale de 1921* (Paris, 1980).
3 C. Tilly and E. Shorter, *Strikes in France: 1830–1968* (London, 1974).
4 M. Perrot, *Les ouvriers en grève 1870–90* (Paris, 1974), C. Tilly and E. Shorter op. cit. (1974).
5 J. Zeitlin, 'Historical Alternatives to Mass Production', in *Past and Present* (1985); M. Lévy-Leboyer 'Le patronat français a-t-il été Malthusien?', in *Le Mouvement Social*.
6 S. Elwitt, *The Making of the Third Republic* (Baton Rouge., 1975). S. Elwitt, *The Third Republic Defended* (Baton Ronge, 1986). H. Lebovics, *The Alliance of Iron and Wheat: The Origins of the New Conservatism* (Louisiana State UP, 1988).
7 P. Stearns, *Paths to Authority* (Urbana, 1978). D. Reid, 'Industrial Paternalism: Discourse and Practice in French Mining and Metallurgy', in *Comparative Studies in Society and History*, (1985). L. Murard and P. Zylberman, *Le petit travailleur infatigable* (Fontenay-sons-bois, 1976). G. Noriel, 'Du "patronage" au paternalisme' in *Le Mouvement Social*, (1988). J. Vichniac, *The Management of Labour in the British and French Iron and Steel Industries 1860–1918* (Greenwich, CT, 1990).
8 Failure rates in strikes against large *Sociétés Anonymes* were very high (57 per cent between 1870 and 1890), see M. Perrot op. cit. (1974).
9 L. Murard and P. Zylberman op. cit. (1976). Nuns were widely used in the textile industry to supervise women workers. In the Lyonnais they ran the notorious silk 'convent-workshop' – functioning as shopfloor and dormitory supervisors. In the Nord Cotton Industry they ran *Notre Dame de L'Usine* prayer groups, visited homes and linked provision of charity to 'moral' family life. See e.g. C. Heywood, 'The Catholic Church and Industrial Discipline in 19th Century France' in *European History Quarterly* (1989). D. Vanoli 'Les couvents-soyeux' in *Les Revoltes Logiques* (1976).
10 R. Trempé, *Les mineurs de Carmaux*, 2 vols (Paris, 1974).

11 J. M. Gaillard, *Un example français de ville – usine: La Grandé Combes et sa compagnie des mines* (thesis, Université de Paris X, 1974).

12 G. Noiriel, *Longwy: Immigrés et Proletaires* (Paris, 1984). J. M. Moine, *Les Barons de fer: Les maîtres de forges en Lorraine 1850–1939* (Nancy, 1989).

13 D. Reid, op. cit. (1985) D. Reid 'Schools and the Paternalist project at Le Creusot 1850–1914' in *Journal of Social History* (1993).

14 C. Johnson, 'Union-busting at Graissesac' in *Journal of Social History* (1985).

15 D. Reid, 'Genèse du Fayolisme' in *Sociologie du Travail* (1986). D. Reid, *The Miners of Decazeville* (Cambridge, Mass. 1985). Fayol's *Administration Industrielle et Generale* was published in 1916. He became an advocate of an organized, bureaucratic State and of larger employer organizations that could catch the ear of government policy-makers.

16 R. Trempé, 'Analyse du comportement des administrateurs de la Société des Mines de Carmaux vis-à-vis des mineurs', in *Le Mouvement Social* (1963).

17 D. Reid, 'The role of mine-safety in the development of working-class consciousness', in *French Historical Studies* (1981).

18 J. Michel, 'Syndicalisme minier et politique dans le Nord/Pas de Calais 1880–1914: le cas Basly', in *Le Mouvement Social* (1974).

19 M. Perrot, 'Ages of Industrial Discipline', in J. Merriman (ed.), *Consciousness and Class Experience in 19th Century Europe* (New York, 1979). P. Fridenson, 'Genèse de l'usine nouvelle', in L. Murard and P. Zylberman (eds.) *Le Soldat du Travail* (Paris, 1978). A. Melucci, 'Règlements d'usine et contrôle de la main d'oeuvre au XIX siècle', in *Le Mouvement Social* (1976).

20 J. Scott, *The Glassmakers of Carmaux.* (Cambridge, Mass, 1974).

21 Y. Lequin, 'Apprenticeship in Ninteenth-Century France', in S. Kaplan and C. Koepp (eds.) *Work in France* (Cambridge, 1986).

22 G. Humphrey, *Taylorism in France 1900–1920* (New York). A. Moutet 'Les origines du système de taylor en France', in *Le Mouvement Social* (1975). P. Fridenson. 'Un tournant taylorien de la societe francaise?', in *Annales E.S.C.* (1987).

23 M. Mottez, Baltimore *Systèmes de salaires et politiques patronales* (Paris, 1966).

24 L. Berlanstein, *The Working People of Paris,* (Baltimore 1984). Y. Lequin, *Les ouvriers de la region Lyonnaise 1848–1914*, Vol. 2 (Lyon, 1977). L. Berlanstein, *Big Business and Industrial Conflict in Nineteenth Century France* (Berkeley, 1991).

25 A. Rabinbach, 'The European Science of Work', in S. Kaplan and C. Koepp (eds.) op. cit., (1986).

26 M. Perrot, op. cit., (1974).

27 P. Schöttler, *La naissance des Bourses du Travail* (Paris P.U.F., 1985).

28 M. Perrot, op. cit., (1974).

29 A. Cottereau, 'Problèmes de conceptualisation comparative de l'indus-trialisation', in S. Magri (ed.), *Villes Ouvrières 1900–50* (Paris, 1989).

30 C. Tilly and E. Shorter, op. cit., (1974).

31 M. Perrot, 'Les patrons français vus par les ouvriers', in M. Levy-Leboyer (ed.) *Le patronat français et la seconde industrialisation* (Paris, 1979).

32 C. Heywood, *Childhood in 19th Century France* (Cambridge, 1989). M. Boxer, 'Protective legislation and home industry: The marginalisation of women workers 1880–1914', in *Journal of Social History* (1986). M. Stewart-Mcdougall, *Women, Work and the French State: Labour Protection and Social Patriarchy* (Kingston, Ont., 1989). The child labour law was quite well enforced, since the proportion of employers reliant on child labour had fallen rapidly since the 1860s. Controls on women's factory condi-tions and hours simply accelerated the transfer of clothing production to domestic sweatshops, however.

33 J. Stone, *The Search for Social Peace: Reform Legislation in France* (Albany, N.Y., 1985).

34 C. Tilly and E. Shorter op. cit., (1974). J. Stone op. cit., (1985).

35 D. Reid, 'Putting Social Reform into Practice: Labour Inspection in France 1892–1914', in *Journal of Social History* (1986).

36 D. Reid, 'The Third Republic as Manager: Labour Policy in the Naval Dockyards', in *International Review of Social History* (1985).

37 P. Stearns, op. cit., (1968).

38 J. Julliard, *Clemenceau, briseur des grèves* (Paris, 1965). A. Calhoun, *The Politics of Internal Order: French Government and Revolutionary Labour 1898–1914* (Princeton University. Ph.D., 1973). P. Stearns, op. cit., (1968). C. Tilly and E. Shorter, 'Le declin de la grève violente en France', in *Le Mouvement Social* (1971).

39 P. Stearns, op. cit., (1968).

40 P. Stearns, op. cit., (1968). M. Stein, 'The meaning of skill: French railway drivers 1837–1917', in *Politics and Society* (1979).

41 N. Papayanis, *A. Merrheim: the emergence of Reformism in Revolutionary Syndicalism* (Dordrecht and Boston, 1985).

42 P. Fridenson, 'The impact of war on French workers', in R. Wall and J. Winter (eds.), *The Upheaval of War.* (Cambridge, 1988).

43 J. Godfrey, *Capitalism at War: Industrial Politics and Bureaucracy in France 1914–18* (Leamington Spa and New York, 1987). G. Hardach, 'La mobilisation industrielle', in P. Fridenson (ed.), *L'Autre Front* (Paris Editions Sociales, 1978).

44 J. Horne, 'Le Comité d'Action CGT/PS et l'origine du reformisme syndicale', in *Le Mouvement Social* (1983). J. Horne, *Labour at War: France and Britain 1914–18.* (Oxford, 1991).

45 N. Papayanis, op. cit., (1983). J. Bond-Howard, 'Le syndicalisme minoritaire dans les usines d'armements de Bourges 1914–18', in *Le Mouvement Social* (1989).

46 R. Huard, 'Les mineurs du Gard pendant la guerre de 1914–18', in *Économie et Société en Languedoc-Roussillon de 1789 a nos jours.* (Montpellier, 1978).

47 G. Hatry, *Renault: Usine de guerre 1914–18* (Paris, 1978).

48 A. Moutet, 'Patrons de progès ou patrons de combat? La politique du rationalisation de l'industrie française au lendemain de la guerre mondiale', in L. Murard and P. Zylberberg (eds.) *Le Soldat du Travail* (Paris, 1978).

49 D. Gallie, *Social Inequality and Class Radicalism in France and Britain* (Cambridge, 1983).

50 J. Godfrey, op. cit., (1987).

51 K. Amdur, *Syndicalist Legacy* (Urbana, III., 1986).

52 J. L. Robert, *Le scission syndicale de 1921* (Paris, 1980).

53 G. Cross, 'Labor Movements, International Reform and the Origins of the 8-hour day in France', in *Journal of Social History* (1985).

54 A. Moutet, op. cit., (1978).

55 D. Simon, 'Le patronat face aux assurances sociales 1920–30', in *Le Mouvement Social* (1986).

56 B. Abhervé, 'Les origines de la grève des métallurgistes parisiens, Juin 1919,' in *Le Mouvement Social* (1975).

57 G. Cross, op. cit., (1985). G. Cross, (1975) 'Redefining Workers' Control: Rationalisation, Labor Time and Workers' Control in France 1900–28', in J. Cronin (ed.), *Work Community and Power* (Philadelphia, 1988).

58 J. L. Robert op. cit., (1980). Union membership sank to 100,000 in 1915, then recovered to reach 598,000 in 1918 and nearly 2 million in early 1920 before declining precipitously. There were 2,026 strikes in 1919 (failure rate 22 per cent), 1832 in 1920 (failure rate 32 per cent) – but only 475 in 1921 (failure rate 50 per cent).

59 J. Jones, 'The French Railway Strikes of 1920', in *French Historical Studies* (1982).

60 J. Michel, 'Les relations industrielles dans les mines françaises de la fin du XIX siècle aux années 1970 (unpublished paper, n.d.).

61 R. Magraw, 'France' in S. Salter and J. Stevenson (eds.) *The Working Class and Politics in Europe and America 1929–45.* (New York, 1990).

62 C. Tilly and E. Shorter, op. cit., (1974).

63 Ehrmann, *Organised Business in France.* (Princeton U.P., 1957).

64 G. Cross, *Immigrant Workers in Industrial France* (Philadelphia, 1983).

65 Y. Lequin, 'Le rationalisation du capitalisme français a-t-il en lieu dans les années vingt?', in *Cahiers d'Histoire de l'Institut Maurice Thorez* (1979),

C. Maier, 'Between Taylorism and Technocracy' in *Journal of Contemporary History* (1970).

66 M. Fine, 'Towards Corporatism; the movement for capital/labor collaboration in France 1914–36. (Wisconsin Ph.D., 1971). M. Fine and H. Dubreuil in *Le Mouvement Social* (1979).

67 Y. Lequin, op. cit., (1979).

68 P. Fridenson, 'Automobile workers in France' in S. Kaplan and C. Koepp (eds.), op. cit. (1986). S. Schweitzer, *Des engrenages à la chaîne: les usines Citroën 1915–35* (Lyon, 1982). J. Depretto and S. Schweitzer, *Le Communisme a l'usine: Renault 1920–39* (Lille, 1984).

69 O. Hardy-Hemery, 'Rationalisation technique et rationalisation de la main d'oeuvre a Anzin 1929–35', in *Le Mouvement Social* (1970). A. Moutet, 'La rationalisation dans les mines du Nord a l'épreuvre du Front Populaire', in *Le Mouvement Social* (1986).

70 D. Reid, op. cit., (1985). D. Reid 'The Limits of Paternalism: Immigrant Coalminers' Communities in France in 1919–45,' in *European History Quarterly* (1985).

71 G. Noiriel, op. cit. (1984). S. Bonnett, *L'homme de fer*, Vol. 1 (Metz, 1975)

72 M. Massard, 'Syndicalisme et Milieu Social 1900–40: Le Creusot', in *Le Mouvement Social*, (1977).

73 J. Sherwood, 'Rationalisation and Railway Workers in France', in the *Journal of Contemporary History* (1980). G. Ribeill 'Politiques et pratiques sociales du logement dans les compagnies de chemin de fer', in S. Magri (ed.) *Villes Ouvrières* (Paris, 1989).

74 A. Moutet, 'La rationalisation du travail dans l'industrie française des années trente', in *Annales E.S.C.* (1987).

75 J. Kolbloom, *La Revanche des Patrons: le patronat français face au Front Populaire* (Paris, 1986).

76 R. Kuisel, 'A. Dutoeuf, conscience of French Industry' in *International Review of Social History* (1975).

77 K. Muller, 'French Fascism and Modernisation', in *Journal of Contemporary History* (1976).

78 B. Badie, 'Les grèves du Front Populaire au usines Renault', in *Le Mouvement Social* (1972).

79 A Rossiter, 'Popular Front Economic Policy and the Matignon Negotiations', unpublished conference paper, n.d.).

80 A Sauvy, *Histoire Économique de la France entre-les deux-guerres* (Paris, 1972)

81 Y. Cohen, 'Mais qui sont donc ces "techniciens sociaux" Peugeot – Sochaux', (unpublished conference paper, n.d.).

82 M. Launay, op. cit., (1986).

83 K. Kolbloom, op. cit., (1986).

84 M. Marguiraz, 'Jean Coutrot et la "Cure Psychoanalytique",' (unpublished conference paper, n.d.).

85 J. Kolbloom, op. cit., (1986). P. Fridenson, 'La patronat français', in R. Remond (ed.), *La France et les Français 1938–39* (Paris, 1986).

86 L. Boltanski, *Les Cadres* (Paris, 1982). J. Kolbloom, 'Patronat et Cadres 1936–38', in *Le Mouvement Social* (1982).

87 M. Seidmann, 'The Birth of the Weekend and the Revolt against Work: Workers of the Paris Region during the Popular Front', in *French Historical Studies* (1982).

88 H. Chapman, 'The political life of the rank and file: French aircraft workers and the Popular Front 1936–38' in *International Labour and Working Class History* (1986).

89 A. Moutet, op. cit., (1986).

90 J. Depretto and S. Schweitzer, op. cit., (1984).

91 J. Colton, *Compulsory Labor Arbitration In France 1936–39* (New York, 1951). J. P. Rioux, 'La conciliation et l'arbitrage obligatoire des conflits du travail', in R. Remond (ed.), *E. Daladier, Chef du gouvernement* (Paris, 1977).

92 S. Berstein, *Histoire du Parti Radical*, 2 Vols (Paris, 1980).

93 R. Magraw, op. cit., (1990).

6 Entrepreneurs and Economic Growth: the Case of Italy

1 See: G. Toniolo, *An Economic History of Liberal Italy* (London, 1990); V. Zamagni, *The Economic History of Italy 1860–1990. From Periphery to Centre* (Oxford, 1994): these debates are also reviewed in J. A. Davis, 'Remapping Italy's Path to the Twentieth Century', *Journal of Modern History* 66 (June 1994) pp. 291–320.

2 On the role of the state and banks, see especially A. Gerschenkron, *Economic Backwardness in Historical Perspective* (Cambridge, Mass., 1962). On the state and the economy during World War 1 and in the interwar period, see: D. Forsyth, *The Crisis of the Liberal Italy: Monetary and Financial Policy 1914–1922* (Cambridge, 1993); Toniolo op. cit., (1990); Zamagni op. cit., (1993).

3 For a recent polemical view, see, for example, Carlo Tullio Altan and R. Scartezzino, *Una Modernizzazione Difficile* (Naples, 1992).

4 For example, P. Corner, 'Italy' in S. Salter and J. Stevenson, *The Working Class and Politics in Europe and America 1929–45* (Longman, London, 1990) pp. 154–69. For a detailed analysis of the reactions of big business to Fascism see R. Sarti, *Fascism and Industrial Leadership in Italy 1919–40* (1971) and M. Abrate, *La lotta sindacale nella industrializzazione in Italia 1906–1926* (Milan, F. Angeli, 1967).

5 A report on European manufacturing industries prepared for the US Bureau of Manufacturers in 1908 described this as one of the most concentrated and advanced industrial regions in Europe and a very promising market for American machine tool exports: see S. Ortaggi Cammarosano, *Il Prezzo del Lavoro. Torino e l'industria italiana nel primo '900* (Turin, 1988) p. 17.

6 G. Baglioni, *L'Ideologia della Borghesia Industriale nell'Italia Liberale* (Einaudi, Turin, 1974) and G. Are, *Alle origini dell'Italia Industriale* (Naples, 1974): see also D. Bigazzi, *Storia dell'impresa in Italia: saggio bibliografico* (Milan, F. Angeli, 1990). On 'entrepreneurial values', the critical observations in A. Gerschenkron, 'Attitudes, entrepreneurship and development' in A. Gerschenkron, op. cit., (Cambridge, Mass, 1962) have not lost their force.

7 See F. Chabod, *Storia della Politica Estera Italiana dal 1870 al 1896* (Bari, Laterza, 1962) pp. 412–49.

8 For example, S. Lanaro 'Il Veneto: Genealogia di un modello' in S. Lanaro (ed.), *Storia d'Italia. Il Veneto* (1984) pp. 60–98.

9 Ibid. and C. Fumian, 'Proprietari, imprenditori, agronomi' and G. Roverato, 'La terza regione industriale' in S. Lanaro (ed.), *Storia d'Italia. Il Veneto* (1984). C. Fumian, *La città del lavoro: Un'utopia agro-industriale nel Veneto contemporaneo*, (Marsilio, 1990).

10 Quoted in L. Cafagna, *Il Nord nella Storia d'Italia* (Bari, Laterza, 1962) p. 48.

11 See A. Cento Bull and P. Corner, *From Peasant to Entrepreneur. The Growth of the Family Economy in Italy* (Berg, Providence, 1993); P. Corner, *Contadini e industrializzazione. Società rurale e impresa dal 1840 al 1940* (Bari, Laterza, 1993), F. Ramella, *Terra e Telai; Sistemi di parentela e manufattura nel Biellese dell'Ottocento* (Turin, 1984); A. Dewerpe, *L'Industrie aux Champs* (Rome, 1985); F. Bettio, *The Sexual Division of Labour: The Italian Case* (Oxford, 1988).

12 For example, Dewerpe, op. cit., (1985).

13 F. Bettio, op. cit., (Oxford, 1988); Dewerpe, op. cit., (1985); and especially R. Romano, *La Modernizzazione Periferica: L'Alto Milanese e la formazione di una società industriale 1750–1914* (Milan, F. Angeli, 1990); id. *I Caprotti; L'avventura economica e umana di una dinastia industriale della Brianza* (Milan, F. Angeli, 1980); id. 'Il Cotonificio Cantoni dale origini al 1900', *Studi Storici* (April–June, 1975).

14 G. Mori, 'Industrie senza industrializzazione 1815–51', *Studi Storici* 30, No. 3 (1989) pp. 603–35.

15 G. Federico, 'Mercantilizzazione e sviluppo economico min Italia', *Rivista di Storia Economica* 2 (1986).

16 S. Lanaro, 'Il Veneto: Genealogia di un modello' in S. Lanaro (ed.), op.

cit., (1984) pp. 60–98; C. Fumian, 'Proprietari, imprenditori, agronomi', in ibid. and G. Roverato, 'La terza regione industriale', in ibid.

17 C. Fumian in S. Lanaro (ed.) op. cit., (1984) p. 151 and also C. Fumian, op. cit. (1990).

18 S. Lanaro (ed.), op. cit., (1984) p. 87; G. Roverato, in S. Lanaro (ed.) op. cit., (1984) p. 171: see also entries on Ernesto Breda, Vincenzo Stefano Breda, in *Dizionario Biografico degli Italiani* (DBI), (Istituto dell'Enicopedia Italiana, Rome, 1966).

19 V. Castronovo, 'La millesima locomotiva di Ernesto Breda', in V. Castrono, *Grandi e Piccoli Borghesi* (Bari, Laterza, 1988) pp. 55–72.

20 G. Roverato in S. Lanaro (ed.), op. cit., (1984) pp. 171–4.

21 A. M. Banti, *Terra e Denaro. Una borghesia padana dell'Ottocento* (Marsilio, Venice, 1989); M. Malatesta, *I signori della terra. L'organizzazione degli interessi agrari padani 1860–1914* (Milan, 1989); and S. Lanaro, *Nazione e Lavoro* (Venice, 1978).

22 A. Bagnasco, *Tre Italie. La problematica territoriale dello sviluppo italiano* (Bologna, 1977). A. Cento Bull and P. Corner, op. cit., (1993). A. Cento Bull 'Proto-industrialization, small scale capital accumulations and diffused entrepreneurship. The case of Brianza in Lombardy (1860–1950)', *Social History* 14, 2 (1989).

23 F. Ramella, (Turin, 1984); A. Dewerpe, (Rome, 1985); F. Bettio, op. cit., (Oxford, 1988).

24 P. Corner, op. cit. (1993); R. Romano, op. cit., (1990).

25 C. Trigilia, *Sviluppo senza autonomia* (Bologna, 1992); E. C. Banfied, *The Moral Basis of a Backward Society* (Glencoe, 1964); R. Putnam, *Making Democracy Work: Civic Traditions in Modern Italy* (Princeton, 1993).

26 A. M. Banti, 'Gli imprenditori meridionali: razionalità e contesto', in *Meridiana* pp. 63–89.

27 M. Petrusewicz, *Latifondo; Economia morale e vita materiale in una periferia dell'Ottocento*, (Marsilio, Venice, 1989).

28 S. Lupo, *Il giardino degli aranci: il mondo degli agrumi nella storia del Mezzogiorno*, (Venice, 1990); see also G. Giarrizzo (ed.), *La modernizzazione difficile: città e campagne nel Mezzogiorno dall'età giolittiana al fascismo* (Bari, De Donato, 1983).

29 L. De Rosa, *Iniziativa e capitale straniero nell'industria metalmeccanica del Mezzogiorno 1800–1904* (Naples, 1968).

30 D. Gambetta, *The Sicilian Mafia; The Business of Private Protection* (Harvard, 1993).

31 V. Castrono, *Giovanni Agnelli* (Turin, 1974).

32 D. Bigazzi, *Il Portello. Operai, tecnici ed imprenditori all'Alfa Romeo 1906–26* (Milan, F. Angeli, 1988).

33 Castronovo, op. cit., (1974) p. 35.

34 L. Bonnefon-Crappone, *L'Italie au Travail* (Paris, 1916) p. 14.

35 M. Abrate, op. cit., (1967) pp. 85–93.

36 M. Abrate, op. cit., (1967) and S. Ortaggi Cammarosano, op. cit., (1989).

37 L. Villari, *Le avventure di un capitano d'industria* (Einaudi, Turin, 1991) pp. 22–7; for the Brescia steel makers see A. A. Kelikian, *Town and Country under Fascism. The Transformation of Brescia 1915–26* (Oxford, 1986).

38 C. Maier *Recasting Bourgeois Europe: Stabilization in France, Germany and Italy in the Decade after World War 1* (Princeton 1975/1988): R. Sarti (1971); V De Grazia *The Culture of Consent: Mass Organization of Leisure in Fascist Italy* (Oxford, 1981). See also P. Willson *The Clockwork Factory: Women and Womens Work in Fascist Italy* (Oxford 1993).

39 See esp D. Bigazzi 'Management and Labour in Italy 1906–45' in S. Tolliday and J. Zeitlin (eds) *Between Fordism and Flexibility* (Berg 1992) pp. 76–96; Sarti (1971); Toniolo (1990).

7 Industrial Workers, Employers and the State in Nazi Germany
1933–1945

This essay is a substantially revised version of the paper I gave on 16 July 1987 to a conference on 'Workers and Managers in the 19th and 20th Centuries' hosted jointly by the Italian Institute for Philosophical Studies and the Centre for Social History in the University of Warwick: I am grateful to both for their hospitality and to Ian Kershaw for his comments on an earlier draft. I have been unable to take account of work which has been published since October 1990, but should draw attention to two studies of one large firm (Siemens) which have much to say about the issues discussed in this essay. These are: T. Siegel & T. von Freyberg *Industrielle Rationalisierung unter dem Nationalsozialismus* (Frankfurt a.M., 1991) and H. Homburg *Rationalisierung und Industriearbeit. Das Beispiel des Siemens-Konzerns Berlin 1900–1939* (Berlin, 1991).

1 For example, T. W. Mason, *Arbeiterklasse und Volksgemeinschaft* (Opladen, 1975); W. F. Werner, *Bleib übrig. Deutsche Arbeiter in der nationalsozialistischen Kriegswirtschaft* (Düsseldorf, 1983); A. von Saldern, *Mittelstand im Dritten Reich* (Frankfurt a.M. and New York, 1979); M. Prinz, *Vom neuen Mittelstand zum Volksgenossen* (Munich, 1986); D. Winkler, *Frauenarbeit im Dritten Reich* (Hamburg, 1986). D. Schoenbaum, *Hitler's Social Revolution* (New York, 1966) must now be regarded as out of date. D. Peukert, *Inside Nazi Germany. Conformity, Opposition and Racism in Everyday Life*

(Penguin Books, 1989) is an impressive synthesis of much recent research, but does not amount to a social history.

2 I. Kershaw, *The Nazi Dictatorship. Problems and Perspectives of Interpretation* (2nd ed., London, 1989) pp. 131–3.

3 D. Petzina, W. Abelshauser and A. Faust (eds.), *Sozialgeschichtliches Arbeitsbuch III* (Munich, 1978), Tables 9(e) and 9(f), pp. 57–8.

4 Ibid. Table 11(d), p. 64.

5 Ibid. Table 9(f), p. 58.

6 T. W. Mason, 'Women in Germany, 1925–1940: Family, Welfare, Work' Pt. 2 in *History Workshop Journal* 2 (1976), pp. 8f.

7 R. Hachtmann, *Industriearbeit im 'Dritten Reich'* (Göttingen, 1989) pp. 68–9.

8 The most recent comprehensive survey of the development of labour and the labour movement in the early Weimar years is H. A. Winkler, *Von der Revolution zur Stabilisierung. Arbeiter und Arbeiterbewegung in der Weimarer Republik 1918–1924* (Berlin, 1985).

9 *Sozialgeschichtliches Arbeitsbuch III*, Table 22(a), p. 111.

10 Ibid. Table 16, p. 84.

11 Ibid. Table 25(a), p. 119.

12 H. A. Winkler, *Der Weg in die Katastrophe. Arbeiter und Arbeiterbewegung in der Weimarer Republik 1930 bis 1933* (Berlin and Bonn, 1987), here p. 23. Mass unemployment and its impact on the German labour movement are also discussed in P. Stachura (ed.), *Unemployment and the Great Depression in Germany* (London, 1986) and R. J. Evans and D. Geary (eds.), *The German Unemployed* (London, 1987).

13 Hachtmann, op. cit., *Industrierarbeit* p. 24.

14 *Sozialgeschichtliches Arbeitsbuch III*, Table 22(a), p. 111.

15 Ibid. Table 25(a), p. 119.

16 Ibid. Table 23(a), p. 114.

17 Winkler, op. cit., *Weg in die Katastrophe* pp. 79–85; Hachtmann, op. cit., *Industrierarbeit* pp. 24–5, Table 21 p. 232; T. W. Mason, *Sozialpolitik im Dritten Reich* (Opladen, 1977) p. 90f. The extent to which rising productivity in some industries was a consequence of the threat of unemployment, how far a consequence of continuing rationalization and mechanization, is difficult to determine.

18 Mason, op. cit., *Sozialpolitik* pp. 81–8.

19 M. Broszat, *The Hitler State* (London, 1981) pp. 140–4; K. Wisotzky, *Der Ruhrbergbau im Dritten Reich* (Düsseldorf, 1983) pp. 57–9, 62f.

20 Mason, op. cit., *Sozialpolitik* p. 107. The text of the Law on Trustees of Labour is translated in J. Noakes and G. Pridham (eds.), *Nazism 1919–1945* vol. 2 (Exeter, 1984) p. 334.

21 Broszat, op. cit., *Hitler State* p. 145f; Mason, op. cit., *Sozialpolitik* p. 115f; Noakes and Pridham (eds.), op. cit., *Nazism* vol. 2 p. 339.

22 The text of the law is translated in Noakes and Pridham (eds.), op. cit., *Nazism* vol. 2 pp. 339–42; Broszat, op. cit., *Hitler State* p. 147f; T. W. Mason 'Zur Entstehung des Gesetzes zur Ordnung der nationalen Arbeit, vom 20. Januar 1934' in H. Mommsen, D. Petzina and B. Weisbrod (eds.), *Industrielles System und Politische Entwicklung in der Weimarer Republik* vol. 1 (Düsseldorf, 1974) pp. 322–51.

23 Broszat, op. cit., *Hitler State* p. 154.

24 Noakes and Pridham (eds.), op. cit., *Nazism* vol. 2 p. 343; Schoenbaum, op. cit., *Hitler's Social Revolution* p. 90.

25 Mason, op. cit., *Sozialpolitik* p. 182.

26 G. Morsch, 'Streik im "Dritten Reich"' in *Vierteljahrshefte für Zeitgeschichte* vol. 36 (1988) pp. 649–89, here pp. 667ff.

27 Monthly unemployment statistics for this period are reproduced in Noakes and Pridham (eds.), op. cit., *Nazism* vol. 2, p. 359.

28 On the development of nominal and real gross and net earnings, see: G. Bry, *Wages in Germany 1871–1945* (Princeton, 1960); T. Siegel 'Lohnpolitik im nationalsozialistischen Deutschland' in C. Sachse et al. *Angst, Belohnung, Zucht und Ordnung. Herrschaftsmechanismen im Nationalsozialismus* (Opladen, 1982); R. Hachtmann 'Lebenshaltungskosten und Reallöhne während des "Dritten Reiches"' in *Vierteljahrsschrift für Sozial- und Wirtschaftsgeschichte* vol. 75 (1988) pp. 32–73; id. *Industriearbeit*, Chapter V; Mason, op. cit., *Sozialpolitik* pp. 147–61, 165–71, 228–31. Of the various attempts to determine levels of real earnings, those of Hachtmann, op. cit., seem to me the most convincing. I follow here the account he gives in *Industriearbeit* Table 4, p. 159 and 'Lebenshaltungskosten und Reallöhne' Tables 4–6, p. 45, 46, 70.

29 Mason, op. cit., *Sozialpolitik* p. 200.

30 On the development of the labour market after 1936, see Mason, op. cit., *Sozialpolitik* pp. 208–37, here p. 215.

31 Tim Mason, 'The Workers' Opposition in Nazi Germany' in *History Workshop Journal* 11 (spring 1981) pp. 120–37, here p. 122.

32 Mason, op. cit., *Sozialpolitik* pp. 229ff; Hachtmann, op. cit., *Industriearbeit* Table 14, p. 159.

33 Hachtmann, op. cit., *Industriearbeit* pp. 231–4; Mason, op. cit., *Sozialpolitik* p. 314f. See also the discussions of the significance of this development in Wisotzky, op. cit., *Ruhrbergbau* pp. 215–20 and H. Yano, *Hüttenarbeiter im Dritten Reich* (Stuttgart, 1986) pp. 86–9. The extracts from the reports of the Labour Trustees reproduced in T. W. Mason, *Arbeiterklasse und Volksgemeinschaft* (Opladen, 1975) and the 'Germany Reports' of the SPD in exile (SOPADE) in K. Behnken (ed.), *Deutschland Berichte der Sozialdemokratischen Partei Deutschlands (SOPADE) 1934–1940* (7 vols, Frankfurt 1980) for 1937–39 provide contrasting contemporary assessments.

34 Hachtmann, op. cit., *Industriearbeit* Chapter VIII; Yano, op. cit., *Hüttenarbeiter* pp. 116–40; Mason, op. cit., 'Workers' Opposition' pp. 125f.

35 Morsch, op. cit., 'Streik im "Dritten Reich" ', pp. 683–9; Mason, op. cit., 'Workers' Opposition', p., 124; U. Herbert 'Arbeiterschaft im "Dritten Reich": Zwischenbilanz und offene Fragen' in *Geschichte und Gesellschaft* 15 (1989) pp. 320–60, here p. 341.

36 Mason, op. cit., 'Workers' Opposition', p. 122.

37 Mason, op. cit., *Arbeiterklasse* p. 667f.

38 Werner, op. cit., *Bleib übrig* pp. 58–72, 81–105.

39 Mason *Arbeiterklasse* Chapters XIX–XXI.

40 Werner, op. cit., *Bleib übrig* pp. 34–41, 105–26; Hachtmann, op. cit., *Industriearbeit* pp. 128–35.

41 Werner, op. cit., *Bleib übrig* pp. 72–80, 171–92; H. Auerbach, 'Arbeitserziehungslager 1940–1944' in *Gutachten des Instituts für Zeitgeschichte* Vol. 2 (Stuttgart, 1966) pp. 196–201.

42 See, for example, the views of employers recorded in reports by the regional armaments inspectorates: Bundesarchiv-Militärarchiv Freiburg, RW20–6/21, reports dated 14.5.41 and 14.6.41; RW20–10/27 reports dated 15.5.41 and 16.6.41; RW20–13/11 report dated 13.12.40.

43 Werner, op. cit., *Bleib übrig* pp. 220–41.

44 Herbert, op. cit., 'Arbeiterschaft' p. 354.

45 Hachtmann, op. cit., *Industriearbeit* pp. 234–47; Werner, op. cit., *Bleib übrig* pp. 166–71, 307–18, 327f.

46 Autorenkollektiv (ed.), *Deutschland im Zweiten Weltkrieg* Vol. 4 (Berlin, 1981), p. 306.

47 Klaus Wisotzky, 'Der Ruhrbergbau am Vorabend des Zweiten Weltkrieges' in *Vierteljahrshefte für Zeitgeschichte* Vol. 30 (1982) pp. 418–61, here p. 420.

48 Mason, op. cit., *Sozialpolitik.*

49 Wisotzky, op. cit., 'Ruhrbergbau am Vorabend', p. 423.

50 Mason, op. cit., *Sozialpolitik* p. 153f.

51 Ibid. pp. 229ff; Hachtmann, op. cit., *Industriearbeit* p. 159.

52 Werner, op. cit., *Bleib übrig* pp. 120–3.

53 Hachtmann, op. cit., *Industriearbeit* Table 9, p. 140.

54 Ibid. Table 8, p. 137; Winkler, op. cit., *Frauenarbeit* pp. 202–4; Siegel, op. cit., 'Lohnpolitik' pp. 119–23.

55 Calculated from figures in A. Milward, *The German Economy at War* (London, 1965) p. 47 and Winkler, op. cit., *Frauenarbeit* p. 201.

56 United States Strategic Bombing Survey, Equipment Division, Machine Tool Section, *The German Machine Tool Industry* Exhibit 12 (Washington?, 1945).

57 Hachtmann, op. cit., *Industriearbeit* p. 68f. On the rationalization move-

ment of the 1920s see R. A. Brady, *The Rationalization Movement in German Industry* (Berkeley, 1933); on rationalization and mechanization in heavy industry, B. Weisbrod, *Schwerindustrie in der Weimarer Republik* (Wuppertal, 1978) pp. 50–62.

58 Hachtmann, op. cit., *Industriearbeit*, p. 76.

59 Ibid. pp. 77–81; A. Milward, *War, Economy and Society 1939–1945* (London, 1977) pp. 188–90.

60 Hachtmann, op. cit., *Industriearbeit* pp. 175–81.

61 Ibid. Chapters VI, VIII; Siegel, op. cit., 'Lohnpolitik' pp. 124–9; Werner, op. cit., *Bleib übrig* pp. 224–34; Yano, op. cit., *Hüttenarbeiter* pp. 116ff.

62 Hachtmann, op. cit., *Industriearbeit* Chapter VII.

63 Ibid. pp. 81–3.

64 Modern features of the development of industrial relations after 1918 are highlighted in: G. D. Feldman, 'The Weimar Republic: A Problem of Modernization?' in *Archiv für Sozialgeschichte* Vol. 26 (1986) pp. 1–26, esp. pp. 10–19.

65 Peukert, op. cit., *Life in the Third Reich* p. 242; Herbert, op. cit., 'Arbeiterschaft' pp. 339–40; J. Mooser, *Arbeiterleben in Deutschland 1900–1970* (Frankfurt, 1984) pp. 213–14.

66 L. Niethammer, 'Heimat und Front' in *idem* (ed.) *"Die Jahre weiss man nicht, wo man die heute hinsetzen soll"*: *Faschismuserfahrungen im Ruhrgebiet* (Berlin/Bonn, 1983) pp. 163–32. M. Roseman 'World War II and Social Change in Germany' in A. Marwick (ed.) *Total War and Social Change* (London, 1988) pp. 58–78 stresses the major social changes brought about by the collapse of the 'Third Reich'.

67 M. Broszat, K.-D. Henke and H. Woller (eds.), *Von Stalingrad zur Währungsreform. Zur Sozialgeschichte des Umbruchs in Deutschland* (Munich, 1989), 'Einleitung' pp. xxv–xlix, here p. xxv.

68 M. Fichter, 'Aufbau und Neuordnung: Betriebsträte zwischen Klassensolidarität und Betriebsloyalität in Broszat et al. (eds.), op. cit., *Von Stalingrad zur Währungsreform* pp. 469–549.

69 G. Hetzer, 'Unternehmer und leitende Angestellte zwischen Rüstungseinsatz und politischer Säuberung' in Broszat et al. (eds.), op. cit., *Von Stalingrad zur Währungsreform* pp. 551–91.

8 Employers and Workers in Japan Between the Wars

1 Chie Nakane, *Japanese Society*, (London, 1974).

2 James Abegglen, *The Japanese Factory* (Glencoe, 1958).

3 See K. Taira, *Economic Development and the Labor Market in Japan* (New

York, 1970). See also Sydney Crawcour, 'The Japanese Employment System' in *Journal of Japanese Studies*, 4–2 (1978).

4 Mikio Sumiya, 'The Emergence of Modern Japan' in Okôchi, Karsh, and Levine (eds.), *Workers and Employers in Japan: the Japanese Employment System* (Princeton, 1974). R. P. Dore, *British Factory–Japanese Factory: the Origins of National Diversity in Industrial Relations* (London, 1973) pp. 375–403. R. Doxe 'Industrial Relations in Japan and Elsewhere' in Albert M. Craig (ed.), *Japan: A Comparative View* (Princeton, 1979).

5 Andrew Gordon, *The Evolution of Labor Relations in Japan: Heavy Industry, 1853–1955* (Cambridge, Mass., and London, 1985), p. 163. This book provides an excellent history of industrial relations in Japan.

6 Stephen S. Large, *The Yûaikai: The Rise of Labor in Japan, 1912–19* (Tokyo, 1972).

7 See Peter Duus, 'Liberal Intellectuals and Social Conflict in Taishô Japan', in T. Najita and J. V. Koschmann (eds.), *Conflict in Modern Japanese History: The Neglected Tradition* (Princeton, 1982).

8 Shinji Sugayama, 'The Interwar Employment System in Japan: A Comparative Study of the Employment Conditions of White-Collar Staff and Workers', in *Shakai Keizai Shigaku* (*Socio-Economic History*) 56–4 (1989) p. 554.

9 Gordon, op. cit., p. 254.

10 Yutaka Nishinarita, *Kindai Nihon Rôshikankeishi no Kenkyu* (Tokyo, 1988) p. 200–1. See also, George O. Totten, 'Collective Bargaining and Works Councils as Innovations in Industrial Relations in Japan during the 1920s' in R. P. Dore (ed.), *Aspects of Social Change in Modern Japan* (Princeton, 1967).

11 A letter from S. Mogi, Japanese Federation of Labour, Tokyo, to Edo Fimmen, International Transport Workers Federation, Amsterdam, 31 March 1933, in *ITWF* papers in *Modern Records Centre*, University of Warwick.

12 Cited in Stephen S. Large, *Organized Workers and Socialist Politics in Interwar Japan* (Cambridge, 1981), p. 203. This is a readable book on labour movements of Japan between the wars.

13 Life in Japan during World War II is well described in Thomas R. H. Havens, *Valley of Darkness: The Japanese People and World War Two* (New York, 1978).

14 *Sanpô*, cf. Gordon, op. cit., Chapter 8 and Stephen S. Large, op. cit., (1981) Chapter 8.

9 The Struggle for Control of the American Workplace 1920–1985

1 R. A. Lester, *As Unions Mature: an Analysis of the Evolution of American Unionism* (Princeton, 1958).

2 R. Edwards, *Contested Terrain: the Transformation of the Workplace in the Twentieth Century* (London, 1979).

3 T. A. Kochan, H. C. Katz and R. B. McKersie, *The Transformation of American Industrial Relations* (New York, 1986).

4 Kochan et al., op. cit., (1986).

5 Edwards, op. cit. (1979).

6 For example, H. C. Katz, *Shifting Gears: Changing Labor Relations in U.S. Automobile Industry* (Cambridge Mass., 1985).

7 R. Herding, *Job Control and Union Structure* (Rotterdam, 1972).

8 Kochan et al., op. cit., (1986).

9 D. Montgomery, 'Thinking about American Workers in the 1920s', *International Labor and Working-class History*, 32 (Fall, 1987), pp. 4–24.

10 S. Meyer, *The Five-dollar Day: Labor Management and Social Control in the Ford Motor Company 1908–21* (Albany, 1981).

11 D. M. G. Raff and L. Summers, 'Did Henry Ford Pay Efficiency Wages?' in *Journal of Labour Economics*, 5, (October), (1987), pp. 557–86.

12 I. Bernstein, *The Lean Years* (Cambridge, Mass., 1960), pp. 52–66; S. M. Jacoby, *Employing Bureaucracy: Managers, Unions and the Transformation of Work in American Industry, 1900–1945* (New York, 1985), pp. 167–70.

13 Jacoby, op. cit. (1985).

14 M. Derber, *The American Idea of Industrial Democracy, 1865–1965*, pp. 260–84 (Urbana, 1970).

15 D. Brody, *Workers in Industrial America: Essays of the Twentieth Century Struggle* (New York, 1980), p. 78.

16 R. Ozanne, *A Century of Labor-management Relations at McCormick and International Harvester* (Madison, 1967), pp. 140–3.

17 R. W. Schatz, *The Electrical Workers: a History of Labor at General Electric and Westinghouse, 1923–60* (Urbana, 1983), pp. 42–6.

18 J. T. Carpenter, *Competition and Collective Bargaining in the Needle Trades 1910–1967* (Ithaca, 1972) B. Ramirez, *When Workers Fight: the Politics of Industrial Relations in the Progressive Era, 1898–1916* (Westport, Conn., 1978).

19 S. Fraser, 'Dress Rehearsal for the New Deal: Shop-floor Insurgents, Political Elites and Industrial Democracy in the Amalgamated Clothing Workers' in M. H. Frisch and D. J. Walkowitz (eds.), *Working-Class America: Essays on Labor, Community and American Society* (Urbana, 1983).

20 G. D. Nash, 'Franklin D. Roosevelt and Labor: The World War I Origins of Early New Deal Policy', in *Labor History* (Winter), 39–52.

21 H. D. Wolf, *The Railroad Labor Board* (Chicago, 1927).

22 D. M. Gordon, R. Edwards and M. Reich, Segmented Work, Divided Workers: the Historical Transformation of Labor in the United States (Cambridge, 1982).

23 P. Nolan and P. K. Edwards, 'Homogenise, Divide and Rule: an Essay on Segmented Work, Divided Workers' in *Cambridge Journal of Economics*, 8 (1984, June), pp. 197–215.

24 Jacoby, op. cit., (1985).

25 R. W. Dunn, *Labor and Automobiles* (New York, 1929).

26 H. A. Millis and E. C. Brown, *From the Wagner Act to Taft-Hartley: a Study of National Labour Policy and Labor Relations* (Chicago, 1950), p. 20.

27 W. E. Leuchtenburg, *Franklin D. Roosevelt and the New Deal, 1932–40* (New York, 1953).

28 J. J. Huthmacher, *Senator Robert F. Wagner and the Rise of Urban Liberalism* (New York, 1971).

29 H. J. Harris, 'The Snares of Liberalism? Politicians, Bureaucrats and the Shaping of Federal Labour Relations Policy in the United States ca. 1913–47' in S. Tolliday and J. Zeitlin (eds.), *Shop Floor Bargaining and the State: Historical and Comparative Perspectives* (Cambridge, 1985).

30 H. J. Harris, *The Right to Manage: Industrial Relations Policies of American Business in the 1940s* (Madison, 1982), pp. 23–34.

31 Schatz, op. cit., 1983.

32 F. Dobbs, *Teamster Rebellion* (New York, 1972).

33 M. Dubofsky, *We Shall Be All: a History of the Industrial Workers of the World* (Chicago, 1969).

34 For example, I. Bernstein, *The New Deal Collective Bargaining Policy* (Berkeley, 1950), though the detailed study of such works is invaluable.

35 S. Lynd, 'The Possibility of Radicalism in the Early 1930s: the Case of Steel', in *Radical America*, 6 (No. 6), (1972), pp. 37–64; A. Preis, *Labor's Giant Step: Twenty Years of the CIO* (New York, 1972).

36 Expressed most clearly by Brody, op. cit. (1980), pp. 121–66, and Harris, op. cit. (1985).

37 P. Friedlander, *The Emergence of a UAW Local, 1936–1939: a Study in Class and Culture* (Pittsburgh, 1975); J. G. Kruchko, *The Birth of a Union Local: the History of the UAW Local 674, Norwood, Ohio, 1933 to 1940* (Ithaca, 1972).

38 T. Skocpol, 'Political Response to Capitalist Crisis: Neo-Marxist Theories of the State and the New Deal', in *Politics and Society*, 10 (No. 2), (1980) 155–201.

39 I. Bernstein, *Turbulent Years* (Boston, 1970), 448–72.

40 W. E. Fisher, 'Bituminous Coal', in Twentieth Century Fund (ed.), *How Collective Bargaining Works* (New York, 1942); M. S. Baratz, *The Union and the Coal Industry* (New Haven, 1955).

41 S. Jefferys, *Management and Managed: Fifty Years of Crisis at Chrysler* (Cambridge, 1986).

42 D. Montgomery, 'To Study the People: the American Working Class', in *Labor History*, 2, Fall (1980), pp. 4–24.

43 R. H. Zieger, *Madison's Battery Workers: a History of Federal Labor Union 19587* (Ithaca, 1977).

44 Schatz, op. cit., (1983), pp. 108–9.

45 Schatz, op. cit., (1983), p. 105.

46 J. W. Kuhn, *Bargaining in Grievance Settlement: the Power of Industrial Work Groups* (New York, 1961).

47 D. E. Pullman and L. R. Tripp, 'Collective Bargaining Developments', in M. Derber and E. Young (eds.), *Labor and the New Deal* (Madison, 1957); N. Lichtenstein, *Labor's War at Home: the OIO in World War II* (Cambridge, 1982).

48 J. N. Baron, F. R. Dobbin and P. D. Jennings, 'War and Peace: the Evolution of Modern Personnel Administration in U.S. Industry', in *American Journal of Sociology*, 92, (1986), (September), pp. 350–83.

49 Harris, op. cit., (1985).

50 J. R. Sperry, 'Rebellion Within the Ranks: Pennsylvania Anthracite, John L. Lewis, and the Coal Strikes of 1943', in *Pennsylvania History*, 40, (May), (1973), pp. 293–312.

51 P. A. C. Koistinen, 'Mobilizing the World War II Economy: Labor and the Industrial-military Alliance', *Pacific Historical Review*, 42, (June), (1973), pp. 443–78.

52 Lichtenstein, op. cit., (1982), pp. 110–12.

53 L. J. Carr and J. E. Stermer, *Willow Run: a Study of Industrialization and Cultural Inadequacy* (New York, 1952).

54 E. Jennings, 'Wildcat: the Wartime Strike Wave in Auto', in *Radical America*, 9, (July–August), 1975, pp. 77–112; Lichtenstein, op. cit., (1982).

55 R. Croucher, *Engineers at War* (London, 1982).

56 K. E. Klare, 'Judicial Deradicalization of the Wagner Act and the Origins of Modern Legal Consciousness', in *Minnesota Law Review*, 62, (March), (1978), pp. 265–339.

57 Harris, op. cit., (1985).

58 C. L. Tomlins, *The State and the Unions: Labor Relations, Law, and the Organized Labor Movement in America, 1880–1960* (Cambridge, 1985).

59 W. T. Dickens and J. S. Leonard, 'Accounting for the Decline in Union Membership, 1950–1980', in *Industrial and Labor Relations Review*, 38, (April), (1985), pp. 323–4.

60 P. Weiler, 'Promises to Keep: Securing Workers' Rights to Self-Organization under the NLRA', in *Harvard Law Review*, 96, (June), (1983), pp. 1769–1827.

61 Kuhn, op. cit., (1961).

62 Jefferys, op. cit., (1985), pp. 111–14.

63 Ozanne, op. cit., (1967), pp. 221–4.

64 Schatz, op. cit., (1983), p. 149.

65 S. Tolliday and J. Zeitlin, 'Shop-floor Bargaining, Contract Unionism and Job Control: an Anglo-American Comparison', in S. Tolliday and J. Zeitlin (eds), *The Automobile Industry and its Workers: Between Fordism and Flexibility* (Cambridge, 1986).

66 D. B. Lipsky and H. S. Farber, 'The Composition of Strike Activity in the Construction Industry', in *Industrial and Labor Relations Review*, 29, (April), (1976), pp. 388–404.

67 T. A. Kochan, *Collective Bargaining and Industrial Relations: From Theory to Policy and Practice* (Homewood, Illn., 1980), pp. 387–8.

68 Tomlins, op. cit., (1985).

69 P. K. Edwards, *Conflict at Work: a Materialist Analysis of Workplace Relations* (Oxford, 1986), pp. 185–92.

70 N. Lichtenstein, 'Auto Worker Militancy and the Structure of Factory Life, 1937–1955', in *Journal of American History*, 67, (September), 1980, pp. 335–53.

71 M. Terry and P. K. Edwards (eds.), *Shopfloor Politics and Job Controls: the Post-war Engineering Industry* (Oxford, 1988).

72 N. Lichtenstein, 'UAW Bargaining Strategy and Shop-floor Conflict: 1946–1970', in Industrial Relations, 24, (Fall), (1985), p. 371.

73 J. T. Dunlop, 'The Function of the Strike', in J. T. Dunlop and N. W. Chamberlain (eds.), *Frontiers of Collective Bargaining* (New York, 1967); H. R. Northrup, 'Management's "New Look" in Labor Relations', in *Industrial Relations*, 1, (October), 1961, pp. 9–24; G. Strauss, 'The Shifting Power Balance in the Plant', in *Industrial Relations*, 1, (May), (1962), pp. 65–96.

74 M. Davis, *Prisoners of the American Dream: Politics and Economy in the History of the US Working Class* (London, 1986).

75 R. Herding, *Job Control and Union Structure* (Rotterdam, 1972); S. Weir, 'Class Forces in the 1970s', in *Radical America*, 6 (No. 3), (1972), pp. 31–77.

76 S. Aronowitz, *False Promises: the Shaping of American Working-class Consciousness* (New York, 1973), pp. 21–50.

77 P. K. Edwards, *Strikes in the United States, 1881–1974* (Oxford, 1981).

78 C. Crouch and A. Pizzorno (eds.), *The Resurgence of Class Conflict in Western Europe Since 1968*, 2 vols. (London, 1978).

79 Davis, op. cit., (1986), pp. 127; Jefferys, op. cit., (1986), Ch. 9.

80 W. Serrin, *The Company and the Union: the 'Civilized Relationship' of the General Motors Company and the United Auto Workers* (New York, 1974).

81 Katz, op. cit., (1985), pp. 32–3.

82 R. Bethell, 'The ENA in Perspective: the Transformation of Collective Bargaining in the Basic Steel Industry', in *Review of Radical Political Economics*, 10, (Summer), (1978), pp. 1–24.

83 P. Cappelli, 'Plant-level Concession Bargaining', in *Industrial and Labor Relations Review*, 39, (October), (1985), pp. 90–104.

84 R. E. Walton, 'From Control to Commitment in the Workplace', in *Harvard Business Review*, 63, (March–April), (1985), pp. 77–84.

85 Kochan et al., op. cit., (1986).

86 B. Bluestone and B. Harrison, *The Deindustrialization of America: Plant Closings, Community Abandonment and the Dismantling of Basic Industry* (New York, 1982).

87 W. Woodworth, 'Promethean Industrial Relations: Labor, ESOPs and the Boardroom', in *Labor Law Journal*, 35, (August), (1985), p. 621.

88 K. Moody, *An Injury to All: the Decline of American Unionism* (London, 1988), p. 142.

89 Davis, op. cit., (1986), pp. 149–51.

90 J. F. Zipp and K. E. Lane, 'Plant Closings and Control over the Workplace', in *Work and Occupations*, 14, (February), (1987), pp. 62–87.

91 S. Wood, 'The Co-operative Labour Strategy in the U.S. Auto Industry', in *Economic and Industrial Democracy*, 7 (December), (1986), pp. 415–47.

92 R. J. Thomas, 'Quality and Quantity? Worker Participation in the U.S. and Japanese Automobile Industries', in M. Dubofsky (ed.), *Technological Change and Workers' Movements* (Beverly Hills, 1985).

93 D. Halle, *America's Working Man: Work, Home and Politics among Blue-collar Property Owners* (Chicago, 1984).

94 H. Shaiken, S. Herzenberg and S. Kuhn, 'The Work Process Under More Flexible Production', in *Industrial Relations*, 25, (Spring), (1986), pp. 167–83.

95 B. Reisman and L. Compa, 'The Case for Adversarial Unions', *Harvard Business Review*, 63, (May–June), (1985), pp. 22–36.

96 Katz, op. cit., (1985).

97 Katz, op. cit. (1985), p. 102.

98 H. C. Katz, 'The Restructuring of Work and Industrial Relations in the US', in M. Ambrosini et al. (eds.) *Transforming US Industrial Relations* (Milan. 1990), p. 100.

99 D. M. Wells, 'Are Strong Unions Compatible with the New Model of Human Resource Management?', in *Relations Industrielles*, 48, (hiver), (1993), pp. 56–85.

100 Edwards, op. cit. (1979), p. 166.

101 B. Harrison and B. Bluestone, *The Great U-Turn* (New York, 1988).

102 L. Haiven, 'Workplace Discipline in International Comparative Perspective', in J. Belanger, P. K. Edwards and L. Haiven (eds.) *Workplace Industrial Relations and Global Change* (Ithaca, 1994).

103 P. C. Weiler, *Governing the Workplace* (Cambridge, Mass., 1990).

104 Ozanne, op. cit., (1967); R. Ozanne, *Wages in Practice and Theory: McCormick and International Harvester, 1860–1960* (Madison, 1968).

105 L. Turner, *Democracy at Work* (Ithaca, 1991).
106 C. C. Heckscher, *The New Unionism* (New York, 1988).
107 A. B. Shostack, *Robust Unionism* (Ithaca, 1991).

Notes on Contributors

John A. Davis was formerly Director of the Centre for Social History at the University of Warwick and is currently holder of the Emiliana Pasca Noether Chair in Modern Italian History at the University of Connecticut. He is joint editor of the *Journal of Modern Italian Studies* and is preparing the volume on Italy for the *Oxford History of Modern Europe*.

Paul Edwards is Professor of Industrial Relations and Deputy Director of the Industrial Relations Research Unit, University of Warwick. He did his doctorate at Oxford, published as *Strikes in the United States, 1881–1974* (1981). He has subsequently studied British work-place industrial relations, most recently in *Attending to Work* (with Colin Whitson, 1993). He is also involved in comparative study of the work place, and is co-editor of *Workplace Industrial Relations and the Global Challenge* (with Jacques Belanger and Larry Haiven, 1994).

Roger Magraw is Senior Lecturer in Modern History at the University of Warwick, England. His recent publications include *A History of the French Working Class 1815–1939*, 2 volumes (Blackwell: 1992)

Peter Mathias was Chichele Professor of Economic History at Oxford 1968–87 and was the Master of Downing College, Cambridge from 1987–95. He has specialized in eighteenth- and nineteenth-century British economic and business history; his main publications include *A History of the Brewing Industry in England, 1700–1830* (1959 and 1993), *The First Industrial Nation* (1969 and 1983), and *The Transformation of England* (1979). He is a Fellow of the British Academy, Hon. President of the International Economic History

Association and Vice-president of the 'Datini' International Institute at Patro, Italy.

Takao Matsumura is a professor in the Department of Economics, Keio University, Tokyo, Japan. His publications include *The Labour Aristocracy Revisited – The Victorian Flint Glass Makers, 1850–1880* (Manchester, 1983) and *The Debate on the United 731* (Banseisha, 1994 – in Japanese).

Dr Stephen Salter has been a Lecturer in Modern History at the University of Sheffield since 1985; and is co-editor (with John Stevenson) of *The Working Class and Politics in Europe and America 1929–1945* (Longman: 1990).

Pat Thane MA (Oxon.) PhD (LSE) is Professor of Contemporary History, University of Sussex. Recent publications include *Maternity and Gender Policies; Women and the Rise of European Welfare States 1880s–1950s* (London, Routledge: 1991), edited with Gisela Bock.

Richard Whipp is Professor of Human Resource Management and Deputy Director of Cardiff Business School, University of Wales. He has taught and researched at the Aston Management Centre, Warwick Business School, and held a visiting professorship at the University of Uppsala, Sweden. He has published widely on the subjects of innovation, the management of strategic change and competition, and the institutional analysis of sectors. His books include: *Innovation in the Auto Industry* (1980), *Patterns of Labour: Work in Social and Historical Perspectives* (1990), *Managing Change for Competitive Success* (1991) and *Competition and Chaos* (1996). In 1992 he was awarded the Thorelli Prize by the *European Journal of Marketing*.

Index

Mathias asserts that this volume represents a <u>histoire intégrale</u>, in trad. of p-i, transcending est^d historiographical compartmentalisation. (p. 2)

Whipp: sceptical about the importance of collective bargaining in early Potteries. Complex division of labour → multiple levels of negotiation and conflict. Industry-wide disputes = v. rare; so too factory disputes. Occupational groups across the district, rather than workplaces, were key. Employers' organisations = weak. GB ind. relations shld be seen "not as a linear progression towards 'formal' maturity, but in terms of cycles of attempted regulation and control of employment triggered by periodic crises of productivity and profit". (p. 82)

NB French propensity for small 'company' towns marked by authoritarian paternalism, or the Italian pattern for dispersed rural ind¹ production.